D1824887

14

April
1992

ECONOMIC
POLICY A European Forum

Cambridge University Press and
Editions de la Maison des Sciences de l'Homme for
Centre for Economic Policy Research and
École des Hautes Études en Sciences Sociales

Panel

Petr Aven
*International Institute for
Applied Systems Analysis, Austria*

Richard Baldwin
Columbia University

Patrick Bolton
Université Libre de Bruxelles

Michael Burda
INSEAD, Fontainebleau

Nicholas Crafts
University of Warwick

John Flemming
EBRD

Martin Hellwig
University of Basel

Arie Kapteyn
Tilburg University

Mervyn King
Bank of England

Gregorz Kolodko
Ministry of Finance, Warsaw

Alan Manning
London School of Economics

Maurice Obstfeld
University of California, Berkeley

Marco Pagano
Università di Napoli

Rafael Repullo
Banco de España

Jean-Charles Rochet
Université de Toulouse

Hans-Werner Sinn
Universität München

Alasdair Smith
University of Sussex

Guido Tabellini
University of California, Los Angeles

John Vickers
Nuffield College, Oxford

Statement of purpose

Economic Policy provides timely and authoritative analyses of the choices which confront policy-makers. The subject matter ranges from the study of how individual markets can and should work to the broadest interactions in the world economy.

Edited in London and Paris, *Economic Policy* offers an independent, non-partisan, European perspective on issues of worldwide concern. It emphasizes problems of international significance, either because they affect the world economy directly or because the experience of one country contains important lessons for policy-makers elsewhere.

All the articles are specially commissioned from leading professional economists. Their brief is to demonstrate how live policy issues can be illuminated by the insights of modern economics and by the most recent evidence. The presentation is incisive and written in plain language accessible to the wide audience which participates in the policy debate.

Prior to publication, the contents of each volume are discussed by a Panel of distinguished economists from Europe and elsewhere. The Panel rotates annually. Inclusion in each volume of a summary of the highlights of the Economic Policy Panel discussion provides the reader with alternative interpretations of the evidence and a sense of the liveliness of the current debate.

Financial support for this special issue from the Pew Charitable Trusts and SPES programme of the Commission of the European Communities is gratefully acknowledged.

Subscriptions: *Economic Policy* (ISSN 0266-4658) is published in April and October, volume 7 (issues 14 and 15) subscription prices, which include postage, valid until 31 December 1992, are per volume £34.00 UK, (US $53.00) for institutions, £19.00 (US $27.00) for individuals ordering direct from the publisher† and certifying that the journal is for their personal use. Single issues cost £18.00 (US $27.00) plus postage. US dollar prices apply to USA and Canada. Copies of the journal for subscribers in USA and Canada are sent by air to New York to arrive with minimum delay. Orders, which must be accompanied by payment, may be sent to a bookseller, subscription agent or to the publishers: Cambridge University Press, The Edinburgh Building, Shaftesbury Road, Cambridge CB2 2RU or 40 West 20th Street, New York, NY 10011-4211, USA.

† When exchange control regulations permit, individuals may pay by any of the following methods: Cheque (made payable to 'Cambridge University Press'), UK Postal Order, International Money Order, bank draft. Post Office Giro (a/c no. 571 6055 – *advice of payment should be sent with the order to the Press*), Barclaycard/Visa/BankAmericard or Access/MasterCard/Eurocard.

Advertising: Apply to Cambridge University Press, UK or North American branch.

14

Contents

Editors' introduction

This special issue is entirely devoted to Eastern Europe. It carries five papers presented at the 14th Economic Policy Panel Meeting held in Prague on 18–19 October 1991.

One way or another, the West will channel resources to help the East. As different official agencies contemplate the appropriate nature and scale of support, there is renewed interest in the role of the Marshall Plan in Western European reconstruction after World War II. We asked Barry Eichengreen, an economic historian, and Marc Uzan, to make an assessment. They begin by observing that the sums involved were small, in total only 2.5% of recipient countries' annual income; nor could they uncover any clear statistical link between Marshall Plan aid and economic performance. In particular, there is no evidence that the Plan significantly mobilized new investment or infrastructure repair that otherwise lacked funding. Does this mean that the Marshall Plan had little effect on post-war European reconstruction? Quite the opposite, Eichengreen and Uzan conclude.

They argue that its most convincing effect lay in its conditionality: the Marshall Plan was more a facilitator than a financier. At each step, for disbursements of aid particular policy actions were required. Usually, these were supply-side friendly, such as the end of price controls or opening up of trade. Getting the market mechanism back into action was thus the main contribution of the Marshall Plan, and Eichengreen sees a direct parallel today in Eastern Europe and the former USSR. A 'marketing crisis' has been induced by price controls. Producers hoard their produce; and, with nothing to buy, the incentive to work or save is eroded. Helping to establish the market securely is one vital task in which external assistance may be important.

Eichengreen and Uzan uncover a second effect of the Marshall Plan, which is explicitly political. Restoration of normal economic conditions required some temporary sacrifices, raising the issue of who would bear these costs. In these politically turbulent years, it may even have been the prospect of Communist successes in France and Italy that triggered the Marshall Plan. Eichengreen and Uzan use some recent theoretical developments to interpret all this as a war of attrition. Social and political groups were delaying much needed policy actions to avoid bearing the costs of adjustment themselves. Outside aid was able to transform a zero-sum game into a situation in which everyone could be a winner, thereby unblocking the path to adjustment. Again, Eichengreen and Uzan conclude that the Marshall Plan's role as facilitator was large although the amount of cash involved was remarkably small.

Some readers will feel that Eichengreen and Uzan's results are insufficient to justify an immediate rerun of Marshall Aid for Eastern Europe. Adequate institutions – economic, legal and political – are first needed to make the best use of fresh funds, and many uncertainties remain. Others will argue that the current situation, particularly in Russia, calls for precisely the kind of external conditional commitment that gave the Marshall Plan its effectiveness.

'Trade not aid' has long been the cry of the less developed countries. However useful any aid package for Eastern Europe and the former USSR, access to Western markets will surely be essential if these latter countries are to flourish. We asked Carl Hamilton and Alan Winters what trade patterns might then emerge and in what areas the comparative advantage of the East might ultimately lie.

They tackle these issues in three stages. First, they develop an empirical model of bilateral trade between market economies which can then be used to make long-run predictions about Eastern trade once adjustment to the market has been accomplished. Some results are obvious: trade between former Comecon members will fall substantially, and trade with nearby Western Europe will expand considerably. Yet the authors emphasize that even far away countries, such as the US, will experience a large growth in their trade with the East. Second, Hamilton and Winters focus more closely on agriculture, borrowing an existing simulation model of this sector. The East will have a clear comparative advantage in agriculture, and this extra supply will bid down world prices of foodstuffs. Eastern prosperity will be greatly enhanced if these potential exports are allowed access to Western markets. Furthermore, as the authors make very clear, since in practice the East will not be allowed to run a massive trade deficit with the West, it is only by admitting imports from the East that the West can simultaneously hope to enjoy an extension of its own export markets.

Third, Hamilton and Winters draw to our attention some evidence which tends to reinforce the emerging view that in manufactures the comparative advantage of the East will lie not in labour-intensive or cheap-labour commodities, but rather in goods of at least medium tech. The authors report the results of a vast multi-country study of the attainment level of scientific education by school children of various ages. The study reveals both breadth and depth of such attainment in the East, which Hamilton and Winters then show is likely to make these countries competitive in medium or even high-tech industries. Thus, it is unlikely that Eastern Europe will become a cheap labour producer on Western Europe's doorstep.

Poland was the first Eastern European country to adopt comprehensive economic reform. While others debated how reforms should be sequenced, Poland opted for 'big-bang': as much and as fast as possible. In just a few weeks, the Solidarity government, and economics minister Balcerowicz, prepared an ambitious programme which took effect on 1 January 1990 against a background of hyperinflation and acute budgetary distress. The effects were massive and controversial. For this reason, we sought two views. Jeffrey Sachs is known for his close involvement with the programme; it is no surprise that his paper, co-authored by Andrew Berg, sees much merit in the Polish approach. More surprising are their new estimates of Polish performance: a much milder recession than hitherto believed, only a small fall in consumption, and merely a return of real wages to the more reasonable levels prevailing before besieged Communists tried to buy their own survival by granting wage increases of 40% or more. Because national statistics inadequately capture the growth of the new private sector – vigorous by all accounts but just how large? – Berg and Sachs' numbers cannot yet be confirmed or disproved. We publish them in the hope that other researchers will thereby be drawn into the long labour of producing statistics.

Berg and Sachs also devote considerable attention to perhaps the most controversial aspect of the Polish programme: the very large zloty devaluation on 1 January 1990 and the inevitability of another depreciation in May 1991, before the adoption of a crawling peg in October 1991. Critics have argued that the zloty's initial devaluation was excessive, with the following adverse effects: an inflationary impact which is still lingering and quickly nullified any competitive advantage; removal of pressure on Polish firms to adapt to international market conditions; and exacerbation of the initial reduction in real wages. Berg and Sachs contend that it was vital to achieve convertibility on day one, and that the exchange rate had to move to the level necessary to eliminate the excess demand generated by the monetary overhang. Put differently, the right level of the exchange rate is determined not by competitiveness but by the money supply. If this implies excessive competitiveness, prices will rise and, in the process, eliminate the monetary overhang.

This argument deserves careful evaluation and will prompt many reactions. Some are already apparent in the discussion we publish after the article.

Our second paper on Poland comes from Washington. Guillermo Calvo and Fabrizio Coricelli have been closely following events in Poland and are puzzled by the behaviour of wages. In January 1990 the government imposed ceilings on wage increases, with heavy penalties for firms exceeding the guidelines. For six months wages remained well below the norm, then forged ahead; and firms seemed prepared to pay the resulting fines. Seriously at variance with the view of Berg and Sachs, Calvo and Coricelli suggest that Poland suffered an early and massive credit squeeze. The combination of tight money, high real interest rates and strict credit ceilings drove firms to borrow elsewhere: through the well-documented phenomenon of interenterprise credit, but also, more surprisingly, from their workers in the form of low wages. When credit conditions eased, and once it became clear that all firms were tied together in a highly unstable web of mutual liabilities which could be unravelled only at the risk of systemic collapse, firms felt more secure and reimbursed their workers. Thus, the authors argue, what ensued was a wage boom financed by borrowing from the government or through interenterprise credit.

This interpretation suggests that the early, dramatic fall in production was at least partly attributable to the supply side. Tight credit so limited the volume of working capital that output fell even below what the market could absorb. Calvo and Coricelli adduce in evidence the fact that inventories fell early during the reforms, not normal behaviour at the start of a demand downturn. Although Berg and Sachs note the same behaviour of inventories, they offer a contrasting explanation: an end to the 'overhoarding' of inventories which was necessary under the vagaries of central planning. These latter authors are adamant that the fall in production is the result of a demand shock deliberately engineered to get to grips with inflation and the budget problem. As Michael Burda notes in his discussion, since Poland began with excess demand, return to equilibrium must have entailed a larger fall in demand than supply. Calvo and Coricelli should therefore be viewed as arguing that supply-side problems exacerbated the required fall in demand.

The final paper of this issue could scarcely be in greater contrast. If Poland has chosen to face gales of creative destruction. Hungary has permitted itself no more than a gentle breeze. We invited Paul Hare and Tamás Révész to explain why, uniquely, the Hungarians have opted for a much slower pace of reform and whether this decision is justified.

Their central argument is that, if a country is fortunate enough already to have achieved much of the necessary institutional change and to have established unambiguously its commitment to the eventual transition, steady progress should always be preferred to upheavals which threaten to destroy nearly as much as they create. This does not in itself imply that neighbouring countries should adopt Hungarian gradualism: Hungary alone had in place many of the crucial institutions and structures, such as a modern income tax and VAT, or a substantial private sector past the first flush of immaturity. Other countries will need to acquire such institutions as quickly as possible. Even so, the authors suggest that there is in practice a distinction between ambition and achievement, and question whether in fact any country is achieving change much more rapidly than in Hungary.

As is well known, in per capita terms Hungary is amongst the most indebted countries in the world, and to date has strenuously resisted any suggestion that it should seek debt relief. Hare and Révész are not completely convinced of the wisdom of this strategy, but observe that even such a very real debt burden need not seriously threaten the success of the transition to the market. As evidence they cite both Hungary's chart-topping performance in attracting foreign investment within Eastern Europe and its recent export success, even during 1991 when Soviet trade was collapsing. Since, until privatization proceeds further, the largest part of output is still produced in state-owned enterprises, this latter success may also call into question the argument that rapid and massive privatization is a prerequisite for success.

Economic Policy   April 1992   Printed in Great Britain

The Marshall Plan

Barry Eichengreen and Marc Uzan

Summary

Europe's post-World War II experience with the Marshall Plan is frequently invoked by advocates of Western aid for Eastern Europe and the former USSR. Yet previous analyses of the Marshall Plan are uniformly sceptical that it had important economic effects. This paper finds, in contrast, that the Marshall Plan contributed importantly to Europe's recovery from World War II. Strikingly, however, the obvious channels through which the Marshall Plan could have affected recovery – stimulating investment, augmenting imports, and financing infra-structure repair – were relatively unimportant. Rather, post-war Europe was suffering a marketing crisis, in which political instability, shortages of consumer goods and fears of financial chaos led producers to hoard commodities and workers to limit effort. The Marshall Plan solved this marketing crisis by facilitating the restoration of financial stability and the liberalization of production and prices; this was its crucial role. These conclusions have obvious implications for Western aid to Eastern Europe and the successor states of the former USSR.

The Marshall Plan: economic effects and implications for Eastern Europe and the former USSR

Barry Eichengreen and Marc Uzan
University of California at Berkeley and Harvard University

1. Introduction

The Marshall Plan is hailed as one of the great foreign economic policy achievements of the 20th century. Between 1948 and 1951 the US transferred $13 bn. to the war-torn economies of Europe. (The Administration requested $14.2 bn., Congress authorized $13.4 bn., and $12.5 bn. was ultimately made available. The $14 bn. figure frequently cited includes appropriations for economic assistance in Asia, mostly to colonial dependencies of the European participants.) This timely and generous programme of aid is said to have solidified US leadership of the Western alliance, buttressed moderate elements in Western European politics, smoothed Europe's labour-management relations, and checked the westward march of communism (Kolko and Kolko, 1972; Patterson, 1973).

Less transparent are its economic effects. Qualitative discussions typically credit the Marshall Plan with a significant impact on Europe's recovery.[1] After stagnating through much of 1947, European growth

Much of the research for this paper was undertaken during Eichengreen's visit to the Research Department of the International Monetary Fund, whose hospitality is acknowledged with thanks. Eichengreen received financial support from the Center for German and European Studies of the University of California at Berkeley, Uzan from the Caisse de Depots. Many colleagues have provided helpful comments. We are especially indebted to Alessandra Casella and Brad De Long, on whose collaboration we have drawn (we hope not too) liberally. We gratefully acknowledge conversations with Jeremy Bulo, Daniel Cohen, Ishac Diwan and Dale Henderson. For comments on the paper we are grateful to our discussants at the Economic Policy Panel meeting, Nick Crafts and Martin Hellwig, and to Michael Bordo, Peter Garber, Douglas Irwin, Charles Maier, Torsten Persson and Charles Wyplosz. We thank Pamela Fox for logistical support.

[1] Views to this effect include Brookings Institution (1951), Ellis (1950), Tinbergen (1954), Mayer (1969), Arkes (1972) and van der Wee (1986). Arkes (1972), for example, asserts that Marshall Plan assistance was 'critical at the margins' and that it had a 'multiplier effect of three or four times its value', but he does not specify the model in which this result obtains. Wallich (1955) similarly concludes that, while several factors contributed to German economic revival, 'by providing key commodities at a critical time foreign aid probably helped to increase output by a multiple of its own value'.

accelerated in 1948, coincident with the release of Marshall aid. The continent then embarked on two decades of sustained high growth. The concurrence of Marshall Plan inflows with the quickening of growth has encouraged observers to attribute European prosperity to the American programme.

Quantitative discussions (e.g. Collins and Rodrik, 1991) are more sceptical. Marshall aid averaged only 2.5% of the combined national incomes of the recipient countries over the period it was in effect. Even at its height it could have financed no more than 20% of their capital formation. There is no obvious correlation across countries between the magnitude of Marshall Plan allotments and the pace of economic growth. Germany grew most quickly during the Marshall Plan years, but its share of American aid was not large. Given the existence of alternative explanations for Europe's rapid growth – notably post-war reconstruction and scope for catching up to the US – there is no *a priori* case for attaching particular weight to the Marshall Plan (Milward, 1984).

In this paper, we challenge this new conventional wisdom. We find that the Marshall Plan's economic effects had a significant impact on Europe's recovery from World War II. The recipients of large amounts of Marshall aid recovered significantly faster than other industrial countries. Strikingly, however, the obvious channels through which the Marshall Plan could have affected European recovery – stimulating investment in plant and equipment, augmenting capacity to import, and financing public investment on infrastructure repair – were relatively unimportant. Post-war Europe's crisis was not a crisis of insufficient investment, inadequate capacity to import raw materials, or inability to repair devastated infrastructure. Rather, Europe was suffering a 'marketing crisis', in which producers refused to bring goods to market, and workers and managers limited the effort they devoted to market activity. Political instability, shortages of consumer goods and fears of financial chaos led them to hoard commodities and withold effort. The Marshall Plan facilitated the restoration of financial stability and the liberalization of production and prices; this was its crucial role. The Marshall Plan thereby allowed Europe to return to its underlying growth path more quickly than would have been possible otherwise. Indeed, one can imagine, had the Marshall Plan not been forthcoming and had the post-war crisis deepened, that democratic institutions and the commitment to the market might have broken down, preventing Europe from returning to that growth path at all.

These conclusions have obvious implications for Western aid to the successor states of the USSR ('the Republics' for short), where uncertainty about the pace of liberalization and about the prospects for monetary stability have given rise to shortages of consumer goods and financial chaos resembling those which plagued Western Europe after World War II. In the absence of a social contract, struggles over income distribution threaten to swamp efforts to raise productivity. Western aid could facilitate solutions to these problems. Equally, there are important differences between the two settings. Compared to Europe a half-century ago, the Republics today possess less experience with and commitment to the market. The institutional infrastructure that is a prerequisite for an aid-instigated acceleration of economic growth is not yet in place. Not even the outlines of a social contract are evident. These considerations militate against a Marshall Plan for the East.

2. Background

European economic recovery from the conclusion of hostilities to the inauguration of the Marshall Plan falls into two phases: six quarters of rapidly rising output achieved mainly through repair of infrastructure and productive capacity, followed by six more difficult quarters when the gains of the preceding period had to be consolidated.

2.1. Recovery before the Marshall Plan: the first phase (mid-1945 through 1946)

The first 18 months of the pre-Marshall Plan period, from mid-1945 through the end of 1946, were marked by rapid output increases. Industrial production had fallen to 30–40% of pre-war levels in Belgium, France and the Netherlands, and to less than 20% in Italy and Germany. The slump in industrial output reflected not the wholesale destruction of capacity, however, but disruption to the channels for obtaining inputs and distributing outputs. In Italy, for example, no more than 20% of industrial capacity had been destroyed by fighting, bombing, sabotage and the removal of plant and equipment to Germany (Grindrod, 1955). The low level of output reflected rather the difficulty of obtaining raw materials, transporting goods and distributing food. The majority of the continent's freight cars were damaged or destroyed. Blocked water-ways and lack of barges and tugs crippled water transportation. At the time of liberation, only 5% of France's inland waterways were open to navigation. Roads, bridges and rail links were out of commission.

These conditions provided scope for rapid output growth through the reconstruction and repair of infrastructure. European industrial production (including mining, manufacturing, building and construction) rose quickly, to 83% of 1938 levels in the fourth quarter of 1946. Sectors producing final goods were fastest to expand. Resuming the

Table 1. Indexes of industrial production in Western Europe (1938 = 100)

Country	1947	1948	1949	1950	1951	Percentage increase 1951 over 1947
Turkey	153	154	162	165	163	7
Sweden	142	149	157	164	172	21
Ireland	120	135	154	170	176	46
Denmark	119	135	143	159	160	35
Norway	115	125	135	146	153	33
UK	110	120	129	140	145	32
Belgium	106	122	122	124	143	33
Luxembourg	—	139	132	139	168	—
France	99	111	122	123	138	39
Netherlands	94	114	127	140	147	56
Italy	93	99	109	125	143	54
Greece	69	76	90	114	130	88
Austria	55	85	114	134	148	269
Germany (Federal Republic)	34	50	72	91	106	312
All participating countries	87	99	112	124	135	55
All participating countries exclusive of Germany (Federal Republic)	105	119	130	138	145	37

Source: US President, *First Report to Congress on the Mutual Security Program* (31 December 1951), p. 75. Drawn from Brown and Opie (1953), p. 249.

fabrication of finished goods required only the repair of some machinery. Manufacturers found a ready market. Often, however, raw material supplies were a binding constraint. Except in Germany, European forests had been overcut during the war, limiting supplies of timber. Coal production remained depressed due to manpower shortages and the destruction of mines. The output of iron and steel recovered only slowly, due in part to the lack of coal. In countries like Germany, the shortage of spare parts for industrial equipment was acute.

The incidence of recovery was uneven. As Table 1 shows, those parts of Europe remote from the main theatres of the war – the UK, Ireland and much of Scandinavia – were most successful at quickly surpassing pre-war levels of industrial activity. Italy, Greece and the Netherlands, along with Germany, in contrast, failed to match pre-war levels of manufacturing. Compared to industry, agriculture recovered slowly from the war. In 1946 European agricultural production was still less than two-thirds that of 1938. (Industrial production outside Germany,

in contrast, had already matched its 1938 peak.) Grain and potato
output recovered quickly, that of meat and dairy products less so.
Wartime slaughtering of livestock, destruction of farm machinery and
inadequate use of fertilizers all hampered European agriculture. Even
where capacity could be restored swiftly, many crops required a 6- or
12-month harvest cycle and livestock a comparable gestation period.
Considerable delay consequently ensued before the appearance of an
output response. Price controls on foodstuffs were kept in place longer
than other price ceilings, discouraging the expansion of production.
Fertilizers and machinery required by agriculture were in particularly
short supply.

2.2. Recovery before the Marshall Plan: the second phase
(1947 through mid-1948)

The second phase of the pre-Marshall Plan period, from the beginning
of 1947 to the release of Marshall aid, was marked by mounting difficulties. According to World Bank experts, 'no further progress was made
in 1947' (IBRD, 1948). Leaving aside Germany, industrial output in
1947-III was no higher than at the end of 1946. The fourth quarter
of 1947 was marked by a growth spurt, with industrial output rising
by 8%. Then, however, stagnation set in again: output in 1948-III was
essentially unchanged from a year before. Europe's recovery seemed
in jeopardy.

We regard this view as overly pessimistic. There is no indication that
the growth process had petered out. Annual averages show, notwith-
standing temporary set-backs, expansion throughout the period. Taking
annual averages, European industrial production (excluding Germany)
was 14% higher in 1947 than in 1946. Observers may have been
generalizing from more serious problems in agriculture. Measured
agricultural output was 3% lower in 1947 than in the preceding year.
Unseasonable weather in the winter and spring of 1947 depressed
yields. Winter frost damaged plants and trees; spring and summer
drought then hindered their recovery.

Pessimism may have also stemmed from developments which bode
ill for the future. Increasingly pervasive shortages threatened to create
disruptive bottle-necks. The fuel shortage associated with the cold winter
of 1947 limited energy supplies to manufacturing and transport. Thaw-
ing snows flooded coal mines, and summer drought reduced supplies
of hydroelectric power. Iron and steel shortages disrupted fabricating
industries requiring metals as inputs. Shortages of industrial raw
materials became increasingly prevalent. Except in the UK, the scarcity
of special-purpose machine tools emerged as a serious problem. The

dearth of foodstuffs limited caloric intake and labour productivity. These developments may not yet have brought growth to a halt, but they threatened to do so.

Such difficulties were thought to reflect three problems: the slump in international trade which tightened the foreign exchange constraint; inadequate fiscal capacity which limited infrastructure repair; and low levels of income which constrained domestic savings. Following an overview of economic growth in the Marshall Plan years, we consider these problems in turn.

2.3. Economic growth in the Marshall Plan years

Discussions of the economic effects of the Marshall Plan (Berolzheimer, 1953; Kirman and Reichlin, 1991) typically compare industrial production at the start and end of the programme. Between 1947 and 1951 industrial output in the participating countries rose by 55%. (See Table 1.) Growth ranged from 7% in Turkey to 269% in Austria and 312% in the FRG. More typical were Denmark, Norway, the UK, Belgium and France, in each of which industrial production rose between 30 and 40% over the four years. Excluding Germany, the rise in industrial production averaged 37%. This was remarkably rapid progress.

The question is how much of this performance is attributable to the Marshall Plan. Variations in the rate of growth of industrial production provide few hints. Europe's industrial output rose by 15% between 1946 and 1947, by 16% between 1947 and 1948 and by 14% between 1948 and 1949.[2] In the aggregate, then, there is essentially no variation in the period spanning the inauguration of the Marshall Plan. Europe's agricultural output also rose impressively over the Marshall Plan years, by 37% in the OEEC countries (Table 2). Again, however, variations in the rate of output growth provide few hints about the role of the Marshall Plan. Measured production rose by 19% between 1945/46 and 1946/47, declined marginally between 1946/47 and 1947/48, but then rose strongly, by 17% between 1947/48 and 1948/49 and by 10% the following year. Unless the rebound from the bad harvest of 1947/48 is attributable to the Marshall Plan, its effect is not obvious.

Nor do cross-country variations in the rate of economic growth strongly support the existence of a Marshall Plan effect. Figure 1 juxtaposes Marshall Plan allotments as a share of GNP against the growth rate. There is considerable variation in the generosity of American aid. Austria and the Netherlands received Marshall transfers

---

[2] These figures exclude the USSR. (UN, 1949a, 1950).

Table 2. Index of total agricultural output for human consumption of OEEC countries (Pre-war = 100)

Country	% of pre-war total European production (a)	1947–48	1948–49	1949–50	1950–51
Austria	1.63	53	66	79	88
Belgium–Luxembourg	2.09 (b)	83	93	116	119
Denmark	1.93	84	92	113	126
France	15.72	78	100	103	111
Germany (Federal Republic)	10.61 (c)	60	76	96	106
Greece	1.21	83	79	110	93
Ireland	1.50	89	88	95	103
Italy	8.42	85	95	103	109
Netherlands	2.58	79	93	116	119
Norway	0.62	86	92	112	120
Sweden	2.08	101	111	115	116
Switzerland	1.38	95	98	98	104
Turkey	2.33	96	120	94	106
UK	5.89	95	111	114	122
All member countries	N.A.	81	95	104	111

Source: OEEC *Statistical Bulletins* (Paris, May 1952), Table II, 1, p. 66. Drawn from Brown and Opie (1953), p. 253. Also UN (1948), p. 11.
Notes: (a) Europe excluding USSR; (b) Belgium only; (c) Three Western Zones.

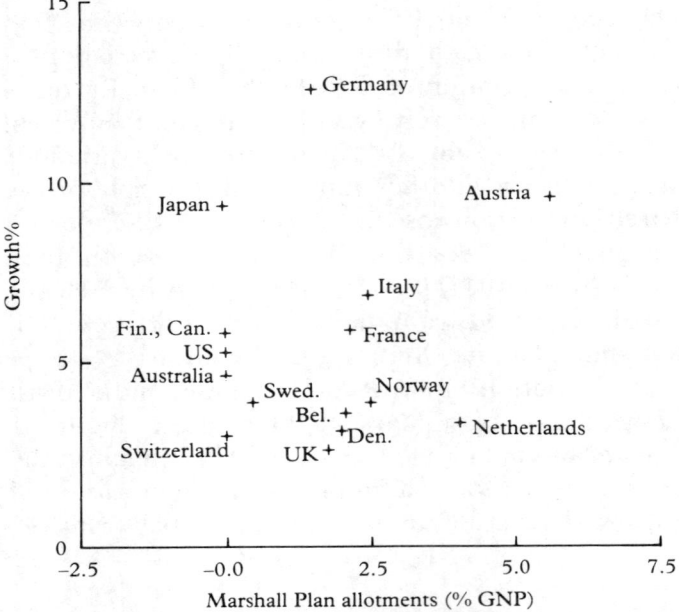

Figure 1. Annual rate of GDP growth and Marshall Plan allotments as a share of GNP, 1948–51

Box 1. The origins of the Marshall Plan

George C. Marshall traced the origins of the plan that bears his name to the failure of the UK and US in the spring of 1947 to win Soviet support for German industrial reconstruction. The Truman Administration was convinced that American prosperity required buoyant export markets, which hinged in turn on European recovery. The 1947 crisis convinced Marshall and other US officials that a viable European economy required a prosperous Germany at its core. Holding down German industrial production limited German imports from the rest of Europe and hindered the continent's recovery. Reversing the policy of limiting German production was necessary to stimulate European growth. Secretary of State Marshall and British Foreign Secretary Ernest Bevin put these points to the Soviets at the Moscow Foreign Ministers Conference of March–April 1947. Soviet resistance was interpreted as a ploy to radicalize Western European politics by destabilizing the continent's economy. This in turn provided the impetus for Marshall's aid proposal.

His June 5th Harvard address offered to include 'everything up to the Urals' so as not to antagonize European governments wishing to avoid a confrontation with the USSR. It seems unlikely that the US was serious about including the USSR. Washington made it clear that the offer was contingent on close cooperation by the participating governments among themselves and with the US, cooperation which extended to the disclosure of detailed information about the operation of their economies. American aid also entailed a commitment on the part of the recipients to economic integration and a willingness to accept American input into the formulation of domestic policy. Once these conditions were spelled out, the Soviets rejected them, to no one's surprise.

The Economic Cooperation Act was passed in April 1948 as part of the Foreign Assistance Act, which included also aid to China, assistance to Greece and Turkey, and funds for UNICEF. In the meantime, an Interim Aid Programme was launched in December of 1947 to provide modest assistance for Austria, France and Italy. The European Recovery Program opened with a 90 Days Recovery Program spanning the second quarter of 1948, followed by the first full ERP year (July 1948–June 1949).

---

amounting to nearly 6 and 4% of GNP respectively, while Sweden's aid was less than 0.5% of national income. More typical were Belgium, Denmark, France, Italy, Norway and the UK, all of which received about 2% of GNP. The figure suggests at best a weak positive correlation between the growth rate and Marshall Plan receipts as a share of national income. A regression of growth on a constant and on Marshall Plan allotments as a share of GNP fails to turn up a statistically significant relationship.

The foreign trade of the participating countries rose even more strongly than their domestic production, in contrast to the preceding depression in intra-European and intercontinental trade. Total exports in constant prices rose at an annual rate of more than 20% between 1947 and 1950. Europe's imports expanded more slowly than its exports, as was desired by those who wished for a strengthening of its current account.

By all three criteria, then – industrial output, agricultural productivity and trade – Europe's economic performance was admirable, absolutely and relative to the preceding period. The problem is to identify the contribution of the Marshall Plan.

3. Short-term effects

We turn now to this problem, concentrating in this section on short-term effects in the period when the Marshall Plan was in operation. Traditional accounts emphasize saving, imports of industrial inputs and public investment as constraints on economic growth. In Appendix A we develop a three-gap model which shows that foreign aid which supplements domestic saving, augments imports of industrial inputs and allows increases in public investment can have a major impact on current levels of output. In fact, however, it turns out that these were not the principal channels through which the Marshall Plan stimulated European economic growth.

3.1. The savings-investment gap

Was investment a significant short-run constraint on European economic growth? Did the Marshall Plan, by boosting investment, significantly raise the level of output? Although qualitative accounts typically answer both questions positively, systematic analysis gives grounds for scepticism.

The notion that the savings gap bound in the aftermath of World War II is implicit in accounts suggesting that the residents of many European countries were living close to subsistence. A physically active man requires 3,200 to 5,500 calories daily, depending on the nature of his work. In 1946 UN experts figured that more than 140 mn. Europeans were receiving fewer than 2,000 calories daily, while an additional 100 mn. Europeans were receiving fewer than 1,500 calories.

Table 3. **Savings rates in the aftermath of**
World War II and the 1950s (%)

Period	1946–51	1948–51	1952–60
Australia	16	20	21
Austria	na	12	23
Belgium	na	na	17
Canada	16	20	21
Denmark	15	23	25
Finland	14	24	27
France	na	18	20
Germany	na	19	27
Italy	15	18	19
Japan	15	18	24
Netherlands	na	20	27
Norway	28	35	34
Sweden	17	21	22
Switzerland	na	10	23
UK	9	13	16
US	14	17	18

Source: Mitchell (1975, 1983).
Note: Saving rates are calculated as the sum of investment
and the current-account surplus.

In Germany, where the official ration was 1,550 calories, the actual ration as late as 1948 was as little as 1,000 calories. The implication, according to N. H. Collision, Deputy Chief of the European Cooperation Agency (ECA) Mission to the Bizone, was that there was 'little savings in Germany' (US House, 1949). Table 3 shows saving rates following the war and compares them with those prevailing in the 1950s. That savings rates were highest in countries with relatively high per capita incomes is consistent with the view that people living close to the margin of subsistence were unwilling or unable to defer consumption to the future. For every European country but Norway, moreover, savings rates were lower prior to 1952, when low incomes and inadequate nutrition were a particular problem. Low recorded rates of saving and investment may also reflect the post-war surge of consumer durables spending, which in reality was a component of investment but showed up in the statistics as consumption. But the implications were the same: less domestic income was left for other forms of capital formation. Strikingly, however, savings rates also were low in the US, Canada and Australia, where they were hardly constrained by low levels of income. The US was pegging interest rates at low levels until the Fed-Treasury Accord of 1951; it could be that low interest rates affected savings propensities. More than low levels of income seem to have contributed, then, to Europe's low savings rates.

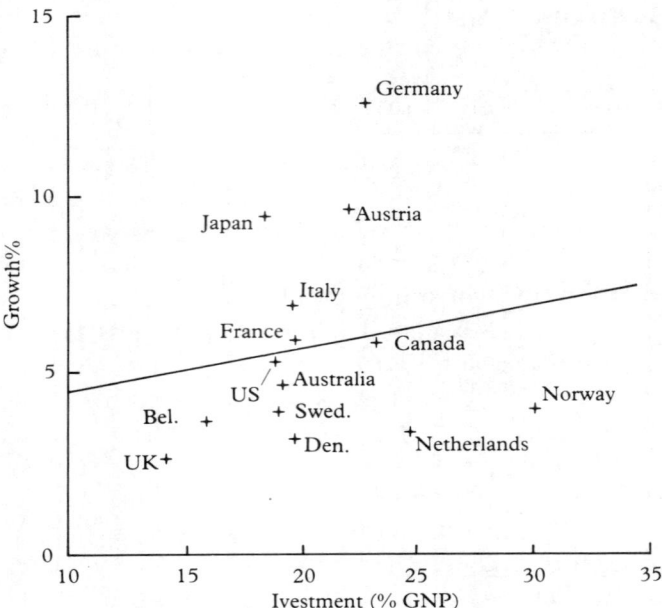

Figure 2. **Growth and investment rates, 1948–51**

Moreover, just because savings and investment rates were low, it does not follow that growth had to be significantly constrained. Figure 2 juxtaposes investment rates in the Marshall Plan years against rates of economic growth. The investment ratios of the high growth countries, Austria and Germany, were unexceptional. Other countries, notably Norway and the Netherlands, placed an even greater emphasis on investment (see Price, 1955). The relationship between the investment share of GNP and the growth rate is weak. Rigourous estimates are obtained from the analysis presented in Appendix B (multivariate regressions linking Marshall Plan allotments to investment) and C (regressions linking investment and growth). We find that Marshall Plan inflows were positively (and significantly) associated with sub-sequent investment, even after controlling for other determinants of capital formation. Transfers equal to 2% of GNP raised investment by 0.7% of GNP in the following year. We also find that the rate of GDP growth was positively related to investment – although the magnitude and significance of the effect depend on the specification. Excluding the special case of Norway (see Box 2), it appears that raising the investment share of GNP by 0.7% would have raised the growth of domestic output by 0.3%.

That $1 of Marshall Plan aid raised domestic investment by as much as 40 cents is striking when it is recalled that the vast majority of

Box 2. The peculiar case of Norwegian investment

In Figure 2, Norway's high investment rate stands out. Norway's capital stock had been devastated by the war. Nearly half the merchant marine fleet had been sunk. In retreating before the Russian Army, Germany adopted a scorched-earth policy and devastated Norway's northern regions. In response, the country embarked on an ambitious investment programme, with the government using every device to stimulate capital formation. Rations of food and consumer goods were kept at exceptionally low levels. The average urban dweller received less than 1 pound of meat a month, fewer than 30 eggs a year, and half a pint of milk a day. Cabinet ministers bicycled to work to encourage citizens to economize on their spending.

Norway's policy of investment promotion stayed in place throughout the 1950s. Large shares of national income were devoted to investment in rebuilding the merchant marine, in hydroelectric power, and in industries producing for export. The principal exports were forest products, fish products, ore, metals and iron and steel products. Metals and engineering accounted for more than a third of Norwegian gross investment in industry in 1947 (UN 1949b, p. 52). Investments in rebuilding the merchant marine were particularly important. The transportation sector accounted for 40% of Norwegian investment in 1947 and 1948, a larger fraction than for any of the other 11 countries for which UN (1949a, p. 50) provided sectoral breakdowns. The UN (1964) devoted an entire subsection of its report on European economic growth in the 1950s to the low productivity of investment in Norway. Norway's investment rate was shown to be higher than for any other European country but Ireland. UN (1964, Chapter IV, pp. 17–22) cited a combination of factors to account for this disappointing performance. Capacity utilization in Norwegian industry declined between 1948 and 1959, which reduced measured productivity. The country was said to have invested in the wrong industries, like herring oil and meal. Investment in the engineering industry significantly exceeded the availability of labour with the relevant skills. Agricultural machinery was underutilized. Investments in transport and hydroelectric power yielded significant increases in output only after an exceptionally long gestation period, and government's efforts to bias investment toward the northern regions of the country exacerbated these tendencies.

aid-financed imports took the form of food and raw materials. Equally, that an additional percentage point of GNP devoted to investment raised the growth rate by more than a third of a percentage point is striking when one observes that we are considering a period as short as a year.[3] Yet even accepting these upper-bound estimates, the combined impact on European economic recovery was small. Marshall aid in the amount of 2.5% of recipient GDP, operating through this channel, would have raised the growth rate by only half a percentage point. While helpful, this is hardly the dramatic stimulus trumpeted by champions of the Marshall Plan.

3.2. The foreign exchange gap

Was capacity to import a significant constraint on European economic growth? Did the Marshall Plan, by providing additional foreign exchange, alleviate bottle-necks that otherwise would have stifled production? Again, while qualitative accounts emphasize the importance of the foreign exchange gap, more systematic analysis challenges the notion that it was a significant constraint on growth.

Imported raw materials were important to the operation of European industry. Cotton for the textile industry was in short supply.[4] So was the coal needed to provide power for manufacturing and to refine petroleum for transportation. The output of Ruhr coal, which 'provided the basis for much of the industrial development on the European Continent', had recovered to only 65% of pre-war levels by the end of 1947 (Federal Reserve Board, 1948). Western European coal production as a whole was still only 80% of pre-war. The current-account gap ostensibly bound not only for intermediate inputs but for foodstuffs as well. The American and British zones of Germany produced less than two-thirds of the modest food ration permitted by the occupation authorities. The rest had to be imported. Paul Hoffman, the ECA administrator, told the Senate Foreign Relations Committee that 'In

---

[3] Romer (1989) and Cohen (1991) find a virtually identical coefficient on the investment share in equations they estimate to explain growth in a cross section of countries, but both authors consider longer time horizons.

[4] As Paul Hoffman described the situation, 'I found last year that supplying cotton, for example, for mills that did not have cotton, was just as much a recovery item as perhaps machine tools to some company that needed machine tools.' Winks (1960) recounts the story of a Dutch bicycle firm saved from having to shut its doors by a mere $1,200 of Marshall Plan aid. Lauritz Hensen, President of Hede Nielsen Ltd., explained that he had the cash to buy bearings, but could not do so where kroner were acceptable currency. He appealed to his government and the $1,200 of ball bearings were flown from the US on an emergency order. Compare the recent story of a sock-making factory in the USSR with 50 'gleaming Italian sock-making machines purchased last year for about $15,000 each by the Soviet Ministry of Light Industry. For much of the time they stand idle because of a shortage of needles that sell in the west for a few cents. 'The ministry paid hard [Western] currency for these machines, and we paid them back in rubles [in the words of the plant manager]. But now they are saying that they don't have enough hard currency to buy the necessary needles and spare parts. As a result, we've already had to stop these machines on the evening shift and will soon have to stop the day shift as well.' Dobbs (1991).

some cases I think the very No. 1 recovery item is a little more food to get a little more work out of people' (US Senate, 1949).

The current-account constraint bound only if reserves were depleted and foreign borrowing was precluded. In fact, reserves had been exhausted in the first post-war quarters, and foreign capital (mainly direct investment) supplemented domestic savings only modestly once aid fell off in 1947 (Table 4). American investors' unsatisfactory experience with foreign lending after World War I surely helped to shape these trends. Two-thirds of the foreign dollar bonds floated in the US in the 1920s lapsed into default in the 1930s, and more than a few remained in default following the war. The disorganization of the European economy and of its finances reinforced US investors' caution.

Figure 3 shows the current-account balances of 16 countries. Austria, Denmark, France, Germany, the Netherlands and Norway all ran substantial current-account deficits. There is a strong positive relationship between the current-account deficit and Marshall Plan receipts. A regression analysis suggests that increasing Marshall aid by 1% of GNP allowed a country to increase its current-account deficit by 0.9% of GNP. This simple correlation exaggerates the impact of the Marshall Plan on the current account, since causality also ran in the other direction: countries with larger current-account deficits received more

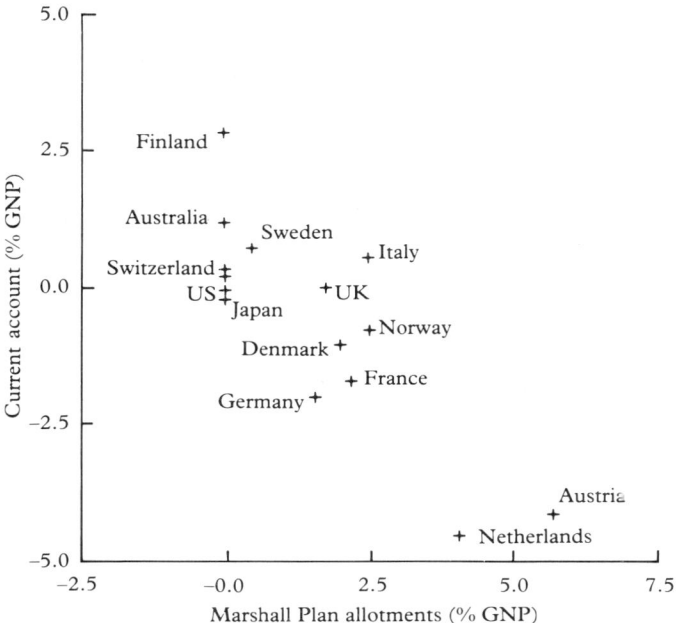

Figure 3. Average annual current-account balance and Marshall Plan allotments, 1948–51

Table 4. The financing of Europe's overseas deficit (billion current US$)

Item	1947			1948			1949			1950		
	US	Other overseas countries	Total	US	Other overseas countries	Total	US	Other overseas countries	Total	US	Other overseas countries	Total
I. Balance on goods and services and other transactions making up the deficit:												
Balance on goods and services	−5.6	−1.8	−7.4	−3.4	−1.5	−4.9	−3.2	−0.6	−3.8	−1.6	−0.9	−2.5
Private donations	+0.4	—	+0.4	+0.4	−0.1	+0.3	+0.4	−0.1	+0.3	+0.3	−0.1	+0.2
Private capital movements	+0.3	−1.1	−0.8	+0.2	−0.1	+0.1	−0.1	−0.4	−0.5	−0.1	−0.1	−0.2
Special official financing (debt settlements, specific investment projects etc.)	−0.6	−0.1	−0.7	−0.2	−0.3	−0.5	+0.2	−0.4	−0.2	+0.5	−0.3	+0.2
Total deficit to be financed:												
Unadjusted	−5.5	−3.0	−8.5	−3.0	−2.0	−5.0	−2.7	−1.5	−4.2	−0.9	−1.4	−2.3
Adjustments	−0.3	—	−0.3	—	−0.1	−0.1	−0.2	+0.7	+0.5	−0.1	+0.5	+0.4
Adjusted	−5.8	−3.0	−8.8	−3.0	−2.1	−5.1	−2.9	−0.8	−3.7	−1.0	−0.9	−1.9

II. Official financing of a compensatory nature:												
Government grants	+1.0	—	+1.0	+3.2	—	+3.2	+4.1	—	+4.1	+2.7	—	+2.7
Long-term capital movement	+3.8	+0.9	+4.7	+1.1	+0.5	+1.6	+0.7	-0.5	+0.2	+0.2	—	+0.2
Financing by International Institutions	+1.1	+0.1	+1.2	+0.3	—	+0.3	—	—	—	—	—	—
Movement in sterling balances	—	-0.6	-0.6	—	-0.2	-0.2	—	-0.5	-0.5	—	—	—
Movement in US dollar balances	+0.8	—	+0.8	-0.3	—	-0.3	-0.1	—	-0.1	-0.2	+0.9	+0.7
Gold movement	+1.9	-0.2	+1.7	+0.9	-0.4	+0.5	+0.2	-0.2	—	-1.3	-0.4	-1.7
Total compensatory official financing	+8.6	+0.2	+8.8	+5.2	-0.1	+5.1	+4.9	-1.2	+3.7	+1.4	+0.5	+1.9
III. Multilateral settlements in US dollars:												
ERP reimbursement for European outside the US	—	—	—	-0.8	+0.8	—	-1.0	+1.0	—	-0.7	+0.7	—
Other dollar settlements by European countries outside the US	-2.8	+2.8	—	-1.4	+1.4	—	-1.0	+1.0	—	+0.3	-0.3	—
Total multilateral settlements in US dollars	-2.8	+2.8	—	-2.2	+2.2	—	-2.0	+2.0	—	-0.4	+0.4	—

Source: UK (1950), p. 116; UN (1951), p. 118.

American aid. Multivariate regression analysis (controlling for simultaneity and for other determinants of the current account) confirms that recipients of Marshall Plan aid were able to run larger current-account deficits, but the incremental effect turns out to be small. Countries receiving $1 of Marshall Plan aid increased their current-account deficits by 12 cents. That current-account deficits did not widen further reflects the fact that one goal of US policy was to produce current-account balance between Europe and the US. The conditions attached to American aid thus may have worked to limit the growth of European trade deficits.

Even if ability to run larger current-account deficits had a major effect on growth by relaxing resource bottle-necks, the growth effect of the Marshall Plan, operating through this channel, still would have been small because the change in current accounts was small. In fact, the regression analysis in Appendix C suggests a negligible relationship between current account balances and growth once other determinants of the change in GDP are controlled for. The explanation for these small effects is that resource bottle-necks had only a small impact on production.[5] For example, coal was critical for the generation of electric power, which in turn was required for the operation of a wide range of industrial sectors. But over the Marshall Plan years, Europe imported only about 7% of its apparent coal consumption. If half of European production took place in sectors that were coal-burning and unable to substitute other sources of fuel, 7% of that half would have had to shut down. European output would have fallen by 3.5%.

This back-of-the-envelope calculation neglects indirect effects and general equilibrium repercussions. One can imagine, for example, a small decline in coal consumption producing a large decline in steel output, which in turn provoked an even larger fall in output in sectors where steel was an essential input. De Long and Eichengreen (1991) use input–output analysis as a check on these calculations. Utilizing an input–output table for Italy in 1950, they eliminate all Marshall-Plan-financed coal imports and assume that all uses of coal would have been proportionately reduced in the absence of Marshall Plan imports.[6] They find that industrial production would have fallen by 6.8% and the supply

---

[5] We owe this argument to Brad De Long. Points made in this paragraph are elaborated in De Long and Eichengreen (1991).

[6] Coal, according to American observers, was 'the major bottleneck of production' in Italy. See Federal Reserve Board (1947). The country imported three-quarters of its coal in 1950. The input–output table used, from Mutual Security Agency (1953), is disaggregated to 16 sectors. Each element in the vector of final demands is reduced by the same proportion until the coal constraint is just binding. The exercise assumes that all resources made slack would have remained idle rather than being redirected to other sectors.

of transportation services by 7.3%, but that agriculture and services would have been unaffected. Since industry and transport account for less than half of national output, the latter would have fallen by 3.2%, close to the previous estimate.

Moreover, in the absence of the Marshall Plan, adjustments in the allocation of foreign exchange would have lowered the need for imports of consumption goods, coal and other intermediate products. Insofar as firms could have adopted less energy-intensive techniques in response to the coal shortage, the decline in production would have been moderated further. Thus, the estimated 3% output decline should be regarded as a generous upper bound on the Marshall Plan's contribution through the elimination of bottle-necks.

3.3. The fiscal gap

Was the capacity to finance spending on infrastructure repair and other public programmes a significant constraint on European recovery? Did the Marshall Plan, by providing governments with additional resources, stimulate growth by relaxing this constraint? While qualitative accounts emphasize this channel, once again systematic analysis refutes the notion that it was a significant constraint on growth.

We do not deny the existence of fiscal problems. Budget deficits in 1946 approached 10% of national income in the UK, Italy and France, and exceeded that threshold in Belgium. Dutch deficits were probably larger still. Given foreigners' unwillingness to lend and the dearth of domestic savings, these budget deficits were financed largely through monetization. Where they were closed, this was accomplished by reducing the government-expenditure share of GNP. The share of public investment in national income was forced to decline. Of 14 European countries, this share rose between 1947 and 1948 only in Belgium, Finland, Italy and Poland. Nor can one deny the destructiveness of the war. In France, 4,000 km of railway track and more than half of all rail yards had been destroyed. In Belgium, France, the Netherlands and Poland fewer than half of all steam locomotives remained in serviceable condition. Vital bridges had been destroyed in operations culminating in the invasion of Germany. It hardly paid to invest in plant and equipment or to produce for the market where roads and railways remained in disarray and goods could not be transported to ports or mercantile centres.

Yet the worst of this damage was repaired before the Marshall Plan came on stream. Railway track and locomotives were quickly restored. By the last quarter of 1946, nearly as much freight was loaded onto railways in Western Europe as had been transported in 1938. In the

British zone of occupied Germany, where only 1,000 km out of 13,000 km of track was usable at the war's end, 12,000 km were back in operation by June 1946. (If ton-kilometres rather than tonnage are used, recovery is faster still.) Water systems and electricity supply were quickly restored. The implications for production were immediate. Excluding Germany's three Western zones, by the fourth quarter of 1946 Europe's industrial output nearly matched 1938 levels.

Regression analysis (Appendix B) lends no support to the notion that the Marshall Plan operated through this channel. There is no indication in that Marshall Plan inflows allowed for increased levels of government spending. Nor is there evidence that government spending in 1948 and after had a significant impact on the rate of economic growth.

3.4. Combined effects

To estimate the combined effects of the Marshall Plan operating through the investment, current account and public spending channels, we simulated a system of four equations: a growth equation determining the percentage change in GDP and three equations determining investment, the current account and government spending respectively.[7] The Marshall Plan affects investment, the current account and government spending with a lag; in turn these variables affect economic growth. To isolate the impact of the Marshall Plan, we simulate the equations using historical values of the exogenous variables, and then set the Marshall Plan variables to zero and compute counterfactual values for GDP growth. The difference between the predicted and counterfactual simulations is the Marshall Plan effect.[8] This effect is shown in Figure 4. The sum of three small numbers is still a small number. Marshall Plan allotments have raised GDP in the recipient countries by an average of less than 0.1% in the two years following its implementation when it should have had its largest effects. The change is largest in Austria and the Netherlands, which received the most aid, and smallest in

---

[7] Investment, the current balance and government spending are all expressed as shares of GNP. The growth equation used was the first equation from Appendix Table C2. In conducting the counterfactual simulation, we allowed only the linear terms in investment (including the separate term for Norway), the current account and government spending to operate. The interactive terms and the direct effect of the Marshall Plan were not allowed to operate. See, however, the simulations below.

[8] It would be possible to add a fourth equation endogenizing Marshall Plan allotments. Given the structure of our model, the current year's Marshall Plan allotment depends on the current balance and other determinants. American aid then affects the subsequent year's current balance, investment and government spending ratios and through them as well as via its direct effects the subsequent year's GDP growth. In theory there exists feedback from the induced change in the current balance to the Marshall Plan allotment; in practice, the coefficients in question are so small that they can be ignored.

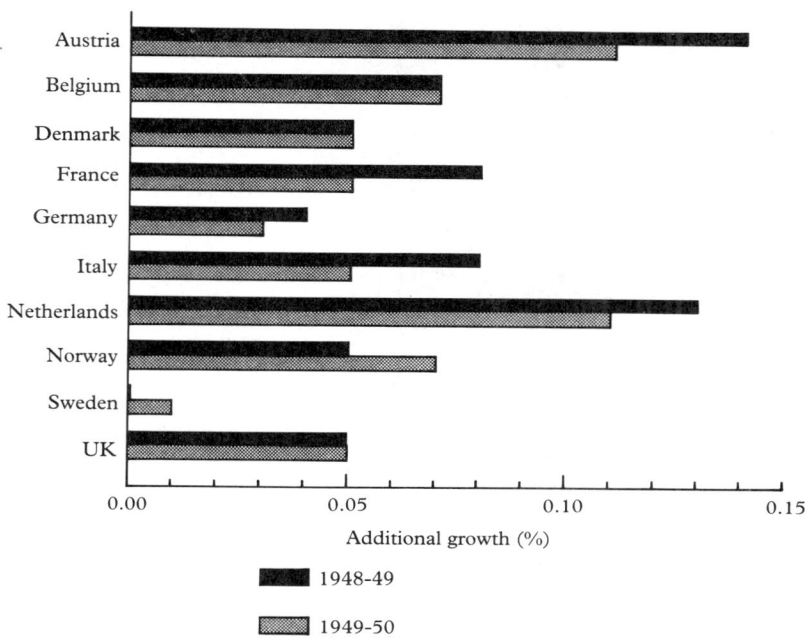

Figure 4. Additional output growth due to the Marshall Plan, including only investment, current account and government spending linkages

Sweden, which received the least (because of the linearity assumed for all equations).

3.5. Is something missing?

Is it correct to assume that the Marshall Plan operated exclusively through the savings, current account and fiscal gaps? To explore the possibility that other channels were also operative, the growth equations have been re-estimated with two modifications. The first one is to include the Marshall Plan allotment directly, to capture other effects of the Marshall Plan not operating through investment, the current account and public spending. The second modification is to interact (i.e. pre-multiply) investment, the current account and government spending with the Marshall Plan allotment. This allows for the possibility that these additional effects opeated most powerfully where investment was low, the current-account deficit was large, or government spending was constrained. The first modification resulted in statistically significant effects: countries receiving large Marshall Plan allotments grew faster, even after controlling for investment and other determinants of growth. The second modification further shows that this direct effect was largest

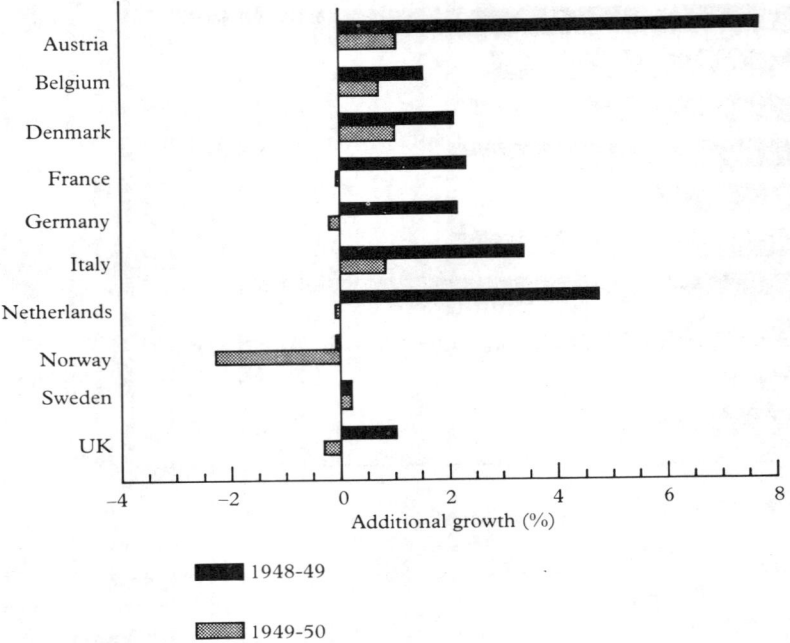

Figure 5. Additional output growth due to the Marshall Plan, including investment, current account and government spending linkages and interaction effects

where investment, the current-account surplus and government spending as shares of GNP were low. The conclusion is that the Marshall Plan mainly operated by means other than altering levels of investment, the current account and government spending.

Figure 5 shows the results of simulations when all channels are allowed to operate. The effects of the Marshall Plan, especially in 1948–49, are an order of magnitude larger than before. Austria, which received Marshall aid equalling 7% of GNP in 1948, grew as a result by an additional 7 percentage points between 1948 and 1949. In Austria, France, Germany, Denmark and the Netherlands, the rate of return on US aid in 1948 was on the order of 100% even if none of the effects lingered! These simulations suggest very large effects of the Marshall Plan. But if those effects did not operate by changing the levels of investment, the current account or public spending, what did they reflect?

4. The Marshall Plan and the marketing crisis

The association of the Marshall Plan with this dramatic burst of growth reflected contributions neglected by the three-gap model and the traditional literature described above. By encouraging the restoration of financial stability and policy reforms allowing the free play of market forces, the Marshall Plan resolved the marketing crisis into which the European economy had sunk. It did so by addressing two problems: shortages due to repressed inflation, and policy uncertainty that prompted producers to delay the delivery of their goods.

4.1. Shortages and repressed inflation

The plight of the European economy in 1947 is best understood as a marketing crisis akin to that afflicting the Republics today. Prices were controlled at unsustainably low levels, encouraging hoarding and inducing producers to withold their goods from market. In France, the interim Blum Government and the Ramadier Government that succeeded it imposed the so-called *baisse Blum*: they rolled back prices by 5% at the beginning of 1947 and froze them at that level, and then mandated another 5% price decline in March. In other countries, controls and rationing, while not universal, were still pervasive. At the end of 1948, bread was rationed in 14 of 21 European countries, butter in 15, meat in 15, sugar in 15, coffee in 12, tobacco in 5, coal in 11, textiles in 11 and gasoline in 14 (UN, 1950). While prompting the growth of black markets, controls discouraged transactions at official prices. The monetary overhang, resulting from the fact that money supplies had increased more rapidly than prices, threatened renewed inflation at any time. With budget deficits deep in deficit, investors were hesitant to purchase government bonds. Inflation consequently threatened to become an explosive spiral rather than a one-time event. Anticipating that prices were soon to rise and that financial assets might lose their purchasing power, producers had every incentive to hoard commodities rather than delivering them to market. Farmers refused to market their produce so long as prices were restricted to artificially low levels. With their receipts vulnerable to inflation, they were better off feeding grain to their livestock. The post-World War II food shortage in many European countries reflected not just bad weather in 1947 but the reluctance of farmers to deliver food to the cities.[9] The manufactured goods farmers might have purchased remained in short supply. Industrial enterprises had the same incentive to hoard inventories. So long as these shortages persisted, workers had little reason to devote their full effort to market work. There is no better way to substantiate

---

[9] Compare the *Financial Times* on 21 August 1991, describing the situation in the USSR. 'The state and cooperative farms, learning from last year, are now keeping their grain in store until the state is willing to pay almost any price to get it.' Lloyd (1991).

this point that to quote a neglected passage from Marshall's (1947) Harvard speech itself:

'There is a phase of this matter which is both interesting and serious. The farmer has always produced the foodstuffs to exchange with the city dweller for the other necessities of life. This division of labour is the basis of modern civilization. At the present time it is threatened with breakdown. The town and city industries are not producing adequate goods to exchange with the food producing farmer . . . The farmer or the peasant cannot find the goods for sale which he desires to purchase. So the sale of his farm produce for money which he cannot use seems to him an unprofitable transaction. He, therefore, has withdrawn many fields from crop cultivation and is using them for grazing. He feeds more grain to stock . . . Meanwhile, people in the cities are short of food and fuel . . .'

Many other examples could be cited on 5 January 1947, the *New York Times* noted that 'It has been a fact for some time that [French] peasants have not been delivering their products to market because of lack of confidence in the money they would get for them.' In its issue of 1 March 1947, *The Economist* commented that the 'main enemy' of French policy-makers was the French farmer, 'whose distrust of his currency makes him loth [sic] to send his produce to market – or at least to the controlled market.'[10] Its issue of 18 October 1947 reported that:

'For more than two months now Parisians have been eating yellow bread. Despite the substantial tonnages of wheat imported into France since the autumn of 1946 and the long prewar years of development towards a position of self-sufficiency in wheat, France has not been forced to turn to maize, and the French officials are seeking large imports of cereals again during the next twelve months . . . One reason for this position is found in the weather of last winter and spring; another in the shortage of tractors, horses and implements. But perhaps the most important reason lies in French policies on prices and control of marketing during the last few years.'

The article then discusses how French wheat prices were kept below world price levels, how the policy of controlling the prices of consumer goods had greatly increased the nominal purchasing power of working-class wages, but how this caused foodstuffs to be in short supply. 'The

[10] *New York Times* (5 January 1947); *The Economist* (1 March 1947). For a French government account to a remarkably similar effect, see INSEE (1958).

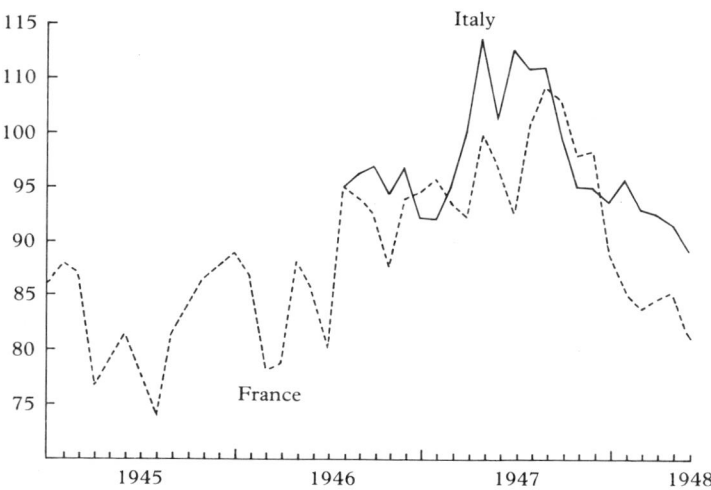

Figure 6. Relative price of food in Italy and France, January 1945–June 1948

Notes: August 1946=100. Wholesale prices for France, retail prices for Italy.

peasant, unable to purchase consumer goods and losing confidence in the currency, eats more himself and feeds wheat to his animals.'[11]

Four separate bodies of evidence support this interpretation. First, the behaviour of food prices is consistent with the view that producers were withholding goods from the market. Farmers, as described above, had exceptional scope for responding to shortages of consumer goods and the threat of inflation by holding back produce and feeding it to their livestock. In both France and Italy the relative price of foodstuffs consequently rose during the period of shortage and financial chaos, but fell during the stabilization. Figure 6 shows that much of the rise in food prices in France occurred *before* the cold winter of 1946–47, as if the problem was more hoarding than prospects of a poor harvest. In both countries the relative price of food fell following the announcement of the Marshall Plan, even though it is hard to find any evidence of 'news' about the harvest.

Second, the recovery of perishable and nonperishable agricultural products supports the interpretation. Grain and potato supplies recovered more quickly than those of meat, as farmers held off slaughtering their livestock. The output of meat remained depressed, even

[11] *The Economist* (26 July 1947). Or, as the *New York Times* (1 January 1949) had put it at the beginning of the year, expectations that prices would have to rise 'caused peasants to withold non-perishable products from the market, and led consumers to spend recklessly in anticipation of further price rises'.

though by early 1947 over much of Europe cattle were as numerous as before the war.[12]

Third, though the prevalence of controls was greatest on foodstuffs, other prices were also controlled, leading firms to hoard stocks. In Italy, the value of inventories rose by 2 bn. lire in 1946 and by 9 bn. lire in 1947, but declined by 1 bn. lire in 1948 (Casella and Eichengreen, 1991, Table 4). In France and Britain inventories of virtually every major good for which data on stocks are available declined following announcement of the Marshall Plan.[13]

Fourth and finally, governments' own policies substantiate the picture of unsustainably low prices giving rise to shortages. In France, Ramadier attacked speculators who were hoarding stocks and withholding goods from the market. He attempted to use the National Council of Credit, a body controlling the nationalized banks, to deny loans to holders of excessive stocks.

4.2. Policy uncertainty and the value of waiting

A dramatic change in the economic environment was imminent, but uncertainty about its nature remained pervasive. The immediate post-war period in many European countries was marked by protracted disputes between the Centre–Right and Left. In Italy, for example, the Liberals and Christian Democrats favoured fiscal discipline and aboli-tion of subsidies and price controls, while the Socialists and Communists favoured capital taxation and extensive social spending. Italian govern-ment was by coalition, and until May 1947 Communist ministers con-trolled the budget. This did not make likely cuts in social spending to balance the budget. At the same time, parliamentary representatives of the propertied classes had sufficient leverage to block initiatives designed to balance the budget through confiscatory capital taxation.

In France, coalition governments were 'perpetually subjected to both political and economic pressures from different sections of the popula-tion, whose demands were often equally urgent and at the same time

---

[12] As the *New York Times* reported of the situation in France on 3 February 1947, 'It is said that cattle are now as numerous as before the war but the situation is such that the producers do not wish to sell. In the first place, they are dissatisfied with controlled prices. Second, as fodder is abundant, they can keep their stock. Third, they have lost confidence in the currency. The uncertainty on future prices and the lack of fertilizer and farm machinery cause the peasant to keep his animals or sell to the black market.'

[13] The only noteworthy exception is stocks of virgin copper. Data on British inventories are from the CSO's *Monthly Business Statistics* (various issues). Data for France are from Bournay *et al.* (1978).

totally irreconcilable' (Pickles, 1953). Having won 185 seats in the 1946 elections, the French Communists were the single largest party in the Assembly. The Socialists occupied an intermediate position between the Communists on the one hand and the Radicals and the clerical party, the Mouvement Republicain Populaire, on the other. Like their Italian counterparts, the French Socialists were 'committed to a directed economy and increased wages for hard-hit workers, while the Radical Socialists have campaigned for moving as rapidly as possible toward freedom of enterprise. . . .' (US Department of State, 1948a). To balance the budget, the left-wing parties favoured a capital levy, their more moderate counterparts cuts in social spending.

Uncertainty surrounding the outcome of this struggle increased the option value of waiting. Investors were reluctant to buy securities, not knowing whether they would be taxed away. Creditors were reluctant to loan money for any length of time, not knowing whether its value would be inflated away. Workers were reluctant to commit to training or apprenticeship programmes or to accept positions in which compensation was deferred, not knowing whether the structure of pay would be changed and job security would be threatened. Absenteeism was rampant.

Alexander (1991) documents the debilitating effects of policy uncertainty in Germany. In the immediate post-war years, uncertainty emanated from the policies of the Allied occupiers, whose goals included dismantling factories that had been integral to Germany's war effort and breaking up the cartels and combines that had been central to the highly-concentrated industrial sector. Until it was known which factories would be dismantled and which firms would be 'deconcentrated', investors held back. Moreover, until it was known whether the lead in the Bizone would be taken by the free-market-oriented US or by the British, whose Labour Government was nationalizing industry at home, property rights remained uncertain. Until the blockade of Berlin, there was even the possibility that Germany's post-war reconstruction would take place only after the four occupied zones had been reunited, which would have spread Soviet influence to the Western zones and lengthened the shadow over private property. Subsequently, however, uncertainty emanated from the clouded political outlook. The largest single German political party, the Social Democrats, advocated nationalization and the maintenance of controls. Its principal opponent, the Christian Democratic Union, preferred a market economy with a social safety net. Which party would dominate was far from clear. As American officials observed, this uncertainty about the nature of the regime created 'a general hesitancy to make any decisions at all' (cited in Alexander, 1991).

4.3. Resolving the crisis

Solving the crisis was straightforward. Prices had to be decontrolled to coax producers to bring their goods to market. Inflation had to be halted for the price mechanism to operate smoothly. Wage demands had to be moderated to relax the profit squeeze on firms and remove demands for government subsidies. Budgets had to be balanced to reduce inflationary pressure. With financial stability restored and market forces given free rein, individuals could direct their attention to market work.

If the solution was clear, why then was it not adopted? The economic model that best answers this question is the war-of-attrition model of Alesina and Drazen (1989). The idea is as follows. Suppose that the sum of notional demands for the national income exceeds 100% and that government is the residual claimant for money income. Demands for transfers exceed the taxes the government can collect. The budget deficit is financed by printing money, and open or repressed inflation results. Now assume that the burden of stabilization, in the form of policies reducing some group's share of the national income, is unevenly distributed. The group conceding first incurs the larger share of the costs. If rival factions differ in their ability to shoulder the costs of inflation and shortages, yet are uncertain about the cost-bearing capacity of the others, each will refuse to concede, hoping to outlast the others. Over time, the costs of inflation and/or shortages rise, and with them the perceived probability that the other factions are in fact more patient. Ultimately, those least able to bear the costs concede, and stabilization occurs. Even if inflation is finally halted by the adoption of policies identical to those deemed unacceptable initially, delay is rational. Different groups still have an incentive to hold out as long as the costs of stabilization are borne unevenly and there is uncertainty about the staying power of their rivals. Until they concede, the probability that others will concede first and bear the costs of stabilization is sufficient to justify the ongoing loss from inflation and shortages.

The distributional nature of the post-war crisis is clearest in the case of France. Successive strike waves punctuated calendar year 1947. When the *baisse Blum* failed to hold, a strike broke out in the Renault works, attracting the support first of the CGT and then of the Communist Party. When the Communist ministers urged the Ramadier Government to reverse its opposition to the strikes, Ramadier dismissed them. The critical question was whether the Socialists would also oppose the policy of pressure for wage moderation, or agree for the first time to support a government that did not include the Communists. Having suffered inflation and financial turmoil for nearly two years, they finally gave in. Real wages then fell continuously through 1950 and unemployment rose, together reflecting labour's acceptance of a smaller distributional share.

Similarly, by the spring of 1947 Italian political leaders agreed that open and repressed inflation were out of control, but they disagreed on policies with which to redress it. The Left favoured credit controls to squeeze the speculators regarded as responsible for the inflation, while the Right favoured fiscal austerity. In April–May 1947 Alcide de Gasperi, the Christian Democratic leader and Italian premier, dissolved the existing coalition and formed a minority government that survived with the support of the small parties. This new government represented a clear shift to the right. The Communists moderated their opposition, hoping that they might be able to re-enter the government in the future. de Gasperi imposed a variety of austerity measures, and unemployment rose dramatically, again reflecting the extent to which the costs were borne by the Left.

Thus, solving the marketing crisis was a problem of political economy, not just a problem of economics. As *The Economist* put it in a discussion of the crisis in France, 'Strictly speaking, the economic answer to all these problems is known – to increase taxation, to ensure investment, to cut state expenditure, to balance the budget and to restore confidence in the franc. But the political answer is one that has eluded Frenchmen for the last 30 years' (*The Economist*, 26 July 1947).

The Marshall Plan played a critical role in ending the war of attrition. It did not obviate the need for sacrifice. But it increased the size of the pie available for division among competing interest groups. Two-and-a-half percent – Marshall aid as a share of recipient-country GNP – was not an overwhelmingly large change in the size of the pie. But if the sum of notional demands exceeded aggregate supply by 5 or 7.5%, Marshall Plan transfers could reduce the sacrifices required of competing distributional interests by a third or a half. They could significantly reduce the costs of compromise relative to the benefits.

In both France and Italy, announcement of the Marshall Plan was accompanied by the exit of Communist ministers from the governing coalition and by the adoption of tax increases and expenditure reductions designed to move the budget toward balance. Subsidies on consumer goods were reduced. Workers moderated their demands for higher wages and government transfers. With the elimination of repressed inflation, goods returned to the market. This role for the Marshall Plan was acknowledged by contemporaries. In July 1947, less than two months after Marshall's Harvard speech, *The Economist* (26 July) noted that the workers were tiring of political strikes and that the unions of the Left were showing new signs of moderation:

'In theory, the economic assistance possible under a Marshall Plan might turn the scale between stability and further disintegration next winter. American assistance could pursue a double policy in attacking the basic problem – lack of confidence in the franc. The provision of dollars or gold could underpin the currency and imports of consumer goods, could begin to create a corrective process by tempting food and goods [to] market, restoring the purchasing power of wages and increasing the incentive to produce more.'

It was not inevitable, of course, that the nations of Western Europe would accept this bargain. Marshall aid was offered to Eastern Europe and even to the USSR. Moscow's rejection of the offer can be understood as unwillingness to allow the US to sidetrack its progress along the road of central planning. It is critical to acknowledge that the prices the US charged for its aid was a price that Western Europe might have paid for its own sake in any event. Support for the market was already widespread; the Marshall Plan only tipped the balance.

5. The role of conditionality

The conditions attached to American aid maximized the likelihood of this outcome. Yet some conditions were more effective than others. American demands that European governments meet specific fiscal and monetary targets were less successful than pressure for price liberalization and economic integration. A number of techniques were used to achieve these ends. First, each recipient was required to sign a bilateral pact with the US agreeing to balance government budgets, restore internal financial stability and stabilize exchange rates at realistic levels. Second, each expenditure of Marshall Plan funds had to be negotiated with the American authorities, a process which afforded the ECA opportunity to influence domestic policy. (For example, the Americans reacted to increasing British government involvement in housing construction by cutting Marshall Plan lumber imports.) Third, for each dollar of Marshall aid, the recipient government was required to place a matching amount of domestic currency in a counterpart fund to be used for purposes approved by the US. Each dollar of Marshall Plan aid thus gave the donor control over two dollars' worth of real resources. In many instances, the US insisted that these funds be used to buttress financial stability by retiring public debt. (See Table 5.) In others, the US authorities prevented the European government from making any use of its counterpart funds at all.

US pressure also operated informally. Marshall Plan administrators took a variety of *ad hoc* steps to encourage price decontrol and

Table 5. MSA/ECA approvals for withdrawal of European Counterpart Funds available for country use, by purpose and country, cumulative, 3 April 1948–30 June 1952 (Dollar equivalents of local currencies, in mn. US$).

Country	Total for production	Promotion of production					
		Electric, gas and other power	Transportation and communications	Agriculture	Manufacturing	Mining	Other production
Total	4,466.3	1,025.5	957.5	817.6	681.7	481.8	502.2
Denmark	62.4	0.6	2.8	11.2	6.7	—	41.1
France	1,925.6	738.4	294.2	234.1	249.2	340.6	69.1
Germany	753.7	182.6	86.8	70.7	218.7	91.8	103.1
Italy	823.8	1.0	348.9	204.8	22.6	—	246.5
Netherlands	212.8	—	13.6	166.5	32.3	—	0.4
Norway	8.4	—	2.7	—	—	5.7	—
Turkey	51.0	0.6	13.9	15.2	8.0	14.7	4.6
UK	2.2	—	—	0.2	—	—	2.0

Country	Monetary and financial stability	For other purposes			Total approved for withdrawal
		Housing and public buildings	Construction production procurement	Other	
Total	2,583.3	757.5	460.9	373.3	8,651.3
Denmark	130.1	—	9.4	2.2	204.1
France	171.4	314.4	283.9	7.5	2,702.8
Germany	—	97.7	—	157.7	1,009.1
Italy	—	172.7	—	45.9	1,042.4
Netherlands	197.4	88.1	46.3	3.0	547.6
Norway	292.7	—	—	—	301.1
Turkey	—	—	60.4	11.0	128.4
UK	1,706.7	—	47.5	6.4	1,762.8

Adapted from Table C-12, p. 13, Mutual Security Agency, *Report to Congress*, December 1952 (seven smaller countries' approvals not shown). Drawn from Mayer (1969), p. 87.

Box 3. The mechanics of the Marshall Plan

The bill passed by Congress authorized US assistance to Europe for four years but insisted that appropriations take place annually. The package authorized $5.3 bn. for the first year, which approximated the Administration's request of $6.8 bn. for 15 months. Congress specified that assistance could take the form of either grants or loans, but placed a ceiling on the loan component of the programme ($1 bn. in the first year). Subject to these limitations, the European Cooperation Agency (ECA) Administrator, heading an independent agency, was authorized to procure commodities and services from all sources for countries in need and to defray the cost of their transportation. The Administrator was instructed to curtail the procurement of American goods in short supply and to encourage the use of surplus stocks. In the case of surplus agricultural commodities, procurement was restricted to the US. When requesting the shipment of foreign merchandise, governments or nationals of the participating countries submitted procurement authorization requests to the ECA. Applications were reviewed to determine whether or not they exceeded the country's allotment, whether they satisfied the criteria set down by the Act, and for their effect on the US economy. Upon approval the ECA issued a letter of commitment to a cooperating bank guaranteeing ECA reimbursement of the credit extended. After the recipient of the merchandise, usually a government agency deposited a matching amount of local currency to a so-called counterpart account, it was able to draw on the credit established in the US.

The US State Department set the interim allocations for the first two ERP quarters (April–September 1948) but insisted that participating governments do so subsequently. For 1948 two US government studies had estimated the dollar deficits of European countries at $5.3 bn. The participating countries, when polled, objected that this figure understated their prospective deficits. In the event, it soon became apparent that Congress would appropriate only $4.9 bn. The OEEC was instructed to reduce country requests so as to produce a total not to exceed the appropriation. That it was able to submit recommendations in September 1948 that were accepted by all member countries but Greece and Turkey was a remarkable achievement. The excess dollar deficit was eliminated by shifting planned imports from the US to non-dollar sources. Priority was given to aid requests that would finance imports of consumption goods needed to keep living standards at 1947 levels, of raw materials needed to keep industry running at existing levels, and of capital equipment and raw materials that would stimulate the production of dollar-earning or dollar-saving commodities. In preparing the second set of allocation requests for 1949–50, the OEEC asked participating countries to assume a reduced level of funding. Its January 1949 submission requested \$4.4 bn. Congress appropriated \$3.7 bn. In August 1949 the OEEC appointed a committee to distribute the shortfall. ECA allotments were cut for all countries except Sweden and Iceland, with some participants (Germany and Belgium) suffering disproportionately. The negotiations were sufficiently difficult that it was decided to divide aid for the third year in the proportions established by the second allocation.

In the early stages of the programme most countries used ECA funds to import foodstuffs and other essential materials. This conformed to American wishes: the ECA's April 1948 order on operating policies and procedures specified that initial procurement should concentrate on food, fuel and fertilizer. But it had also urged participating countries to emphasize the procurement of commodities needed to facilitate industrial and agricultural production. With the recovery of domestic production, ECA aid was used increasingly to finance the importation of capital equipment for investment projects.

---

discourage nationalization. For example, they viewed with alarm British schemes for unifying and nationalizing the coal industries of the Ruhr, then part of the British zone of occupation. Such schemes were dropped once ECA administrators made their opposition known. Similarly, Hoffman lobbied against the nationalization of the British steel industry and at least delayed this eventuality. Washington, D.C. also pressed continuously for economic integration. Each aid recipient was required to develop a schedule for liberalizing its foreign trade. The recipient governments were forced to decide among themselves the international allocation of US aid and to coordinate their national recovery programmes so as to ensure that their combined current-account deficits *vis-a-vis* the dollar area did not exceed the aid the US was willing to make available. Their discussions, in conjunction with US pressure, led to the formation of the CEEC and the OEEC, way-stations along the route to the Schuman Plan, the European Payments Union and the EEC.

The question is how successful US conditionality ultimately proved to be. While much of the older literature (e.g. Price, 1955; Arkes, 1972) uncritically accepts the importance of conditionality, some recent revisionists (e.g. Esposito, 1985, Wall, 1991) dismiss it as ineffectual. In part, this dispute reflects the different countries and issues upon which these authors focus. That there were limits on what could be achieved by conditionality is apparent even from the bilateral agreements that

Table 6. US conditionality in France, 1948–50

Quarter	American demand	French response
1948-I	Refrain from inflationary finance.	Fix 200 bn. franc ceiling on Bank of France advances.
1948-II	Eliminate budget deficit, end use of Bank of France advances to cover budget deficit.	None.
1948-III	Eliminate budget deficit, end use of Bank of France advances to cover budget deficit.	Increase taxes on tobacco, and income, increase postal rates, impose credit controls.
1948-IV	Pass balanced budget for 1949, maintain credit controls.	Reduce ceiling on Bank of France advances to 175 bn. francs, limit government expenditure.
1949-I	None.	None.
1949-II	Eliminate prospective 100 bn. franc budget deficit.	Increase gasoline tax.
1949-III	None.	None.
1949-IV	Eliminate prospective 120 bn. franc budget deficit, do not increase ceiling on Bank of France advances.	New taxes imposed, capital controls maintained, advances ceiling left unchanged.
1950	Invest 20 bn. francs in low cost housing.	20 bn. francs invested in low income housing.

were a prerequisite for the receipt of aid. These agreements were the subject of protracted negotiations. London and Paris acceded to American demands to control the allocation of counterpart funds but resisted giving Washington control over their monetary and fiscal policies. An American-authored provision allowing the IMF to veto European exchange rate changes was eliminated. So was a provision that would have given the US first call on strategic materials possessed by the recipients. American demands for measures to balance budgets and restrict domestic credit creation also led to extended negotiations and, sometimes, political crises. Repeatedly, the US demanded tax increases, expenditure reductions and new restrictions on domestic credit creation. It threatened to impound counterpart funds unless these steps were taken. Table 6 shows the course of Franco-American negotiations over French macroeconomic policies. Strictly speaking, the US failed to achieve its stated targets. Not only was there no quarter in which the US target was fully met, but there was no quarter in which release of counterpart funds was actually suspended.

Yet if the ECA's stated target is viewed as the opening bid, there is reason to think that conditionality still had some effect. Stated targets were not achieved, but concessions were obtained. French budget deficits were smaller and monetary policies were less inflationary than they would have been otherwise. Analysis of a variety of episodes leads to this conclusion. For example, in the autumn of 1948, when the US threatened to withhold counterpart funds, Prime Minister Henri Queuille moved to impose new taxes and to raise the prices of transport, postage and tobacco. The *loi des maxima* of December 1948 did much to stabilize the French public finances (Wall, 1991). Although the Americans were not fully satisfied with the outcome, it is likely that more movement in the direction of budget balance occurred than would have in the absence of American intervention.

In other countries, American conditionality operated more powerfully. In Italy, counterpart releases were delayed. Italian economic policy was modified. As James Clement Dunn, the American ambassador to Italy, put it, 'He who controls the so-called lire fund will control the monetary and fiscal, and in fact the entire economic policy of Italy' (cited in Hogan, 1987). In Greece, the US withheld the release of counterpart funds because it felt that the economy was operating under excessive pressure of demand. American control over economic policy was extensive. The treaties signed in conjunction with the extension of Marshall aid explicitly gave the US supervisory powers over domestic as well as foreign resources. The treaties 'ensured that no economic or military decision of any consequence could be taken by the Greek Government without the prior approval or consent of the US Administration or its representatives in Athens' (Freris, 1986).

What accounts for these different outcomes? American conditionality was least effective in countries that were strong fiscally and large economically. France and the UK were in a stronger fiscal position than Greece. France's fiscal position was more tenuous than the UK's, but her economy was large and therefore critical to European recovery. French officials, aware of this fact, played this card to their advantage. The UK's fiscal position was sufficiently secure that she required no counterpart releases for investment in housing or industrial investment. Brown and Opie (1953) conclude that countries like the UK utilizing counterpart funds to retire public debt eluded the influence of the ECA, but that for other countries counterpart releases gave US administrators significant leverage. Regression analysis supports this speculation. We added to the basic growth equation estimated in Appendix C counterpart funds withdrawn for 'productive purposes' (the ECA term for funds spent on investment or the purchase of inputs). We found that a Marshall Plan allotment of 2% GNP would have raised output by 4.6% in the next year if and only if the matching 2% of GNP was withdrawn from the counterpart accounts for use in production.

Otherwise, output would have risen not by 4.6% but by 0.3%.[14] Clearly, US decisions regarding the counterpart accounts mattered for recipient-country welfare and endowed US policy-makers with leverage.

Where political support was closely divided between Left and Right, extreme monetary and fiscal austerity might undermine Socialist support for moderate governments, leading to their downfall and playing into the hands of the Communist Party. This was especially true when austerity measures could be blamed on American interference. French politicians invoked this danger repeatedly. They warned that acceptance of American demands would lead to the government's downfall, and the Americans moderated their demands. In contrast, in countries where centrist governments were more firmly entrenched, the threat that conditionality would create political instability was less credible.

If the overall record of conditionality regarding fiscal and monetary policy was mixed, informal pressure for market liberalization and economic integration was more successful. These more abstract principles were less intimately connected to the public purse. Their distributional consequences were less transparent. Hence they were less likely to occasion a government's downfall or provoke complaints of American intervention. As a condition for receiving Marshall aid, each country was required to develop a programme for removing quotas and other trade controls. Even where domestic markets were highly concentrated, competition could be injected via international trade. Government intervention and other efforts to interfere with the operation of markets would be disciplined by foreign competition. American insistence that aid recipients coordinate their national recovery programmes led to regular meetings of the OEEC and to increasingly frequent bilateral consultations. They culminated in the creation of the Coal and Steel Community and the European Payments Union.

6. Enduring effects

The evidence presented so far indicates that the Marshall Plan *initiated* Europe's recovery from World War II earlier than otherwise. Less certain is whether US aid had a *permanent* impact on the level of output. In principle, both outcomes are possible. In traditional growth theory (in the tradition of Solow) diminishing returns to capital imply that it is impossible to increase permanently the capital/labour ratio. The steady-state level of output per capita depends exclusively on parameters

---

[14] This example considers, for simplicity, a country whose investment, current account and government spending ratios are zero. Some of this growth would have been given back in the succeeding year: see Appendix C for further details.

like the population growth rate, the rate of time preference and the rate of technological change. Since there is no reason why an injection of foreign aid should affect any of these parameters, there is no reason why it should permanently affect the level of output. If the aid arrives when the capital/labour ratio is below normal levels, then the fact that some part of the transfer is invested will allow the capital/labour ratio and output per person to rise toward their steady-state values faster than otherwise. But since their ultimate destination is unchanged, faster growth initially implies slower growth subsequently. The impact of aid on the *level* of output is temporary. In contrast, in endogenous growth theory (following Romer, 1990) there are no diminishing returns to capital so that a one-time injection of foreign aid may raise permanently the capital/labour ratio, and therefore output and savings proportionately. The higher capital/labour ratio can be fully financed with higher savings, so that the level of output can remain higher permanently. A temporary injection of foreign aid can have a positive initial impact on growth without being subsequently reversed.

To separate out these two hypotheses, we analysed quarterly data on industrial production and receipts of US foreign aid from 1948 through 1955 for the 10 principal beneficiaries of the Marshall Plan. The time pattern of foreign aid effects is captured by three lags. The results showed a positive impact effect followed by a negative subsequent effect. The three lagged terms summed to zero.[15] According to this evidence, recovery commenced earlier than it would have otherwise, but the Marshall Plan did not have enduring effects.

Still, one wonders whether American aid had enduring effects of a subtler nature. Perhaps the Marshall Plan permanently affected European economic growth in ways that did not materialize at the time of foreign aid receipts. (If so, its enduring effects would not be captured by our econometric techniques.) This would be the case, for example, if the Marshall Plan provided the solution to a coordination problem.

---

[15] Industrial production was expressed in logs, foreign aid in real terms by converting it into local currency and deflating it by the consumer price index. The countries were Austria, Belgium, Denmark, France, Germany, Italy, the Netherlands, Norway, Sweden and the UK; the sample period was 1948Q4 through 1955Q4. The coefficients on the three lags of foreign aid were constrained to be the same across countries but the constant and three lags of industrial production were allowed to differ across countries. A typical estimate (for Austria) was (with *t*-statistics in parentheses):

$$IP = 0.56 + 0.74\ IP(-1) + 1.58\ IP(-2) - 1.44\ IP(-3)$$
$$\quad (0.12)\ (0.28) \qquad (0.59) \qquad (0.62)$$

$$\quad + 0.22\ FA(-1) - 0.17\ FA(-2) - 0.02\ FA(-3)$$
$$\quad (3.23) \qquad (2.78) \qquad (0.42)$$

$$DW = 2.00$$

Imagine that European labour and management were faced with choosing between two equilibria after World War II. In one – the interwar equilibrium – each faction tried to maximize its current share of national income. Intense distributional struggles would have produced wage inflation, a profit squeeze, low levels of investment and lagging productivity. In the other – the post-war equilibrium – all parties agreed to trade current compensation for faster longer-term growth and ultimately for higher living standards. Workers deferred their wage demands, management its demands for higher profits. Higher investment and faster productivity growth ensued, ultimately rendering everyone better of.[16] The second equilibrium may not arise without some form of coordination. Indeed if workers press for higher wages, management has little incentive to plough back earnings in expectation of higher future profits. If management fails to plough back profits, workers have little incentive to moderate wage demands in return for the promise of higher future living standards. If workers and management in some sectors refuse to follow policies of moderation, reducing the supply of investible funds to the economy, those in other sectors have less incentive to do so.

The Marshall Plan could have shifted Europe from one equilibrium to the other. Until 1948, European labour-management relations were conflictual. Pressures for real wage increases were intense. At that point, the Marshall Plan administrators urged European unions and governments to focus on raising productivity rather than current compensation (Maier, 1977). They pressed governments to adopt a variety of investment-friendly policies (Esposito, 1985). European nations had an incentive to shift to the high-investment, deferred-compensation equilibrium in order to obtain Marshall aid. Once there, they had no reason to deviate.

The two most prominent features of the dramatic acceleration in European growth that began in 1948 and lasted for more than two decades – high investment rates and wage moderation – are consistent with this interpretation. The investment share of GNP in Europe was nearly twice as high as it had been between the wars (Table 7). Labour's share of national income was stable or falling. Workers consciously allowed real wage increases to lag behind productivity to provide the incentives and resources for investment. In Britain, for instance, the Trades Union Congress cooperated with management and with the

---

[16] This is how some historians view the high growth of the first post-World War II decades. For example, Maier (1981) concludes, 'For society as a whole, the politics of productivity meant simply the adjournment of conflicts over the percentage of national income for the rewards of future economic growth.'

Table 7. Non-residential fixed investment as percent of GNP at current prices

	1920–38	Average of ratios for years cited	
		1950–60	1960–70
Austria	6.1[a]	16 4	20.2
Belgium		12 4	15.5
Denmark	8.9	14 0	16.9
Finland		19 6	20.0
France	11.8	13 7	17.4
Germany	9.7	16.1	19.3
Greece	7.5[b]	11.7	18.2
Ireland		13.1	15.1
Italy	13.6	15.1	14.5
Netherlands		18.0	20.3
Norway	12.4	23.7[c]	23.8[c]
Sweden	10.5	15.5	17.3
Switzerland		14.1	20.0
UK	5.7	11.6	14.2
Average for Western Europe	9.6	15.4	18.1

[a] 1924–37.
[b] 1929–38.
[c] Includes some elements of repair and maintenance excluded by other countries.
Source: Maddison (1976), p. 487.

Conservative governments that ruled from 1951 through 1964, deliberately moderating their wage claims (Flanagan *et al.*, 1983). In the Netherlands, unions allowed wages to lag behind productivity in the 1950s 'so that industry could earn profits which would pay for expansion and modernization of the productive apparatus' (a quote from a *union publication,* cited in Windmuller, 1969). Industrial relations specialists like Barkin (1983) lay great stress on this growth-oriented consensus. Of course, other explanations exist for the high investment rates and labour-market flexibility that characterized Europe's first two post-war decades.[17] But the fact that dramatic shifts in the pattern of investment and in labour market conduct both surfaced during the Marshall Plan years lends credence to the idea that the American programme contributed to solving a coordination problem.

---

[17] International monetary stability and the absence of major supply shocks are two popular explanations for high investment in this period (Boltho, 1982). Similarly, the availability of elastic supplies of underemployed labour in Europe's rural sector, in conjunction with the influx of refugees from Eastern Europe and guestworkers from the Continent's southeast, may have enhanced labour market flexibility (Kindleberger, 1967).

7. Implications for Eastern Europe and the former USSR

Are conditions like those that made the Marshall Plan a success present in Eastern Europe and the Republics today? Consider first the Republics' predicament. As in Europe in 1947/48, ceilings on food prices are discouraging cultivators from bringing their produce to market.[18] As in Europe in 1947/48, the traditional division of labour between town and country has broken down; not just the fuel, fertilizer and tractors required for agricultural production but the televisions and refrigerators offered as incentives to farmers have not been made available. Shortages of consumer goods are increasingly pervasive, as enterprises hold back stocks in anticipation of higher prices once controls are relaxed. Workers hold back effort until policy uncertainty is resolved.[19] Excess liquidity and government budget deficits create the spectre of rampant inflation.

As in post-war Europe, foreign aid could help in principle to resolve these problems. Support for living standards could contain public opposition to economic reform if output falls during the transition to a market economy. Hard currency would enable the Republics to import much-needed equipment from the West or, better still, from its Eastern European neighbours. Reserves of foreign exchange would enable the authorities to stabilize the ruble once it is rendered convertible.

On the other hand, very important differences weaken – in our view, seriously – the case for a Marshall Plan for the Republics. In post-war Europe there existed widespread support for the market economy. The Marshall Plan only tipped the balance. The social contract upon which the subsequent generation of prosperity was based was a compromise between positions that were only a moderate distance apart. Hence a modest side payment could make the difference between chaos and stability. The same is not true of the Republics today. Powerful elements in government and the military – certainly not all of which were eliminated by the failure of the August 1991 coup – oppose serious economic reform. Much of the public understands only dimly what a free market entails. The choice is not between a heavily regulated mixed economy and a lightly regulated mixed economy, or between a distributionally neutral fiscal system and a moderately redistributive fisc, but between

---

[18] 'It is the farmers' decision to hang on to their grain, rather than any absolute shortage, which as much as anything underlies the latest US estimates that the Soviet Union will this year need to import 37 mn. tonnes of grain.' Nicholson *et al.* (1991).

[19] Consider the following first-hand description of the situation in Lithuanian agriculture. 'Since independence nobody at the Kolkhoz wants to work. Everyone is waiting. Production is falling. We do not know what is going to happen.' (Ignatieff, 1991).

public and private property and between prices and commands. With the cleavage between views so pronounced, it is unlikely that a limited amount of foreign aid would significantly speed the emergence of a consensus favouring rapid liberalization. In post-war Europe, the administration of US aid encouraged the reductions in government spending needed for financial stability. It is far from certain that aid for the Republics would have the same effect. Aid transfers could place additional resources in the hands of the very individuals most opposed to scaling back the public sector, accelerating privatization and creating a market economy.

For those committed to aid, these arguments highlight the need for conditionality and specifically for conditioning aid on actions rather than promises. An area in which there exists a special opportunity for conditionality is relations among the Republics. Disputes among them threaten to derail the reform process. Free trade among the Republics will speed reform; otherwise comparative advantage will be squandered, local monopolies will gain power and traditional economic relationships will be disrupted.

Intervening in this process through the administration of aid might be regarded as meddling in the domestic politics of another country. Recall, however, that after World War II the US laid down as a condition for aid that the recipients collectively decide on the allocation of the funds. Trade liberalization and economic integration were explicit conditions of Marshall Plan aid. The OEEC and the EEC – two examples of the type of loose federations to which the Republics aspire – were established in response to this impetus. What worked once could work again. There is no reason why the US and the EC could not require the Republics to negotiate the formula according to which foreign aid would be allocated. The donors could make free trade among the Republics a condition for the receipt of Western aid, or press for establishment of a fiscal system like the US and other federal entities possess.

More specific forms of conditionality are more problematic. In principle, quarterly targets could be set for number of farms and firms privatized, number of goods freed from tariff or quota and progress on the fiscal and monetary fronts, with the release of aid conditioned on whether those targets are met. America's experience with the Marshall Plan indicates that such conditionality, while sure to produce controversy, can also produce results. But experience with the Marshall Plan suggests as well that aid conditioned on nuts-and-bolts issues of everyday politics is more likely to provoke a firestorm of protest and to backfire on the donor than is aid conditioned on high principles like openness and integration. A lesson of the Marshall Plan is that specific monetary and fiscal targets are especially difficult to impose on a large country to which the prosperity of an entire region is linked.

In Eastern Europe, the situation is simpler. In most cases, the central government remains a logical recipient of the foreign aid. In some countries a commitment to liberalization and meaningful reform already exists. But hard times threaten to fuel opposition. We believe that there exists a strong case for foreign aid to Eastern European countries precisely in order to minimize this danger. So long as reform continues, aid to solidify support for current programmes by easing the transition, however slightly, can only help. Its extension must be made contingent upon conditions, but if this is done it is hard to see how aid could be counterproductive.

One final caution. In post-war Europe, foreign aid could promote adjustment and growth because Europe had experience with markets and possessed the institutions needed for their operation. Property rights, a bankruptcy code and courts to enforce contracts, not to mention generations of accumulated entrepreneurial skills – were all in place. None of this is true today of the successor states to the USSR, and as yet it is true of only parts of Eastern Europe. Even under the best circumstances the donors should therefore not expect that the impact on economic growth will match that of the Marshall Plan.

Discussion

Nicholas Crafts
University of Warwick and CEPR

This is a very welcome and useful contribution on a topic neglected for too long by economists. I find myself agreeing with many of the conclusions though it might be useful to develop a wider historical perspective.

The approach through a three-gap model gives a good way of addressing the historical literature and quantifying arguments made by Maier, Milward and others to the effect that the impact directly on investment and the balance of payments of the grants under the ERP was modest. The econometric analysis also says that these peter out in a Solovian world, a result which does not surprise me. The authors are ingenious in supplementing this conventional analysis, which does not account for the revealed importance of the ERP, by suggesting its main effects came through solving a marketing crisis and/or by aiding the resolution of conflicts between capital and labour. Both these channels of influence might matter to Eastern European countries struggling with the political economy of transition.

In terms of perspective, I would argue for something of a shift of emphasis. First, the Marshall Plan was part of a grander American design or foreign policy strategy. The end result of this was greater European integration to which European governments were credibly committed. Such commitment surely had a significant impact on subsequent rent-seeking (see Adams, 1989, on France). American leverage came from its German occupation, not from the Marshall Plan *per se*, and the outcome was not completely controlled by the US (c.f. Milward 1984). Second, in terms of the post-war dollar gap, it seems odd that the 1949 devaluations are not integrated into the tale more explicitly. Third, more might be made of the contrasts with Allied policy toward Germany in the early 1920s.

Mention of these aspects suggests there is a complementary account of the Marshall Plan impact, which is hinted at several times here, but could be drawn out more fully. This would involve explicitly linking the ERP – and more importantly American policy overall – to the optimal sequencing of reform in the transition from war to peace. This would seem a useful further exercise if lessons for Eastern Europe are to be learnt.

Finally, I have two doubts about the findings of the paper. First, I think the argument about ERP's role in solving the 'coordination dilemma' is oversold. Isn't this more a story about the changes in the natural rate of unemployment than about growth? Moreover, productivity and growth depend on bargaining structures: for Germany it may be that achieving (Olson-like) industrial unions was an important outcome from the war – but it was not a result of the ERP. Again, the American achievement through its 'Pax Americana' in destroying protectionism may be at least as important and was at least as clear an *ex-ante* objective. Second, the paper says relatively little about how Marshall Aid was allocated. In the growth equations, is it conceivable that 'Catch-Up' and 'Reconstruction' are not adequately normalized for and that 'Marshall Plan' is a surrogate for these variables? I think some further sensitivity analysis may be in order.

To conclude, this paper is highly informative and very nicely argued. It takes the literature on the Marshall Plan forward substantially.

Martin Hellwig
University of Basel

The paper by Eichengreen and Uzan presents an impressive and comprehensive assessment of the economic effects of the Marshall Plan. According to the authors, the Plan's direct economic effects were significant, but not overwhelming. Instead, they suggest that the Plan's secular importance stems from its impact on the political process in Western Europe: by tipping the balance of political discussion, the plan set the stage for a new social consensus which in turn provided the basis for the sustained growth of the 1950s. By and large, I agree with the authors' assessment. Even so, there are a few points where the analysis could be sharpened.

First, I am uneasy about the role of macroeconomic aggregates in the analysis. In particular, I wonder whether the foreign exchange problems of the time are adequately captured by aggregate export, import and balance-of-payments data. After all, apart from the Swiss Franc, European currencies were not freely convertible, and trade was covered by multiple bilateral agreements with only limited credit agreements (which had largely been exhausted by 1947; see Kaplan and Schleiminger, 1989, p. 23). For a country like Belgium, the shortage of dollars to pay for raw materials from outside Europe was not alleviated by its exports of coal and steel to other European countries. Italy's surplus in its trade with the UK could not automatically be used to finance its deficits with other European countries or the US. In contrast, Marshall Plan aid came in a currency that was fully convertible and everybody wanted to have. To assess the significance of this advantage, a more disaggregated analysis of international trade relations in the late 1940s is needed.

Second, while I share the authors' views about the indirect, political effects of the Marshall Plan, I find it difficult to identify these effects (separating them, for instance, from the effects of changes in US military stance at the onset of the Cold War). If the political situation in Western Europe did change in the late 1940s, it is hardly possible to distinguish the effects of the Marshall Plan from the effects of the Cold War or, more vaguely, the effects of the American commitment not to leave Europe alone. Even in terms of direct economic consequences, in the case of Germany, it is difficult to determine the effects of the Marshall Plan from the effects of currency reform and economic reform – including the abandonment of the immediate post-war deindustrialization programmes.

A distinct role of the Marshall Plan is evident in the creation of the European Payments Union (EPU), the multilateral trade and payments agreement that replaced various bilateral agreements in 1950, providing for trade liberalization as well as multilateral clearing with certain credit facilities. Throughout the negotiations that eventually led to the EPU, the Marshall Plan administration played a leading role. Marshall Plan money provided a large part of the initial reserve of the EPU. Perhaps even more importantly, Marshall Plan money was instrumental in buying off British resistance against the move from bilateral to multilateral clearing (Kaplan and Schleiminger, 1989). To the extent that European growth in the 1950s is ascribed to the growth in intra-European trade, this effect of the Marshall Plan is important. Conditionality here was even more concrete than Eichengreen and Uzan's discussion suggests.

In contrast, I am sceptical about a more general linking of European integration to the Marshall Plan. To be sure, closer cooperation within Europe was one of the objectives which distinguished the Marshall Plan from earlier forms of American aid to Europe. However, the institutions of the OEEC – and later the EPU – were fairly weak, reflecting British insistence on national sovereignty rather than a substantial move towards integration (Monnet, 1976, pp. 321ff, 329ff). The creation of supranational institutions, which are the hallmark of the European Communities, seems to have had little to do with the Marshall Plan. Indeed, if we follow the account of Monnet (1976, pp. 341ff), the immediate motivation for the Schuman Plan came from a fear that the emancipation of Germany, which followed the onset of the Cold War, might re-establish national institutions and national patterns of behaviour, which reinforce old animosities and disadvantage French industry (see also Schwartz, 1986, pp. 716ff).

Third, it is not clear that the economic and political changes induced by the Marshall Plan were actually *sufficient* to propel Europe into the sustained growth of the 1950s. The German experience suggests that up to 1951 the situation may have been quite fragile. To be sure, the 'economic miracle' of 1948/49 solved what Eichengreen and Uzan call a 'marketing crisis' and led to a drastic increase in production. At the same time though, unemployment also rose drastically, reaching 9.5% in 1950, with a fair amount of social and political unrest. Later in 1950 and in early 1951, the problem was compounded by a balance-of-payments crisis, induced by panic buying of raw materials after the beginning of the Korean War (Stolper *et al.*, 1964, pp. 263ff). Policy advice to Germany in these years reads like a rehearsal for later 'go–stop–go . . .' routines, and the situation was anything but settled. The improvement in 1951 owed a lot to the Korean War boom and the concomitant increase in exports of final products i.e. a new and largely exogenous event. (The liberalization of intra-European trade through the EPU may have played a role as well.) Would the economic and political situation have been stabilized without the additional impulse from the Korean War?

To conclude my comment, I want to endorse the authors' warnings about any comparison of Eastern Europe or the former USSR today with Western Europe in the late 1940s. Eichengreen and Uzan stress the difference in the political constellations then and now. To this concern, I would like to add the observation that Western Europe in the late 1940s had firms with well-defined property rights and a functioning legal and fiscal system as well as the managers, lawyers and administrators required to run these systems. In Eastern Europe today these preconditions of a functioning market economy are lacking. Also, if aspiration levels are guided by the comparison with Western standards of living, distributional conflicts in Eastern Europe today may be rather harder than in Germany in 1950 where people were happy merely to get out of the rubble of the war and its aftermath.

One aspect of the Marshall Plan that does seem relevant today is its limited time horizon. Accounts of the period give the clear impression that the limited duration of the Marshall Plan provided people with a sense of urgency. The idea that by 1951/52 Western Europe would have to stand on its own without Marshall Plan aid seems to have dominated people's thinking, sparked their imagination and increased their willingness to accept institutional reforms.

General discussion

Discussion focused both on the historical analysis of the paper and on the lessons for Eastern Europe today. Angus Maddison thought the authors underestimated the role of the Organization for Economic Co-operation, which reduced pressures for beggar-my-neighbour policies. He also thought it was easy to forget how many governments had been inclined towards highly dirigiste approaches to recovery, and thought that US pressure for more liberal policies had been of great though unquantifiable importance. Richard Portes found the evidence that the Marshall Plan ended a war of attrition weak; he also stressed the importance of the Korean War in changing the outlook for Germany. Maurice Obstfeld argued that policy-makers had indeed perceived a liquidity crisis and had proceeded cautiously as a result; the Marshall Plan had helped to change their behaviour even if the direct evidence for a liquidity crisis was now hard to discern.

There was disagreement about the effects of the European Payments Union. Georges de Menil thought that even with deeper devaluations it would still have been needed. Maurice Obstfeld was convinced that, despite its evident faults, the EPU had helped with settlements and promoted trade. Jeffrey Sachs argued that, though it had represented a major advance on earlier institutions, the EPU remained a poor model for the present day. This led on to a discussion of the lessons of the Marshall Plan for present-day Eastern Europe and the former USSR. Sachs pointed out that the problem with all major structural reforms lay in winning enough time for their beneficial effects to come through. Every successful structural reform had passed through a precarious phase (he mentioned the Japanese general strike of 1947). The point of a present-day Marshall Plan, which he strongly supported, was not so much to create present growth but to win time, to create the necessary institutions to enable future growth. This was made more urgent by the very high aspiration levels characterizing Eastern European societies.

Other panellists drew attention to important respects in which Eastern Europe today differed from Western Europe after the war. Richard Portes thought that, while there might be evidence of a marketing crising in the former USSR and perhaps in Bulgaria and Romania, it was irrelevant to Poland, Hungary and Czechoslovakia. Charles Wyplosz pointed out that international capital markets were much better developed now than in the 1940s; furthermore, private institutions were good at making conditionality credible. John Black stressed that conditionality was crucial: the scale of the problem was so great that aid could make no difference unless there was additional associated leverage: aid should consequently be linked to trading access. Petr Aven pointed out serious dangers in conditionality; they might be difficult to enforce, and if the policies failed might elicit a xenophobic response. However, both he and Jan Svejnar urged the need for a modern Marshall Plan. Svejnar argued that the present accommodating response of the trade union movement to the reforms could not be expected to last indefinitely. Aven said that it was hard to overestimate the psychological impact of Western aid upon the patience of those undergoing reforms. Michael Burda agreed that the distributional conflicts in Eastern Europe were very significant, and that the potential value of aid in buying time was extremely important.

Appendix A: A three-gap model for analysing the macroeconomics of foreign aid

To analyse the macroeconomics of foreign aid, we utilize the two-gap model of Chenery and Bruno (1962), as extended by Bacha (1990) to incorporate fiscal constraints on public capital formation. Our formulation has much in common with the treatment of McKinnon (1964).

We start with the savings-investment identity for an open economy:

$$S - I = X - M \tag{1}$$

where S is saving, I is investment, and X and M are exports and imports of goods and services. Imports are of two types: consumption goods M_c and capital goods M_k.[20] (Abstracting from changes in relative prices, we set all prices to unity.) The balance of payments, which is the current account plus net capital transfers F, must equal zero. (We treat net transfers interchangeably with foreign aid because significant foreign borrowing was not possible in the immediate post-war years.)

$$X - M_c - M_k = -F \tag{2}$$

Domestic production is a function of the capital stock:

$$Y = \alpha K \tag{3}$$

A fixed fraction of investment requires imported capital goods:

$$M_k = m_k I \tag{4}$$

where I is investment. In addition, a fixed fraction of investment must take the form of public capital formation G_k:

$$G_k = g_k I \tag{5}$$

where g_k (like m_k) is taken as less than one.

To keep the model simple, we adopt the following functional forms for the behaviour of the household and government sectors. Aggregate savings S is a linear function of national income in excess of consumption necessary for subsistence:

$$S = s(Y + F - C) \tag{6}$$

where s is the savings rate and C is subsistence consumption. Total tax revenues T depend on the tax rate on income above subsistence t_y and the share of foreign aid accruing to the government t_f:

$$T = t_y(Y - C) + t_f F \tag{7}$$

The government budget constraint is:

$$G_k + G_c = T + D \tag{8}$$

G_c is the exogenous level of government consumption and D is the exogenous level of government spending financed from sources other than current taxation. For simplicity, we set $D = 0$.

Equation (1) can be solved for the relationship between the rate of growth γ ($\gamma = I/K$) and foreign aid as a share of GDP (denoted f, $f = F/Y$):

$$\gamma = [\alpha/(1 - m_k)][-x + s(1 + f - c) + m_c] \tag{9}$$

---

[20] The model is easily generalized to incorporate imports of intermediates used by industry. See Bacha (1984).

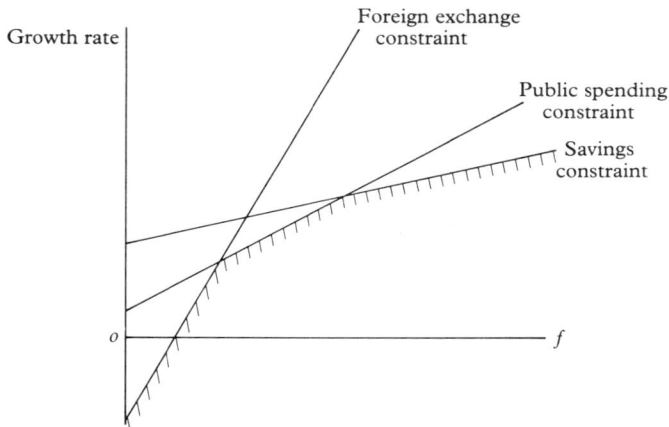

Figure A1. Three-gap model of constraints on growth

where x is the export share of GDP $(x = X/Y)$ and c is subsistence consumption relative to GDP $(c = C/Y)$. This relationship has a positive slope $(\alpha s/(1 - m_k))$ and intercept as depicted in Figure A1. It shows the familiar McKinnon-style relationship between aid and growth in an economy whose growth is constrained by a low level of saving. The innovation here is that the intercept can shift, and with it the likelihood that the savings gap binds, as the economy moves further from subsistence. If the savings gap binds, then $\partial\gamma/\partial f = s\alpha/(1 - m_k)$.

Similarly, Equation (2) can be solved for the relationship between growth and aid:

$$\gamma = (\alpha/m_k)[x - m_c + f] \tag{10}$$

This is the relationship between growth and aid in an economy constrained by the availability of imported capital goods. Equation (10), the foreign exchange constraint, is steeper than Equation (9). Its intercept is negative if $m_c > x$, which is appropriate to our circumstances. If the foreign exchange constraint binds, then $\partial\gamma/\partial f = \alpha/m_k$. This is larger than in the case where the savings constraint binds, under the plausible assumptions that the savings propensity is small and that only a minority of capital goods are imported. Then foreign aid has a larger growth effect in a foreign-exchange-constrained economy than in one that is savings-constrained because only a fraction less than one of foreign aid is saved, while all of f can be used to finance additional imports.

Finally, Equation (8) can be solved in a similar fashion:

$$\gamma = (\alpha/g_k)[-g_c + t_y(1 - c) + t_f f] \tag{11}$$

This is the relationship between aid and growth in an economy constrained by public capital formation. The likelihood that this constraint

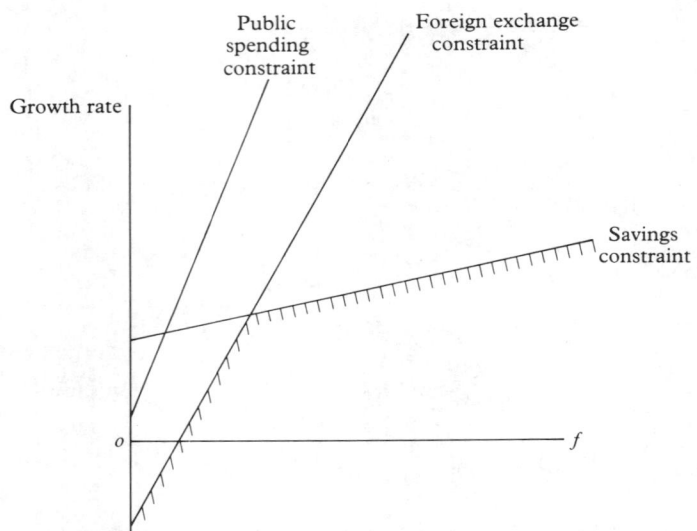

Figure A2. The case where only two constraints bind

will bind depends both on the intercept (and hence on proximity to subsistence c) and on the slope of $\partial \gamma / \partial f$ (namely $\alpha t_f / g_k$). The growth effect of foreign aid may be larger or smaller than in savings- and foreign-exchange-constrained economies. If $t_f > g$, which is plausible for the Marshall Plan period, and if m_k and g_k are small, then the effect of foreign aid in a public-spending-constrained economy will be larger than that in a savings-constrained economy. There is no obvious presumption about the relative size of the effect in foreign-exchange and public-spending constrained economies, which depends mainly on the relative magnitude of g_k and m_k.

Figure A1 shows the case where g_k is large relative to m_k, for a poor economy (one just above subsistence in the absence of foreign aid). The foreign exchange constraint cuts the public spending constraint from below. Additional foreign aid produces progressively smaller increments to growth, depending on whether the foreign exchange, public spending or savings constraints bind. Figure A2 shows the case where g_k is small relative to m_k. Here public spending is never a binding constraint.

How does the level of income influence the growth effects of foreign aid? As c declines from unity (the economy moves away from the margin of subsistence), the savings and public-capital-formation constraints shift up. For a given range of foreign aid, it becomes more likely that the foreign exchange gap binds, implying a large growth effect. Thus, the effects of the Marshall Plan should have depended in part on which of these three constraints were binding, which should have depended in turn on the initial level of income.

Appendix B. Regression analysis of investment, current balance and public spending

Data for the immediate post-World War II period have serious limitations. Statistical agencies were in disarray in 1945–46, but some scattered data are available even for this early period. Estimates of economic aggregates consistent with those for subsequent years and compatible across countries become available only around 1948, however, when statistics were first gathered and processed into consistent form by the OEEC. Most data used in this analysis are drawn from the OEEC's *Statistics of National Product and Expenditure* and cover the period 1948–55. The major exceptions are the rate of growth of GDP and Marshall Plan allotments.[21] Marshall Plan allotments were drawn from Mutual Security Program (various issues). We include funds made available in 1951–55 under the provisions of the Mutual Defence Assistance Program.[22] Data on the growth of GDP are from Maddison (1982), who drew figures from national sources and adjusted them for consistency. Maddison's sample therefore defines the 16 industrial countries forming our international cross section: Australia, Austria, Belgium, Canada, Denmark, Finland, France, Germany, Italy, Japan, the Netherlands, Norway, Sweden, Switzerland, the UK and the US.[23]

Investment, the current account and government spending are all assumed to depend on the economy's underlying rate of growth, proxied by per capita GDP relative to the US and by GDP growth since 1938. In addition, they are determined by the rate of population growth, the rate of consumer price inflation and the openness of the economy.

---

[21] Using the growth of GDP rather than the growth of GDP per capita as the dependent variable made no difference for any of the empirical results. We replicated the regressions reported below using GDP per capita, and found only the slightest changes in point estimates and levels of statistical significance.

[22] The MDAP was established by the Mutual Security Act of 1951, passed by the US Congress in response to the outbreak of the Korean War. For 1951–52 Congress authorized $4.92 bn. in military assistance and $1.02 bn. in economic and technical assistance (known as 'defense support'). Our data for foreign economic aid include only economic and technical assistance.

[23] For the non-European members of this group, ancillary variables were gathered from other sources. These came from Butlin (1962) for Australia, Ohkawa and Rosovsky (1975) for Japan, and Mitchell (1983) for Canada and the US, supplemented by the IMF's *International Financial Statistics* for later years. Annual population estimates for all countries were drawn from Liesner (1989).

Table B1. Channels linking the Marshall Plan to growth, 1948–54

(Dependent variables expressed as shares of GDP)

	Investment	Current account	Government spending
Constant	0.21	−0.16	0.37
	(5.42)	(3.16)	(2.84)
GDP relative to US	−0.10	0.17	−0.28
	(2.42)	(3.20)	(2.11)
GDP growth since 1938	0.10	−0.05	0.01
	(6.79)	(2.41)	(0.29)
Terms of trade	−0.01	0.01	0.01
	(1.98)	(0.37)	(0.34)
Pop growth	1.08	−0.24	1.95
	(2.42)	(0.39)	(1.25)
CPI inflation	0.06	−0.55	−0.13
	(2.73)	(1.63)	(1.75)
Openness	−0.03	0.48	−0.01
	(0.64)	(7.35)	(0.03)
Marshall Plan lagged	0.36	−0.12	−0.31
	(2.53)	(2.28)	(0.63)
n	122	113	125
S.E.	0.02	0.02	0.06

Source: See text.
Note: t-statistics in parentheses. Country dummy variables are included in all equations.

Marshall Plan allotments are entered with a one-year lag to minimize simultaneity.[24]

The first column of Table B1 reports the results on the determinants of investment. Investment ratios were higher in countries with rapidly growing populations, which had already restored output to 1938 levels, and which were far from the technological frontier as defined by the US. There is no indication that monetary stabilization, openness or the terms of trade (export prices relative to import prices) had a strong impact on investment.[25] In contrast, Marshall Plan transfers equal to 2% of GNP raised investment by 0.7% of GNP in the subsequent year.

[24] We experimented with a second lag of Marshall Plan allotments but found that it had a small coefficient, was uniformly insignificant and had no discernible impact on the other terms, including the first lag of Marshall Plan transfers. Hence we report only equations including the first lag. To test the exogeneity of lagged Marshall Plan receipts, we added the fitted value from a first-stage regression designed to explain Marshall Plan receipts. The fitted value consistently displayed a t-statistic smaller than unity.

[25] The result for openness is in contrast to Romer's (1990) finding for 90 countries over the period 1960–85, that more open economies had higher investment rates. The contrast may be explicable in terms of the slower and more troubled growth of international transactions immediately after World War II.

This suggests a significant impact of the Marshall Plan. The second column reports results for the current-account balance. Relatively poor countries (those with per capita incomes far below America's) and countries that succeeded in restoring output to 1938 levels tended to run current-account deficits. Openness is associated with current-account surpluses. High inflation countries ran current-account deficits, which is plausible insofar as inflation signals excess demand. There is evidence, moreover, that Marshall Plan inflows permitted the maintenance of larger current-account deficits. Transfers equal to 2% of GNP were associated with an additional current-account deficit equal to 0.25% of national income in the subsequent year. The third column reports results for government spending. This is the least robust of the three equations. Marshall Plan receipts enter with a negative coefficient, suggesting declines in the public spending share in countries receiving US aid. This may be plausible insofar as the US pressured recipients to reduce government spending and to the extent that some countries, notably Britain, used counterpart funds to retire public debt, reducing debt service charges. In any case, the evidence on government spending provides little support for the notion that the Marshall Plan operated by bridging the fiscal gap.

Appendix C. Regression analysis of growth

Table C1 reports the simplest possible convergence and catchup regressions that might be used to analyse the Marshall Plan. These are descriptive correlations rather than tests of a particular model. The growth rate for each year from 1948 through 1954 is regressed on per capita GDP relative to the US, the GDP growth rate since 1938, and Marshall Plan allotments as a share of GNP in the current and immediately preceding years. Faster growth is exhibited by countries farther from the technological frontier as defined by the US, and by countries whose output had fallen most from pre-war levels.[26] Marshall Plan effects are substantial and significant at the 95% level; the negative lagged term is about half the size of the positive contemporaneous one. (Subsequent lags never approached statistical significance.) A coefficient

---

[26] Since 1938 was a recession year, we reran all regressions substituting GDP growth since 1936 for GDP growth since 1938. This substitution reduced the *t*-statistic on the change in output since the late 1930s below two in the third equation in Table C1 (without changing the magnitude or significance of any of the other variables). But in none of the subsequent regressions reported in this paper did this substitution alter the magnitude or statistical significance of the variable discernibly.

Table C1. Catchup and convergence regressions
(dependent variable is growth rate of real GDP)

	(1)	(2)	(3)
Constant	0.08	0.06	0.07
	(9.04)	(7.94)	(9.02)
GDP relative to US	−0.06		−0.09
	(3.38)		(3.91)
GDP growth since 1938		−0.01	−0.03
		(0.74)	(2.04)
Marshall Plan	1.29	1.43	1.41
	(4.55)	(4.73)	(4.92)
Marshall Plan lagged	−0.67	−0.59	−0.67
	(2.44)	(2.08)	(2.46)
n	126	126	126
S.E.	0.04	0.04	0.04

Source: See text.
Note: t-statistics in parentheses.

of unity suggests that a transfer of 2% of GDP raised the growth rate
of domestic output by two percentage points in the same year.

A reason to hesitate before drawing such inferences is the possible
endogeneity of Marshall Plan allotments. To test for this possibility,
using a procedure suggested by Hausman (1978), we added to the third
equation in Table C1 the fitted values of Marshall aid (current and
lagged one year) derived from regressing it on the current balance and
per capita GDP.[27] While the lagged value of Marshall aid had a small
t-statistic, that on the current value was significantly greater than zero
at the 95% confidence level, supporting our suspicion of the endogeneity
of Marshall Plan allotments.

---

[27] The Marshall Plan allotment was expressed as a share of GNP, as was the current account
balance. Consistent with specifications reported below, per capita GDP was expressed as a
proportion of US per capita GDP, where all income estimates were converted to US dollars
using Summers and Heston's purchasing-power-parity exchange rates. The equation, estimated
only on the subsample of countries receiving ECA aid, was:

ECA Aid = 0.035 − 0.313 Current balance/GNP − 0.067 Relative per cap GDP
      (7.02) (5.74)   (4.94)

$R^2 = 0.48$ $N = 73$

with t-statistics in parentheses. For countries not included in the subsample, fitted values were
taken as zero.

**Table C2. Additional growth regressions for 1948–52
(dependent variable is growth rate of real GDP)**

	(1)	(2)	(3)	(4)	(5)	(6)
Constant	0.08	0.09	0.10	0.08	0.09	0.07
	(8.81)	(7.85)	(1.99)	(5.02)	(4.89)	(1.00)
GDP relative to US	−0.09	−0.10	−0.09	−0.09	−0.10	−0.05
	(5.24)	(5.25)	(1.44)	(4.72)	(3.61)	(0.66)
GDP growth since	0.05	0.05	0.04	0.04	0.05	0.02
1938	(4.61)	(4.13)	(1.79)	(3.76)	(3.61)	(0.67)
Openness	−0.10	−0.10	−0.15	−0.10	−0.11	−0.09
	(3.98)	(3.99)	(1.78)	(3.26)	(3.30)	(0.86)
Export growth	0.05	0.04	0.04	0.05	0.04	0.04
	(4.72)	(2.99)	(3.66)	(4.27)	(2.76)	(3.18)
Marshall Plan	0.59	0.85	0.38	0.58	0.73	0.38
lagged	(2.85)	(3.10)	(1.47)	(2.52)	(2.48)	(1.39)
Marshall Plan	−0.41	−0.83	−0.45	−0.49	−0.78	−0.58
lagged twice	(1.95)	(3.09)	(1.88)	(2.18)	(2.69)	(2.29)
Investment				0.01	0.01	−0.01
				(0.20)	(0.16)	(0.28)
Current account				−0.05	−0.03	−0.06
				(0.47)	(0.30)	(0.44)
Government				0.01	0.01	0.02
spending				(0.06)	(0.35)	(0.29)
Year dummies		×			×	
Country dummies			×			×
n	112	112	112	112	112	112
S.E.	0.03	0.03	0.03	0.03	0.03	0.03

Source: See text.
Note: *t*-statistics in parentheses.

Table C2 therefore lags Marshall Plan aid one and two years to redress problems of simultaneity.[28] In addition, it augments the basic regression with measures of economic structure and policy, a la Barro (1989) and Romer (1989). GDP per capita relative to the US continues to enter with a negative sign, as if countries far from the technological threshold had the greatest scope for growth subsequently, but GDP growth since 1938 no longer exhibits a negative sign. Openness, measured as exports

[28] In some early regressions we included also the current year's Marshall Plan allotments, instrumenting them with the current balance and per capita GDP. In no case was the coefficient on the current value significantly different from zero. Thus, it appears that aid affected growth only with a lag. We therefore dropped the current value from subsequent regressions. We also conducted Hausman tests of the hypothesis of exogeneity of the remaining (lagged) allotment variables by adding their fitted values to the various equations reported in Table B1. In no case did the fitted values have *t*-statistics as large as unity. We also experimented with additional lags, but in no case was the coefficient of Marshall Plan allotments lagged two years statistically different from zero at standard confidence levels.

as a share of GNP, enters negatively, indicating slower growth in more open economies (which plausibly suffered most from bilateral clearing arrangements, non-tariff barriers and the slow recovery of trade). As in previous studies like Michaely (1977), the growth rate of exports (in constant prices) enters positively. The coefficients on Marshall Plan allotments lagged one and two years both differ from zero at the 95% confidence level. Those on Marshall aid lagged one year are between 0.5 and 1, suggesting that allotments equal to 2% of European GNP raised European output by 1 to 2 percentage points in the subsequent year. Now, however, the coefficient on the second lag is as large in absolute value as the coefficient on the first. (We cannot reject the hypothesis that the two coefficients are equal and opposite in sign at the 95% confidence level.) This suggests that the effect of the Marshall Plan was temporary. The last three columns add investment, the current-account surplus and central government expenditure as shares of GNP. None appears to have had a statistically significant impact on growth.

A possible explanation for the small and statistically insignificant coefficients on investment, the current account and government spending is simultaneity bias. We tested for the endogeneity of these variables using the Hausman test described above, adding the fitted values for investment, the current account and government from the equations reported in Table B1 to the growth equations just reported, together and separately. In no case did the fitted values have t-statistics as large as one, supporting our treatment of these variables as exogenous with respect to growth.

Our three-gap model suggests that aid transfers to countries with low levels of investment, large current-account deficits and limited capacities to finance additional government spending may have had a disproportionately large impact on growth. To test this hypothesis, Marshall Plan allotments as a share of GNP lagged one year were interacted with the investment, current account and government spending ratios. (We also interacted Marshall Plan allotments lagged two years with the investment, current account and government spending variables, but the second lags were not statistically significant.) The estimated equations are reported in Table C3. The coefficient on Marshall aid lagged one year is now significantly greater than zero at the 99% confidence level. That on Marshall aid lagged twice differs significantly from zero at the 95% level in one of the three cases; in all three equations it is significantly smaller (at the 95% level) than the coefficient on the first lag. The interaction terms often display coefficients significantly different from zero at the 95% level. Their negative coefficients accord with the intuition provided by the three-gap model. That on the Marshall Plan

**Table C3. Growth equations with interactive Marshall Plan
effects, 1948–54 (dependent variable is growth rate of real GDP)**

	(1)	(2)	(3)
Constant	0.06	0.06	0.07
	(3.29)	(3.24)	(1.15)
GDP relative to US	−0.08	−0.09	−0.09
	(4.28)	(4.45)	(1.43)
GDP growth since 1938	0.04	0.04	0.01
	(3.32)	(3.35)	(0.48)
Openness	−0.10	−0.10	−0.23
	(3.25)	(3.33)	(2.30)
Export Growth	0.04	0.03	0.03
	(3.98)	(2.51)	(2.67)
Marshall Plan lagged	2.86	2.96	5.36
	(2.43)	(2.39)	(4.12)
Marshall Plan lagged twice	−0.26	−0.54	−0.23
	(1.18)	(1.91)	(0.92)
Investment	0.10	0.11	0.35
	(1.40)	(1.48)	(1.96)
Current account	0.09	0.12	0.25
	(0.89)	(1.11)	(1.74)
Government spending	0.02	0.03	0.04
	(0.49)	(0.74)	(0.75)
Investment*	−6.91	−7.29	−9.16
Marshall Plan	(2.10)	(2.21)	(2.64)
Current account*	−14.35	−14.69	−15.12
Marshall Plan	(2.61)	(2.67)	(2.78)
Government spending*	−5.83	−5.29	−16.50
Marshall Plan	(1.48)	(1.27)	(3.49)
Year dummies		×	
Country dummies			×
n	112	112	112
S.E.	0.03	0.03	0.03

Source: See text.
Note: *t*-statistics in parentheses.

interacted with investment suggests that American aid provided the
least stimulus to growth in countries where investment was already
high. That on the Marshall Plan interacted with the current-account
ratio suggests that it boosted growth least in countries whose current-
account position was strong. That on the Marshall Plan interacted with
government spending suggests that American aid stimulated growth
least in countries where government spending was already high. This
supports the notion that the Marshall Plan had the largest impact on
growth in countries for which the savings, current account and fiscal
gaps were binding.

Table C4. Growth equations distinguishing counterpart funds used for production

	(1)	(2)	(3)	(4)	(5)	(6)	(7)	(8)	(9)
Constant	0.06	0.06	0.05	0.08	0.08	0.05	0.05	0.06	0.04
	(3.28)	(3.27)	(0.91)	(4.65)	(4.61)	(0.72)	(0.84)	(1.06)	(0.61)
GDP relative to US	-0.08	-0.09	-0.08	-0.08	-0.09	-0.04	-0.08	-0.09	-0.04
	(4.09)	(4.18)	(1.25)	(4.43)	(4.52)	(0.59)	(1.27)	(1.44)	(0.06)
GDP growth since 1938	0.04	0.04	0.01	0.04	0.04	0.06	0.01	0.01	0.01
	(3.18)	(3.10)	(0.24)	(3.42)	(3.29)	(0.22)	(0.13)	(0.13)	(0.08)
Openness	-0.09	-0.09	-0.21	-0.09	-0.09	-0.09	-0.21	-0.24	-0.10
	(2.81)	(2.82)	(2.05)	(2.78)	(2.74)	(0.91)	(2.08)	(2.39)	(0.94)
Export growth	0.05	0.03	0.03	0.05	0.03	0.04	0.03	0.03	0.04
	(4.08)	(2.51)	(2.83)	(4.30)	(2.62)	(3.29)	(2.89)	(2.74)	(3.31)
Marshall Plan lagged	3.74	3.62	5.75	2.30	2.40	1.53	5.58	5.05	1.65
	(2.93)	(2.71)	(4.02)	(4.10)	(4.03)	(2.29)	(3.93)	(3.91)	(2.49)
Marshall Plan lagged twice	-1.05	-0.97	-1.48	-1.62	-1.74	-2.26	-1.43	-0.32	-2.26
	(1.74)	(1.45)	(2.30)	(3.29)	(3.30)	(4.08)	(2.23)	(1.29)	(4.13)
Investment	0.09	0.09	0.39	0.04	0.04	0.19	0.42	0.40	0.24
	(1.31)	(1.31)	(2.21)	(0.66)	(0.59)	(1.06)	(2.42)	(2.25)	(1.36)
Investment for Norway	—	—	—	—	—	—	-1.35	-1.60	-1.57
							(1.54)	(1.85)	(1.70)

	(1)	(2)	(3)	(4)	(5)	(6)	(7)	(8)	(9)
Current account	0.08 (0.72)	0.10 (0.93)	0.22 (1.54)	0.02 (0.18)	0.02 (0.22)	0.04 (0.31)	0.22 (1.56)	0.25 (1.76)	0.04 (0.26)
Government spending	0.02 (0.49)	0.03 (0.73)	0.04 (0.76)	0.01 (0.18)	0.01 (0.40)	0.02 (0.39)	0.04 (0.85)	0.04 (0.87)	0.03 (0.50)
Investment* Marshall Plan	−5.57 (1.62)	−5.77 (1.65)	−8.64 (2.39)	—	—	—	−7.96 (2.20)	−8.61 (2.51)	−8.64 (2.39)
Current account* Marshall Plan	−8.24 (1.25)	−10.55 (1.55)	−8.31 (1.29)	—	—	—	−9.67 (1.50)	−16.16 (2.99)	—
Government spending* Marshall Plan	−5.22 (1.29)	−5.24 (1.22)	−14.72 (3.07)	—	—	—	−14.53 (3.05)	−15.78 (3.38)	—
Counterpart for production Marshall Plan	1.37 (1.74)	1.08 (1.29)	0.90 (1.07)	2.16 (3.34)	2.13 (3.19)	1.57 (2.12)	0.97 (1.15)	—	1.70 (2.30)
Counterpart for production Marshall Plan lagged	−0.62 (1.01)	−0.20 (0.30)	−1.35 (2.08)	−0.99 (1.81)	−0.77 (1.29)	−1.87 (3.00)	−1.15 (1.74)	—	−1.69 (2.71)
Year dummies	—	×	×	—	×	×	×	×	—
Country dummies	—	—	—	—	—	×	×	×	×
n	112	112	112	112	112	112	112	112	112
S.E.	0.03	0.03	0.02	0.03	0.03	0.03	0.02	0.02	0.03

Source: See text.
Notes: t-statistics in parentheses.

To test whether the use of counterpart funds had a significant impact on growth, we added counterpart withdrawals for productive purposes (investment and purchases of intermediates). Since counterpart authorizations followed Marshall Plan allotments with a lag of several quarters, we used the current year's authorizations rather than authorizations lagged. To make the effect of counterpart funds as transparent as possible, we defined the variable as counterpart withdrawals for production minus Marshall Plan allotments lagged. Table C4 reports the results. Both Marshall Plan allotments and counterpart withdrawals have economically important and statistically significant effects. But with the addition of measures of the use of counterpart funds, the interaction terms introduced in Table C3 matter less than before. Their coefficients are uniformly smaller and only the interaction terms involving the investment and government spending ratios in the equation with country dummy variables differ significantly from zero at standard confidence levels. Given the insignificance of the majority of these terms, we excluded the interactions from the equations reported in the middle three columns of Table C4. The coefficients on Marshall Plan allotments remain statistically significant. The same is true of the first lag of counterpart withdrawals. Evidence on the second lag on counterpart withdrawals is mixed. The results in the fourth column suggest that a Marshall Plan inflow of 2% of GNP raised output in the next year by 4.6% when a matching amount of counterpart funds were withdrawn for productive purposes. When counterpart funds were used for other purposes, however, the impact on output growth was only 0.3%. About two-thirds of the first year's output growth was given back in the second year. The fifth equation, which includes dummy variables for years, is essentially identical. Once again, however, the equation including dummy variables for countries (in the sixth column) tells a different story. A Marshall Plan allotment raises the growth rate in the first year after which it is received but reduces growth by a matching amount in the second subsequent year. This is true regardless of the disposition of counterpart funds.[29]

Thus, these results support the view that the Marshall Plan had important economic effects. Conditionality played an important role in shaping the effects of American aid. To determine the robustness of the results, we undertook a number of sensitivity analyses. We first reestimated the model containing counterpart effects but omitting interaction terms (the fourth equation of Table C4) eliminating each observation in turn. In no case did the omission of a single observation produce

----

[29] We tested for the equality, in absolute value terms, of the coefficients of Marshall Plan allotments lagged once and twice and of counterpart withdrawals lagged once and twice, and were unable to reject the hypothesis of equality at standard confidence levels.

a noticeable change. Next we explored whether the results were driven by the observations for a particular country. In no case did the omission of a single country have much impact on the coefficients on Marshall Plan allotments and counterpart withdrawals. (That the results survive Germany's exclusion reassures us that they are not picking up the effects of American occupation or of currency reform.) A potentially troubling aspect of these equations is the small size and statistical insignificance of the investment ratio. Our scatter plot of investment and growth suggests that the absence of a relationship may be due to the exceptionally high investment rate in Norway. We therefore added to our growth equations the product of the investment ratio and a dummy variable for Norway – which allowed the investment rate for this country to differ. The relevant regressions are shown in the last three columns of Table C4. This greatly increased the magnitude of the investment coefficient for the remaining countries. When the interaction term for Norway was included along with the vector of country dummy variables, the investment rate was generally statistically significant at the 95% confidence level. The coefficient on the investment rate, now in the neighbourhood of 0.4, is similar to those obtained in other recent studies. Of the other coefficients, the principal change is in the magnitude of the current-account ratio. This now has a larger effect and in one case is statistically significant at the 90% level. The other coefficients remain essentially unchanged. In particular, the effects of the Marshall Plan and counterpart withdrawals are no different than before.

References

Adams, W. J. (1989). *Restructuring the French Economy.* The Brookings Institution, Washington, D.C.

Alesina, A. and A. Drazen (1989). 'Why Are Stabilizations Delayed'? unpublished manuscript, Harvard University and Tel Aviv University.

Alexander, L. (1991). 'Radical Economic Reform in Germany, 1948 and 1990: Similarities, Differences, and Lessons for the Soviet Union', unpublished manuscript, International Finance Division, Board of Governors of the Federal Reserve System.

Arkes, H. (1972). *Bureaucracy, the Marshall Plan and the National Interest,* Princeton University Press, Princeton.

Bacha, E. L. (1984). 'Growth with Limited Supplies of Foreign Exchange: A reappraisal of the Two-Gap Model', in M. Syrquin *et al.* (eds.) *Economic Structure and Performance,* Academic Press, New York.

—— (1990). 'A Three Gap Model of Foreign Transfers and GDP Growth in Developing Countries', *Journal of Development Economics.*

Barkin, S. (1983). 'The Postwar Decades: Growth and Activism Followed by Stagnancy and Malaise', in Barkin (ed.) *Worker Militancy and its Consequences,* Praeger, New York.

Barro, R. (1989). 'A Cross-Country Study of Growth, Saving and Government Spending', NBER Working Paper no. 2855.

Berolzheimer, J. (1953). 'The Impact of U.S. Foreign Aid Since the Marshall Plan on Western Europe's Gross National Product and Government Finance', *Finanzarchiv.*

Boltho, A. (1982). 'Growth', in A. Boltho (ed.) *The European Economy,* Clarendon Press, Oxford.

Bournay, J., O. Maigne and G. Laroque (1978). 'Comptes trimetriels 1949–1959' *Collections de l'INSEE.*

Brookings Institution (1951). *Current Issues in Foreign Economic Assistance*, The Brookings Institution, Washington, D.C.
Brown, W. A. and R. Opie (1953). *American Foreign Assistance*, The Brookings Institution, Washington, D.C.
Butlin, N. G. (1962). *Australian Domestic Product, Investment and Foreign Borrowing*, Cambridge University Press, Cambridge.
Casella, A. and B. Eichengreen (1991). 'Halting Inflation in France and Italy After World War II', in Michael Bordo and Forrest Capie (eds.) *Monetary Regimes in Transition*, Cambridge University Press, Cambridge (forthcoming).
Chenery, H. and M. Bruno (1962). 'Development Alternatives in an Open Economy: The Case of Israel', *Economic Journal*.
Cohen, D. (1991). 'Slow Growth and Large LDC Debt in the Eighties: An Empirical Analysis', CEPR Discussion Paper No. 461.
Collins, S. and D. Rodrik (1991). *Eastern Europe and the Soviet Union in the World Economy*, Institute for International Economics, Washington, D.C.
Committee of European Economic Cooperation (1947). *General Report*, U.S. Department of State, Washington, D.C.
De Long, J. Bradford and B. Eichengreen (1991). 'The Marshall Plan: History's Most Successful Structural Adjustment Program', in R. Dornbush, R. Layard and W. Nolling (eds.) *Postwar Reconstruction 1945-9: Implications for Eastern Europe* (forthcoming).
Dobbs, M. (1991). 'In Moscow, Running out of Socks: Factory's Woes Reflect Breakdown of Soviet Economy', *Washington Post* (22 June).
Economic Cooperation Administration (various years), *Report*, GPO, Washington, D.C.
Ellis, H. (1950). *The Economics of Freedom*, Harper and Row, New York.
Esposito, C. (1985). 'The Marshall Plan in France and Italy, 1948-1950: Counterpart Fund Negotiations', Ph.D. dissertation, State University of New York at Stony Brook.
Federal Reserve Board (1947). 'France and Italy: Patterns of Reconstruction', *Federal Reserve Bulletin*.
——— (1948). 'Recovery in Western Europe', *Federal Reserve Bulletin.*
Flanagan, R. J., D. W. Soskice and L. Ulman (1983). *Unions, Economic Stabilization, and Incomes Policies*, The Brookings Institution, Washington D.C.
Freris, A. F. (1986). *The Greek Economy in the 20th Century*, Croom Helm, London.
Grindrod, M. (1955). *The Rebuilding of Italy*, Royal Institute of International Affairs, London.
Hausman, J. A. (1978). 'Specification Tests in Econometrics', *Econometrica*.
Hogan, M. J. (1987). *The Marshall Plan: America, Britain and the Reconstruction of Western Europe, 1947-1952*, Cambridge University Press, Cambridge.
Ignatieff, M. (1991). 'In the New Republics', *New York Review of Books* (21 November).
INSEE (1958). *Situation Economique de la France, 1944-57*, INSEE, Paris.
International Bank for Reconstruction and Development (1948). *Summary of the United Nations Economic Commission for Europe Report Entitled 'A Survey of the Economic Situation and Prospects of Europe'*, Economic Department, GdeF/cstp, IBRD, Washington, D.C.
International Monetary Fund (1949), *Balance of Payments Yearbook, 1938, 1946, 1947*, IMF, Washington, D.C.
——— (various years). *International Financial Statistics*, IMF, Washington, D.C.
Kaplan, Jacob J. and Günther Schleiminger (1989). *The European Payments Union*, Oxford University Press, Oxford.
Kindleberger, C. (1967). *Europe's Postwar Growth*, Oxford University Press, London.
Kirman, A. and L. Reichlin (1991). 'The Marshall Plan', in J.-P. Fitoussi (ed.) *A L'est en Europe: Des Economies en Transition*, Presses de la Fondation Nationale des Sciences Politiques, Paris.
Kolko, J. and G. Kolko (1972). *The Limits of Power: The World and United States Foreign Policy, 1945-54*, New York.
Liesner, T. (1989). *One Hundred Years of Economic Statistics*, Economist Publications, London.
Lloyd, J. (1991). 'Triple Panic that Sparked Kremlin Putsch', *Financial Times* (August 21).
Maddison, A. (1976). 'Economic Policy and Performance in Europe, 1913-1970', in C. Cipolla (ed.) *The Fontana Economic History of Europe*, Vol. 5, Pt. 2, Fontana, London.
——— (1982). *Phases of Capitalist Development*, Oxford University Press, Oxford.
Maier, C. S. (1977). 'The Politics of Productivity: Foundations of American International Economic Policy After World War II', reprinted in *In Search of Stability*, Cambridge University Press, Cambridge (1987).
——— (1981), 'The Two Postwar Eras and the Conditions for Stability in Twentieth-Century Western Europe', *American Historical Review*, reprinted in *In Search of Stability*, Cambridge University Press, Cambridge (1987).

Marshall, G. C. (1947). 'European Initiative Essential to Economic Recovery', *Department of State Bulletin* (15 June).

Mayer, H. C. (1969). *German Recovery and the Marshall Plan, 1948–1952,* Atlantic Forum, Bonn, Brussels and New York.

McKinnon, R. (1964). 'Foreign Exchange Constraints in Economic Development and Efficient Aid Allocation', *Economic Journal.*

Michaely, M. (1977). 'Exports and Growth: An Empirical Investigation', *Journal of Development Economics.*

Milward, A. (1984). *The Reconstruction of Western Europe, 1945–51,* Methuen, London.

Mitchell, B. R. (1975). *European Historical Statistics,* Macmillan, London.

—— (1983). *International Historical Statistics,* Macmillan, London.

Monnet, Jean (1976) *Mémoires,* Fayard, Paris.

Nicholson, M., C. Freeland and G. Tett (1991). 'A Long and Hungry Ride to Market', *Financial Times* (1 October).

Ohkawa, K. and H. Rosovsky (1975). *Japanese Economic Growth,* Stanford University Press, Stanford.

Organization for European Economic Cooperation (1957). *Statistics of National Product and Expenditure,* vol. 1, OEEC, Paris.

Patterson, T. G. (1973). *Soviet-American Confrontation: Postwar Reconstruction and the Origins of the Cold War,* Johns Hopkins University Press, Baltimore.

Pickles, D. (1953). *French Politics: The First Years of the Fourth Republic,* Royal Institute of International Affairs, London.

President's Committee on Foreign Aid (1947). *European Recovery and American Aid* GPO, Washington, D.C.

Price, H. H. (1955). *The Marshall Plan,* Cornell University Press, Ithaca, New York.

Romer, P. (1989). 'Cross-Country Determinants of the Rate of Technological Change', unpublished manuscript, University of Chicago.

—— (1990). 'Capical, Labor and Productivity', *Brookings Papers on Economic Activity.*

Schwartz, Hans-Peter (1986). *Adenauer: Der Aufstieg 1876–1952,* Deutsche Verlags-Anstalt, Stuttgart.

Stolper, Gustav, Karl Hauser and Knut Borchardt (1964). *Deutsche Wirtschaft seit 1870,* J. C. B. Mohr Siebeck, Tübingen.

Tinbergen, J. (1954). 'The Significance of the Marshall Plan for the Netherlands Economy', in Ministry of Finance, *Road to Recovery: The Marshall Plan, its Importance for the Netherlands and European Cooperation,* Ministry of Finance. The Hague.

United Nations (1948). *A Survey of the Economic Situation and Prospects of Europe,* UN. Geneva.

—— (1949a). *Economic Survey of Europe in 1948,* UN, Geneva.

—— (1949b). *World Economic Report, 1948,* Lake Success, UN, New York.

—— (1950). *Economic Survey of Europe in 1949,* UN, Geneva.

—— (1951). *Economic Survey of Europe in 1950,* UN, Geneva.

—— (1964). *Some Factors in the Economic Growth of Europe During the 1950s,* UN. Geneva.

United States Department of State (1948a). *The European Recovery Program: Introduction to Country Studies,* US Department of State, Washington, D.C.

—— (1948b). *Foreign Relations of the United States in 1947,* GPO, Washington, D.C.

United States House of Representatives (1948). *Final Report on Foreign Aid,* Select Committee on Foreign Aid, GPO, Washington, D.C.

—— (1949). *Hearings Before the Committee on Foreign Affairs,* 81st Congress, 1st Session, on H.R. 2362, A Bill to Amend the Economic Cooperation Act of 1948, Part 1, GPO, Washington, D.C.

United States Mutual Security Agency (1953). *The Structure and Growth of the Italian Economy,* MSA, Rome.

—— (various years). *Report to Congress,* GPO, Washington, D.C.

United States Senate (1948). *Administration of United States Aid for a European Recovery Program,* Report to the Committee on Foreign Relations, 80th Congress, 2nd Session, GPO, Washington, D.C.

—— (1949). *Hearings on the Extension of ERP,* Foreign Relations Committee, 81st Congress, 1st Session, GPO, Washington, D.C.

van der Wee, H. (1986). *Prosperity and Upheaval,* University of California Press, Berkeley.

Wall, I. M. (1991). *The United States and the Making of Postwar France, 1945–1954,* Cambridge University Press, Cambridge.

Wallich, H. (1955). *Mainsprings of the German Economic Revival,* Yale University Press, New Haven.

Windmuller, J. P. (1969). *Labor Relations in the Netherlands,* Cornell University Press, Ithaca, New York.

Winks, R. W. (1960). *The Marshall Plan and the American Economy,* Holt, Rinehart and Winston, New York.

Economic Policy April 1992 Printed in Great Britain

Trade with Eastern Europe

Carl B. Hamilton and L. Alan Winters

Summary

Previous economic policy in the Soviet Union and Eastern Europe sought to restrict international trade with market economies. Hence, liberalization and reform should now lead to a huge increase in such trade. This will have a major impact both on the reforming economies and on their new trade partners.

First, we develop an empirical model of trade flows between existing market economies, and use this to forecast long-run trade flows as the former Soviet Union and Eastern Europe are reabsorbed into the world economy. Second, we provide a more detailed analysis of one key sector, agricultural trade. We compare and contrast three regime changes: reform in the East, admission of the East to the EC CAP and worldwide success on agricultural liberalization in the GATT. Third, we adduce evidence of high quality human capital in Eastern Europe and argue that this will tend to confer a comparative advantage in quite sophisticated products.

We conclude by stressing that since trade cannot be permanently and profoundly unbalanced, Western market economies can enjoy potential gains from trade only if they allow market access to emergent producers from the former Soviet Union and Eastern Europe.

Opening up international trade with Eastern Europe

Carl B. Hamilton and L. Alan Winters
Institute for International Economic Studies, Stockholm,
and University of Birmingham

with the assistance of Per Lundsjo and Zhen Kun Wang

1. Introduction

One explicit goal of economic policy in the former Soviet Union and Eastern Europe (henceforth SUEE) during the communist period was to limit economic dependence on the West. Hence, opening up these economies is now expected to lead to a huge increase in their trade with Western market economies. Opening up the SUEE, accounting for about 15% of world income, would introduce new supplies of goods and export market opportunities on a scale and speed unprecedented in modern history. How and with whom this trade will evolve is a question of major significance.

This paper offers some answers. First, we estimate the eventual volume and direction of SUEE trade. Trade within the SUEE will remain static or fall, but, even with the present low levels of national income, trade with Western markets could increase up to fivefold. West European trade with the SUEE will increase very significantly, especially in Germany, the gateway to the East. However, Western Europe cannot hope to retain its current dominant share of trade with the East: as market forces take hold, SUEE trade with Japan and the US will increase sharply, albeit from a low baseline. Overall, we estimate that SUEE trade will raise US exports and imports by 20% and 11%, German trade by 24% and UK trade by about 14%.

Increases in exports and imports must broadly balance. Hence, if Western producers are to reap opportunities for higher exports and investment, Western consumers and firms must be allowed to benefit

Part of this work was supported by CEPR's programme 'The Economic Transformation of Eastern Europe' funded by the Ford Foundation and the SPES programme of the European Commission. We are grateful to the editors and members of the Economic Policy Panel for comments on an earlier draft, and to Tina Attwell for typing.

from increased imports from the SUEE. It is through this route – and this route alone – that the West as a whole can benefit from SUEE liberalization and growth. Any attempt to boost Western exports without a corresponding increase in imports is bound to fail, because SUEE demand will be frustrated, either immediately or as SUEE countries fall ever further into debt.

The second issue is to identify the sectors most affected, both in Eastern and Western economies. We consider two aspects of this question. The first is agriculture. The inefficiency of SUEE agriculture is well known. Farmers the world over, however, are among the most flexible of producers: we anticipate that better incentives and the import of Western technology and organization will stimulate agricultural production. With rising incomes, domestic consumption will also increase. Section 3 examines the implications for agricultural production, export supply and prices both at home and in world markets.

We are especially interested in closer integration of Eastern Europe with the EC's Common Agricultural Policy (CAP), and in the effects of a worldwide trade liberalization as under discussion in the Uruguay Round of the GATT. We conclude that in either case developments in the SUEE will put considerable strain on the CAP, essentially because additional world supply inevitably reduces world prices. We also note, however, that the effects of higher SUEE supply are themselves substantially smaller than those that would emanate from a desirable reform of the CAP itself.

Section 4 of the paper turns from agriculture to manufactures and considers one important aspect of comparative advantage. The present low wage costs in the SUEE, coupled with pessimism about possible inflows of capital, have led some to conclude that its manufactured exports will be concentrated on unsophisticated labour-intensive goods, as presently produced in parts of Southern Europe and the NICs. This may be correct in the short run. However, as we argued in CEPR (1990), human capital statistics rank Eastern Europe above the NICs and Southern Europe in skill and education. SUEE long-run strength is likely to lie in more sophisticated goods. We now develop this theme. First, we examine data suggesting that the quality of scientific education in Poland compares with that in several industrial countries, while that in Hungary is among the very best in the world. Second, we show that these quality indicators correlate well with comparative advantage in sophisticated engineering goods. Third, recent research identifies the proportion of school children in secondary education, another aspect in which the SUEE looks more like Western than Southern Europe or the NICs, as a key determinant of an economy's ability to grow.

2. The size and direction of SUEE trade

Economic theory has much to say about the composition of international trade, but much less about its volume and direction; yet these are issues of considerable political and economic importance. In this section we explore the potential volume and direction of SUEE trade using a simple but robust model of trade flows, the gravity model.[1]

2.1. The gravity model

The gravity model (Linnemann, 1966) pragmatically combines three determinants of the size of bilateral international trade flows: the importer's demand, the exporter's supply and the costs of doing business. Its theoretical foundations have never been entirely secure (Wang and Winters, 1991) yet it has intuitive appeal and has been used for a wide range of tasks – e.g. Aitken (1973), Bergstrand (1985), Slama (1983) and Brada and Mendez (1985). We use it to characterize the trading patterns of a large sample of market economies and then assume that eventually the SUEE will slot into the same pattern.

The gravity model refers to countries' total trade and may be estimated on cross-section data. It is best interpreted as providing a long-run equilibrium view of trading patterns; hence for now we ignore the issue of how the SUEE makes the transition to that pattern.

The trade flow from country of origin i to country of destination j is viewed in terms of the framework of Table 1. Country i's potential supply of exports depends on its GNP and on its 'openness ratio' (total exports to total production) which tends to vary inversely with population. Population proxies the physical size of an economy. Larger economies have less need to trade in order to gain from specialization or scale economies. Similar arguments apply to imports: higher GNP suggests higher demand, larger population suggests greater self-sufficiency.

The remaining variables reflect the costs of trade, or trade barriers. The main natural obstacles to trade are transport and transactions costs. The former are related to distance, while the latter are partly related to the 'economic horizon' of a country. People are better informed about, and have closer ties with, nearby countries. We use geographic distance to measure both the natural obstacles to trade. This is supplemented, however, by an adjacency dummy which is non-zero if i and j share a common land border; it reflects reductions in both cultural

----

[1] The model used here was developed by Zhen Kun Wang.

Table 1. The gravity model of exports from country i to country j

Variable	Sign	Reason
GNP of i	+	Export supply; number of varieties available
Population of i	−	Larger countries more self-sufficient
GNP of j	+	Import demand; demand for variety
Population of j	−	Self–sufficiency, less specialized
Distance	−	Transaction costs; 'economic horizons'
Adjacency	+	Common borders cut costs, increase contacts
Trade preferences	+	Reduced trade costs

Note: We assume the logarithm of the trade flow is linearly related to logarithms of explanatory variables.

and transportation frictions between adjacent countries over and above the effect of distance. The main artificial or strategic obstacle to trade is trade policy itself. We omit from our sample trade distorted for political reasons (e.g. Iran–Iraq, China and the SUEE), and proxy preferential trading arrangements by a series of dummy variables.

The gravity model does not relate trade directly to prices, which are endogenous and adjust to equate supply and demand. As Leamer and Stern (1970) observe, this does not imply that prices are ineffective in allocating resources. Rather the model should be viewed as a reduced form in which GNP, population and distance are the ultimate determinants both of trade and of prices (and exchange rates).

We estimate a (log-linear) form of the relationship in Table 1. We use data only from market economies to describe 'normal' trade patterns. Data, averaged over 1984–86 to reduce the effects of temporary distortions, refer to 76 countries (19 industrial and 57 LDCs) which account for about 80% of total world trade during 1984–86.[2] Trade data describe total merchandise imports ($US mn.) from the IMF *Direction of International Trade*; we use export data only to fill in gaps.[3]

GDP data (in $US mn.), from the World Bank's *World Development Indicators*, are also averaged over 1984–86. Population data (millions), from the same source, are for 1985. Distances are in nautical miles (1 nautical mile = 1.15 land miles) for the shortest navigable distance between countries' main ports, plus the overland distance from the ports to the economic centres of the countries concerned. For countries

---

[2] The chief omissions are oil exporters, SUEE (except Yugoslavia) and China.

[3] Very small trade flows are recorded as zero in *DIT*, which creates a problem in log-linear equations. We omit all such flows, and hence estimate the size of trade conditional on its being large enough to be recorded. Wang and Winters (1991) consider other solutions.

Table 2. Estimates of the gravity model of trade flows
(Dependent variable: natural log of exports from *i* to *j*)

Explanatory variable	Coefficient	*t*-statistic
Constant	−12.5	34.3
GNP of *i*	1.2	58.2
Population of *i*	−0.4	15.7
GNP of *j*	1.0	42.8
Population of *j*	−0.2	8.2
Distance from *i* to *j*	−0.8	22.3
Dummy variables:		
adjacency	0.8	3.3
EC	0.7	2.2
EFTA	0.0	0.1
ECOWAS	−0.3	0.3
SADCC	1.3	1.0
CACM	2.1	1.3
AG	0.4	0.6
LAIA	1.0	2.9
ASEAN	2.3	5.2
UK Ex-Colonial	1.9	5.0
French Ex-Colonial	0.7	1.2
GSP	0.4	2.9
ACP	0.9	4.2
ACP*	1.1	5.3

Notes: 4,320 observations. The dummy variables take the value 2
when *i* and *j* satisfy the criterion and 1 otherwise. The preference
dummies refer to the European Communities (EC), European
Free Trade Association (EFTA), the Economic Community of
West African States (ECOWAS), the South African Development
Coordination Conference (SADCC), the Central American Common Market (CACM), the Andean Group (AG), Latin American
Integration Association (LAIA) and Association of South East
Asian Nations (ASEAN). Unilateral preferences include the Generalized System of Preferences (GSP), and EC preferences under
the Lome convention (ACP for such exports to the EC, ACP* for
the reverse flow).

in continental Europe, however, where overland transport predomi-
nates, the direct rail or road distance between economic centres is used.[4]
Trade preference dummies refer to ex-colonial relationships, economic
integration schemes, unilateral preferences from industrial countries
to LDCs and EC preferences to certain LDCs.

The estimates in Table 2 confirm our hypotheses above. All the
coefficients except for two dummy variables have the expected signs.
All the gravity model variables, and many of the trade preference
dummies, are also highly statistically significant. The relationship of

---

[4] For continental Africa, where road transport is poor and therefore expensive, we use sea distances.

Table 2 explains over 70% of the variation in bilateral trade flows between the 76 market economies in the sample. It provides the desired basis for thinking how the SUEE economies may behave once they become market economies.

Table 2 reports strong income effects on trade, and mild, but well defined, population effects. Rewriting the trade equation in terms of income per head and a size variable (either total GNP or population), both affluence and size affect trade positively, as is predicted by modern trade theory, such as Barker (1977), Krugman and Helpman (1985) and Krugman (1989).

We do not wish to make too much out of the precise estimates of region-specific effects, nor shall we make use of them below; but in passing we discuss briefly their general implications for SUEE trade. The strongest and best-defined effect refers to a regional grouping of relatively small countries (ASEAN); effects of other regional groupings are much harder to detect. Hence, while history and geography may encourage Eastern European cooperation, such cooperation cannot be guaranteed to stimulate trade. Moreover, the gravity model cannot distinguish between trade creation and trade diversion. The increases in intra-bloc trade recorded in Table 2 may reduce rather than increase welfare. LDC groupings aside, Table 2 finds strong trade linkages between the former British colonies, but only weak effects from wider preferential trade arrangements. Making the latter effective, especially between richer and poorer countries, may be hard because of the complex restrictions and reservations embodied in the typical arrangements (Svedberg, 1981). Hence, short of full accession, Eastern Europe should not expect a substantial boost to trade from favoured access to the EC or other markets.

2.2. Predicting trade in the SUEE

We now apply the estimates in Table 2 to SUEE data to estimate those countries' trade potential based on data from 1985. We also compare this estimate of long-run potential trade with actual trade in 1985.

2.2.1. Data for the SUEE. There is great ignorance about the levels of SUEE GNP. Estimates by different international agencies for the same country's GNP can vary by a factor of five (CEPR, 1990; Collins and Rodrik, 1991). Since incomes matter in the gravity model, there is an unavoidable uncertainty about our estimates. Here we report results based on GNP data in Summers and Heston (1988), which fall in the middle of the range of published estimates. Wang and Winters (1991) repeat the exercise using a wider range of GNP data.

There are also severe problems with the estimates of actual SUEE trade in 1985. As with market economies, Hungary, Poland and Romania are included in the *Direction of International Trade*. However, for bilateral trade between other SUEE economies, we have to rely on data from various issues of *PlanEcon*. These latter data, reported in transferable roubles, depend on two potentially very distorted exchange rates: conversion of transferable roubles into local currency and then into dollars according to conversion factors provided by *PlanEcon*.

The implied exchange rates between the transferable rouble and the dollar vary considerably by country. For Hungary and Poland, the countries most integrated with the West and adopting IMF statistical norms, the transferable rouble/dollar rates were 1.94 (Hungary) and 2.16 (Poland), in contrast to 0.64 (Bulgaria), 1.38 (Czechoslovakia), 0.63 (East Germany) and 0.61 (USSR). Hence, we suspect that the 'actual' trade data between these latter countries quoted below are seriously exaggerated.[5]

2.2.2. Potential trade. Tables 3 and 4 report our estimated potential trade flows for each SUEE country, and 'actual' trade flows for 1985. For trade within the SUEE, reported trade greatly exceeds predicted potential trade for the USSR, Czechslovakia, Bulgaria and East Germany, the countries with the most serious data problems. On the other hand, Poland seems not to have achieved its potential, while Hungary and Romania seem to be roughly in line with trade potential with their SUEE partners.

Overall, then, we believe that while Comecon caused a huge increase in the share of intra-CMEA trade in total trade, it probably did not increase the absolute level of intra-bloc trade much above 'normal' levels. Until the valuation of intra-bloc trade can be put on a sounder footing, this conclusion, though interesting, must remain tentative.

Clearly, SUEE trade with market economies currently falls dramatically short of its potential. Hungary and Romania have trade volumes of about 30% of potential; other SUEE countries only about 20%. Notice next the impact of politics on SUEE trade: trade with LDCs is least below potential, then trade with EFTA (in which Finland is very strongly represented), while trade with the EC and other industrial countries is much more restricted. It is striking that while SUEE trade with LDCs broadly matches potential, the shortfalls with other industrial countries,

---

[5] Imagine an item traded among Eastern-bloc countries for 1 transferable rouble. If it were exported by Poland it would be valued at 201 zloty (201 zloty per rouble) and hence $0.46 (434.6 zloty per dollar). If it were exported by Bulgaria, however, the sequence would be 1.3 leva (1.3 leva per rouble) and $1.26 (1.028 leva per dollar).

Table 3. SUEE potential trade and actual 1985 trade
($ bn., A = actual, P = potential)

		EC	EFTA	Other indust.	LDCs	76 countries	SUEE
Bulgaria	exports A	0.4	0.1	0.1	0.6	1.1	9.9
	P	2.5	0.6	1.7	0.7	5.6	2.6
	imports A	1.3	0.4	0.3	0.7	2.7	10.1
	P	2.7	0.7	2.0	0.6	6.0	2.7
CSFR	exports A	1.5	0.6	0.2	1.2	3.3	12.5
	P	15.2	2.2	4.2	1.7	23.3	7.4
	imports A	1.6	0.5	0.2	0.6	2.9	13.4
	P	15.7	2.4	4.6	1.3	24.0	7.2
GDR	exports A	4.7	0.7	0.2	1.2	6.7	25.0
	P	23.6	4.1	6.4	2.2	36.3	9.0
	imports A	4.3	0.5	0.3	1.1	6.2	24.1
	P	23.9	4.3	6.8	1.7	36.7	8.4
Hungary	exports A	1.3	0.8	0.3	0.9	3.2	4.5
	P	6.5	0.9	2.4	1.2	10.1	4.1
	imports A	1.8	0.8	0.4	0.7	3.8	4.0
	P	6.9	1.1	2.7	1.0	11.6	4.1
Poland	exports A	2.5	0.7	0.3	1.4	4.9	6.0
	P	12.7	2.6	5.9	2.0	23.2	9.2
	imports A	2.1	0.6	0.5	1.1	4.1	6.4
	P	13.9	3.1	6.9	1.7	25.6	9.5
Romania	exports A	2.6	0.3	0.8	1.9	5.6	4.0
	P	5.3	1.3	3.1	1.5	11.1	4.4
	imports A	0.8	0.2	0.4	1.6	3.1	3.7
	P	5.8	1.5	3.7	1.3	12.4	4.6
USSR	exports A	14.1	4.6	1.7	4.7	25.1	33.4
	P	66.9	15.3	37.7	12.8	132.6	16.1
	imports A	10.3	4.7	7.8	9.5	32.2	40.3
	P	72.7	17.7	43.3	10.7	144.4	16.4
Total SUEE	exports A	27.2	7.0	3.6	12.6	50.3	95.2
	P	132.6	27.0	61.4	22.1	243.2	52.8
	imports A	22.2	7.7	9.9	15.3	55.1	101.9
	P	141.7	30.7	69.9	18.4	260.7	52.8

Source: IMF *Direction of International Trade, 1989*; *PlanEcon 1987*; authors' calculations.
Note: 76 countries refers to total trade with the sample of countries used in estimating the gravity model in Table 2.

of which the US and Japan are the principal components, are by factors of 20 and 30.

Table 3 predicts large increases in the trade/output ratio or openness of SUEE economies. Table 5 compares the reported shares of exports in GDP in 1985 with those predicted by our model. The 'adjusted' figures make allowance both for the inadequate treatment of zero trade flows by the gravity model and the omission from our sample of certain countries (see Wang and Winters, 1991, for details). If the reported

Table 4. SUEE potential and actual 1985 trade with individual countries ($ bn., A = actual, P = potential)

		France	Germany	Italy	UK	Japan	US
Bulgaria	exports A	0.1	0.2	0.1	0.0	0.0	0.0
	P	0.5	0.7	0.5	0.4	0.3	1.2
	imports A	0.2	0.6	0.2	0.2	0.1	0.1
	P	0.6	0.7	0.5	0.4	0.4	1.4
CSFR	exports A	0.2	0.8	0.2	0.1	0.1	0.1
	P	2.6	4.8	2.2	1.9	0.8	2.9
	imports A	0.2	0.9	0.2	0.2	0.1	0.1
	P	2.7	5.0	2.2	1.8	0.8	3.2
GDR	exports A	0.3	3.6	0.1	0.2	0.0	0.1
	P	3.4	10.9	2.6	2.6	0.9	4.7
	imports A	0.2	3.5	0.1	0.1	0.2	0.1
	P	3.5	11.2	2.5	2.5	1.0	5.0
Hungary	exports A	0.1	0.7	0.3	0.1	0.0	0.2
	P	1.1	1.5	1.2	0.8	0.4	1.6
	imports A	0.2	0.9	0.2	0.2	0.1	0.3
	P	1.2	1.6	1.2	0.8	0.5	1.8
Poland	exports A	0.3	1.0	0.3	0.4	0.1	0.2
	P	1.6	4.6	1.9	1.8	0.9	4.3
	imports A	0.2	1.0	0.2	0.2	0.1	0.2
	P	1.8	5.3	2.1	2.0	1.0	5.1
Romania	exports A	0.3	0.8	0.8	0.3	0.1	0.7
	P	1.1	1.4	1.0	0.8	0.6	2.1
	imports A	0.1	0.3	0.1	0.2	0.1	0.3
	P	1.2	1.6	1.1	0.7	0.9	2.5
USSR	exports A	2.3	4.3	2.7	0.9	1.3	0.4
	P	10.1	25.6	8.1	8.0	5.5	27.3
	imports A	2.1	4.0	1.7	0.8	3.1	2.7
	P	11.0	28.6	8.5	8.4	6.1	31.5
Total SUEE	exports A	3.4	11.2	4.5	2.1	1.6	1.7
	P	20.4	49.4	16.7	16.3	9.4	44.0
	imports A	3.1	11.2	2.8	1.7	3.7	3.7
	P	22.0	54.0	18.0	16.6	10.7	50.4

Source: As in Table 3.

'actual' data are exaggerated by overvaluation of intra-CMEA trade, the required increases in openness are greater than implied by the table.

Table 5 confirms the importance of international trade to the emergent economies; failure to realize the potential increases in trade could have serious implications. The estimates of Tables 3–4 confirm that sound international trade relations are likely to offer a far greater stimulus to the SUEE than could any conceivable aid flow.

Table 6 adopts the spectacles of the SUEE's major trading partners in the EC, US and Japan. The relative success of West Germany in Eastern European markets (other than the USSR) is clearly evident; the difference between potential and actual trade is 'only' about three

Table 5. Openness ratios (exports as % of GNP)

	Potential		Reported 1985 actual
	Crude	Adjusted	
Bulgaria	18	21	24
CSFR	26	28	14
GDR	31	33	19
Hungary	25	31	14
Poland	17	19	6
Romania	16	23	11
USSR	8	9	3

Source: As in Table 3.

Table 6. Potential extra trade with the SUEE

		France	Germany	Italy	UK	Japan	US
Potential minus actual, $ bn.							
exports	E. Europe	10.0	18.1	8.3	7.3	3.9	17.9
	USSR	9.0	24.6	6.8	7.6	3.1	28.9
imports	E. Europe	9.3	16.8	7.6	7.1	3.7	15.5
	USSR	7.8	21.4	5.4	7.1	4.2	26.8
Increase as multiple of current trade							
exports	E. Europe	9.7	2.5	7.4	7.7	5.9	17.6
	USSR	2.8	6.2	4.0	10.1	1.0	10.8
imports	E. Europe	8.1	3.4	4.3	5.9	14.0	12.1
	USSR	3.4	5.0	2.0	8.4	3.2	66.6
Increase as % of total actual trade							
exports	E. Europe	9.8	9.9	10.6	7.0	2.2	8.4
	USSR	8.9	13.4	8.6	7.5	1.7	13.5
imports	E. Europe	8.6	10.6	8.3	6.5	2.8	4.3
	USSR	7.2	13.5	5.9	6.5	3.2	7.4

Source: As in Table 3.

times actual trade in aggregate; in fact, Germany's ratio of actual to potential exports exceeds the corresponding ratio for the EC as a whole for every Eastern European partner. Hence, German exports will benefit *proportionately less* from liberalization than will those from other countries, as this initial distortion is removed. Even so, in *absolute* terms, German trade with the East is a major beneficiary of liberalization. Of course, part of these gains – those with East Germany – will now be recorded as internal German trade, but they are real enough; and, even without them, German trade receives a strong stimulus. Germany's trade with the former USSR also looks set for a large expansion, but in this case from a more modest base.

Table 6 also shows that the US has a very large stake in the liberalization of SUEE trade, and even Japan, by far the least affected major country in absolute terms, has increases amounting to 6% and 4% to total imports and exports respectively.[6] Such figures suggest strong adjustment pressures in the industrialized countries. We cannot expect the achievement of potential trade volumes to take less than two or three decades, however, so even for the US and West Germany we are considering increases in the growth rates of trade of perhaps only 1% per annum.

Table 3 implies that rather than their actual mere 7% of world merchandise trade, the SUEE could, even at their current income levels, account for 18% of such trade. Table 2 implies that both exports and imports grow at almost the same rate as income. Thus, as SUEE incomes increase, trade potential will become substantially greater than that shown in Table 3.

2.2.3. Other approaches. It will take a long time to discover if these long-run predictions are fulfilled. It is interesting, however, to compare them with other approaches to the same question. Collins and Rodrik (1991) fit relationships for aggregate exports and imports with respect to countries' GNP and population and apply these to SUEE data to obtain total trade potential. After adjusting our own results to allow for our incomplete country coverage and our treatment of null trade flows, the two approaches are fairly similar in this regard.

For the direction of trade, however, there is a marked contrast between our results and those of Collins and Rodrik. The latter estimate partners' shares in each SUEE country's total exports by updating a 1928 trade matrix. For a sample of six comparator countries – Austria, Finland, Germany, Italy, Portugal and Spain – they explain each partner country's share in total exports in 1989 as the sum of a fraction of its share in 1928 plus an effect specific to the partner but common to all sample countries.[7] Applying the model to SUEE export shares in 1928 generates shares for 1989. They conduct a similar exercise for imports.

This approach has two implications. First, because the comparator countries all experienced strong European integration between 1928 and 1989, this is built into predictions for the SUEE. Second, their method tends to predict similar shares for all Eastern European countries: the only thing that varies between countries – the 1928 share – is

---

[6] Trade with Japan may in fact be higher: Japan has a large trade potential with nearby areas of the USSR which is not adequately captured by the gravity model.

[7] Collins and Rodrik estimate an equation of the form $X_{89,ij} = a + b_j + cX_{28,ij}$ for i sample countries with j partners. $X_{89,ij}$ is j's share of i's exports in 1989, and a, b_j and c are parameters.

multiplied by a fraction before entering the 1989 share. The remaining component of the 1989 share – the partner effect – is common to all countries. As a result, Collins and Rodrik predict a greater concentration of Eastern trade on the EC than we do. For example, according to Collins and Rodrik the EC share of Eastern imports falls below 50% only for Hungary, and for exports only for Hungary and Czecho-slovakia. In contrast, we find only Czechoslovakia records EC shares of 50%, followed by Hungary and the USSR at around 44% and other countries below 40% (Table 3). Moreover, recognizing that countries are excluded from our sample of 76, would reduce the range of EC shares to 45% for Czechoslovakia down to 23% for Romania. Our approach also finds much greater potential for an expansion of SUEE trade with countries outside the EC, notably with the US.[8]

2.2.4. Implications for OECD countries. First, our implied long-run increases in OECD countries' SUEE trade are huge – exports up by 24% for West Germany, 22% for the US and 15% for the UK, and imports by similar amounts. This offers scope for new specialization and scale economies to an extent akin to the opening up of the New World, only more rapid.

Second, we expect a change in the composition of SUEE–OECD trade: the share of the US and Japan should increase and the share of the EC and EFTA should decrease. This in no way indicates any economic failure within Europe, nor does it call for a policy response.

Third, a weakness of the gravity model is that the increased trade we predict between, say, the UK and Poland, has no implications for the UK's other trade: it apparently neither diverts imports from other sources nor absorbs exports destined for elsewhere. This implies that the new imports displace only domestic sales, while the new exports are met by curtailing domestic sales or increasing output. This is not necessarily a bad approximation (see Winters, 1984; Brenton and Winters, 1990), but it is rather extreme. Hence, overall we should expect some spillover from the growth of SUEE trade to declines in intra-industrial country flows: market economies may face extra competition in export as well as home markets.

It cannot be overemphasized that these opportunities for buying and selling cannot be decoupled. Any attempt by industrial countries as a whole to export in SUEE markets without accepting imports in return is destined to fail. Our model in fact predicts that at current income levels, the SUEE should in equilibrium run small trade deficits. But if SUEE economies grow relative to other countries, this imbalance will

------

[8] Our results for trade shares come closer to Collins and Rodrik's if we allow, as they implicitly do, for preferential trade with the EC, but in that case, our total trade volumes then exceed theirs.

gradually disappear. Foreign investment can of course finance some trade imbalances, especially during the transition, but it is simply implausible that such imbalances could be permanent and substantial.

Hence, Western economies must offer decent market access to the East; otherwise, *neither* West nor East can hope to benefit from liberalization. This entails not only immediate access, even to sensitive markets such as steel and agriculture, but also accepting large imports of goods the exact nature of which we cannot yet be sure. The consequent changes in the sourcing of Western production and consumption will require flexibility and adjustment, but will be spread over several decades, not least because the largest SUEE effects emanate from the former USSR, which seems likely to be among the slowest to emerge from the legacy of communism.

3. Eastern European agriculture

3.1. Introduction

The previous section analysed the volume of trade. We turn now to the possible composition of East European (EE) trade.[9] Historically, the EE countries were large agricultural exporters. The inefficiency of their agriculture under central planning is notorious. Together, these observations now suggest the likelihood of a substantial increase in EE agricultural output. What might occur when the EE starts exploiting its comparative advantage in agriculture? This section concentrates on Eastern Europe alone (to be defined precisely below) in order to avoid the even greater uncertainties about the future of Soviet agriculture.

An obvious tool for such analysis is a computable partial equilibrium model of international trade in agricultural commodities. We use a modified version of the well-known model by Tyers and Anderson (1986, 1988, 1992). The actual numbers from the simulations should be treated with caution, but we believe that the basic message robust.

Two important conclusions emerge from this analysis. First, for agriculture both in EE and the EC the change in trade regime is more important than productivity catchup or income growth. Second, the liberalization of Eastern Europe is another nail in the CAP's coffin. Even if Eastern Europe was denied free market access to the EC, EC farmers would still face lower domestic prices as additional EE output forced down world prices. The EC could avoid such an outcome only by spending more of its budget on export subsidies, incurring yet

---

[9] Per Lundsjo undertook the modelling work for this section.

stronger protests from other GATT members. Conversely, if Eastern Europe is allowed access to EC food markets, EC farmers again face lower prices and greater competition. Either way, EC farming output will fall and EC consumers will gain through lower prices. We now develop more carefully the basis for these conclusions.

3.2. The model

The Tyers and Anderson (TA) model is a comparative-static, 7-commodity simulation model of world trade in agriculture among 30 countries/country groups. The commodities are rice, wheat, coarse grains, sugar, dairy products, beef and pigs/poultry. We focus on the four most vital for Europeans: wheat, dairy products, beef and pork. Among the 30 countries and country groups, the USSR is one group, Eastern Europe (Poland, Czechoslovakia, Hungary, Romania and Bulgaria) another. The model captures interactions of consumption and production in each region, and cross-effects between the markets for the seven commodities.

For each country and commodity there is a production and consumption equation. Long-run production levels depend on a trend term reflecting the growth in agricultural productivity, and on changes in the real prices of farm output. Consumption is both direct and indirect: in addition to consumers' direct demand for food, there is a demand for fodder in animal production. Consumers' demand is determined by the long-run price and income elasticities of demand, and by population growth. Consumption of fodder (maize, barley and oats) is modelled as an input into the production of dairy, beef and pig/poultry, and depends on (a) the long-run price elasticity of demand for the final commodity in question; (b) the quantity of commodity i (a fodder) in the production of one unit of dairy, beef and pig/poultry, respectively; (c) the fraction of the livestock product in question that is fodder-fed (grazing can be an alternative); and (d) the long-run productivity growth in the production of dairy, beef and pig/poultry. For details of the model, see Tyers and Anderson (1992).

The model is partial equilibrium in the sense that exchange rates are exogenous and changes in export earnings influence neither real exchange rates nor demand. This would be an awkward assumption if agriculture was a major part of SUEE trade, but it currently accounts for only about 10% of such trade, (GATT, 1990).

For each country domestic and world prices are linked by a price transmission equation. The 'nominal protection coefficient' in that equation measures, crudely speaking, how protectionist the importing country is. However, some of the change in world prices filter through the trade barriers, causing changes in the domestic price. This effect is measured by an 'insulation coefficient'.

3.3. The scenarios

Our scenarios can be viewed as 'reruns of history', with and without liberalization. What could EE production, consumption and trade have been with and without the economic liberalization around 1990? We consider consumption, production, exports and prices and focus on the differences in these variables relative to a reference scenario reflecting the late 1980s in the absence of liberalization. In the reference scenario ('without liberalization') we assume that EE agriculture would have experienced its actual productivity level of the 1980s. In the alternative ('liberalization') scenarios, we assume EE agriculture enjoys a 15% productivity catchup from the import of Western technology and organizational skills. This assumption is motivated in more detail in the Appendix. The elasticities of demand and supply in each sector are assumed to be those of the US in the 1980s: we try to model the eventual behaviour of a market-oriented agricultural sector.

For EE, we reduce the cross-price supply elasticities to 30% of those used by TA; otherwise major price increases induce very substantial changes in the mix of products. Since these effects are not generally well estimated and our interest is more in overall farm output than the product mix, we preferred to attenuate these distracting effects. A side effect of the changes made is that the overall elasticities of supply are increased somewhat from TA's estimates. Details are given in Appendix Table A1. We now turn to our scenarios. In agriculture, the key issue is whether or not the EC allows EE free access to the EC food market.

3.3.1. Scenario 1: Integrating EE into the CAP. We assume that EE liberalization allows a 15% productivity catchup in agriculture and a more modest 10% rise in GNP. The effects of these changes are shown in Table 7. EE agricultural output increases except for dairy products, and net exports increase except for dairy and beef. World prices are depressed for all four commodities, forcing the EC to reduce production and net exports, except for dairy products, even through there is no change in the Common Agricultural Policy.

In the next phase (see Table 8), it is assumed that the liberalized EE is then integrated into the CAP, with EE farmers facing CAP prices and enjoying EC market access. To avoid bankrupting the EC, Table 8 assumes that the combined net export volume of each commodity from EE and the EC is the same as in the reference scenario. The resulting price increases for EE farmers would be significant, 40% for wheat and

Table 7. EE agricultural liberalization with unchanged world trade regime (% increase from reference scenario)

		Prices to		Farm		Net	World
		Farmers	Consumers	output	Consumption	exports	price
EE	wheat	11	11	24	0	219	−5
	dairy	−28	−28	−12	15	−360	10
	beef	−9	−9	7	8	−4	−1
	pork	21	21	42	−12	452	−5
EC	wheat	−1	−1	0	0	−3	
	dairy	3	3	2	−1	26	
	beef	0	0	1	0	776	
	pork	−4	−4	−4	3	−85	

Notes: 'Beef' includes veal; 'pork' includes poultry, lamb and mutton; 'dairy' is in milk equivalents.

Table 8. Integration of a more productive EE into the CAP (% increases)

		Prices to		Farm		Net
		Farmers	Consumers	output	Consumption	exports
EE	wheat	41	41	47	−2	450
	dairy	16	15	26	0	370
	beef	85	85	78	−23	1,030
	pork	32	32	54	−13	570
EC	wheat	−26	−29	−21	11	−100
	dairy	−10	−12	−5	6	−100
	beef	−19	−20	−18	14	−530
	pork	−17	−17	−17	17	−450

Notes: Scenario adjusts CAP to reduce EC exports by same amount as SUEE exports increase; hence world prices constant. See also notes to Table 7.

over 80% for beef. Thus, almost all the price effect comes from EE joining the CAP, not from the prior liberalization inside EE.

Enjoying these higher CAP prices, EE farmers increase their supply between 26% (dairy) and 78% (beef), and prices to EE consumers increase by between 15 and 85%. As a consequence consumption of beef and pork is reduced between 13 and 23%, while consumption of wheat and dairy products remain almost unchanged. Table 8 also shows the export volume increases (between 15 and 85% for EE).

Within the EC, the CAP accession of EE reduces farm prices in Western Europe by 10–26%, depending on the commodity, and also causes agricultural production to fall, most for wheat (21%) and least for dairy products (5%). EC net exports also fall significantly (remember the hard budget constraint on the CAP!) Apart from EE farmers, the 'winners' are EC consumers who face cheaper agricultural products.

3.3.2. Scenario 2: A successful GATT round. Suppose the Uruguay Round of multilateral trade negotiations results in a liberalization of world trade in agriculture. Would that benefit EE? If so, by how much?

Suppose the OECD and EE countries liberalize all agricultural trade (no import barriers), and that EE enjoys the agricultural productivity catchup and GNP growth discussed above. Unlike scenario 1, however, there is now no constraint on European net exports.

Table 9 presents the first part of this scenario, the GATT liberalization. The new world prices mean price increases for EE farmers, leading to higher EE output and net exports. The opposite effect occurs in the EC as previous protection is removed: farmers face lower prices and reduce production. EE consumers suffer from the world price increases, whereas EC consumers enjoy significantly lower prices for much of their food.

When additionally we assume higher EE productivity and income, the price increases to EE farmers are reduced slightly. However, the differences made by such growth to production and consumption are small both in EE and the EC.

Just how competitive can EE agriculture be expected to be in the next few years? Our results are more optimistic than some other studies (e.g. Hughes and Hare, 1991), but we feel that this optimism is justified provided EE is allowed access to Western European markets. First, there is considerable scope for productivity increases, not only on farms themselves but also in supporting infrastructure (communications, schooling, etc.). Second, price liberalization will affect EE factor productivity and use of intermediate inputs as well as trade. Third, for some considerable time to come, rural wages in EE will be low compared with the wages paid by major producers in Western Europe; this is particularly true of wages in Poland, Romania and Bulgaria. Fourth, if EE were given access to Western European markets it would have the clear advantage relative to overseas competitors (especially with regard to perishable products) of being situated right on the doorstep of one of the world's most affluent and densely populated markets.

To conclude, not only are Eastern nations being reborn as democracies and market economies, but this rebirth may have an important side effect, accelerating the demise of agricultural protection, perhaps the most inefficient of all Western economic institutions. A successful conclusion to the GATT round would give this process an important boost, but also directly benefit agricultural producers in EE.

Table 9. Liberalization of OECD trade and EE agriculture (% increases)

		Prices to		Farm output	Consumption	Net exports	World price
		Farmers	Consumers				
EE	wheat	36	36	25	−3	250	16
	dairy	16	16	12	−4	220	80
	beef	35	35	23	−12	360	48
	pork	39	39	43	−21	540	10
EC	wheat	−30	−33	−22	12	−110	
	dairy	−11	−13	−5	6	−110	
	beef	−42	−42	−40	42	−1,320	
	pork	−13	−14	−11	12	−290	

Notes: As in Table 7.

4. Eastern European schooling

In CEPR (1990) we argued that, contrary to the popular view, Eastern Europe's comparative advantage will eventually lie not in simple labour-intensive goods but in more sophisticated goods. The basis of this claim was a series of human capital statistics placing Eastern Europe between Southern Europe and the NICs on the one hand, and Western Europe on the other: for example, in the share of the workforce in professional occupations; the share having particular levels of educational qualification; the share engaged in R&D; the enrolment ratios in primary and secondary education; and the percentage of GDP devoted to education.

This section develops two aspects of schooling in Eastern Europe in more detail – the quality and quantity of secondary school outputs. First, we consider the achievement levels in science in Polish and Hungarian schools and find the latter very impressive indeed. We also show that, in market economies, such achievement levels correlate with comparative advantage in sophisticated products. Second, we briefly consider the importance of skilled labour in economic development and the apparent significance of secondary education in providing that labour. The proportion of the population receiving secondary schooling in Eastern Europe already apparently challenges the West.

There is currently concern about the migration of skilled labour from East to West Europe, especially if the latter maintains trade restrictions. Implicit in the analysis of this section, however, is the presumption that such migration does not reach such proportions as effectively to denude the Eastern economies of skills. It is not that we find this possibility inconceivable, but because it is useful to ask what trade patterns would be if the West adopts a moderately liberal stance.

4.1. The level of skills

4.1.1. The supply of skills. The data and interpretation in CEPR (1990) were subject to two major concerns. First, many of them are input measures, whereas what really matters is the output of skilled services from the work force. Differences in the productivity of skilled workers across countries, however, owe more to economic organization and incentive systems than to the workers *per se* once we normalize for their skill levels. We assume that eventually SUEE workers with particular skill levels and combinations of other factors to work with should be expected to be, ceteris paribus, as productive as those in market economies. The second concern was about the skill levels themselves. How do we know formal qualifications are of comparable levels to Western qualifications?

These are complex and sensitive issues, not yet close to being resolved. We offer a small contribution making use of a data source not normally studied by economists. Our results suggest that for Hungary skill levels may be higher than previously suspected. For Poland, on the other hand, they are perhaps lower.

4.1.2. School science scores. The data we examine are scores of school children on a series of internationally standardized science tests. The data, compiled by the International Association for the Evaluation of Educational Achievement (IEA), may be the largest social science research project ever undertaken. In the exercise, conducted during the 1970s – see Comber and Keeves (1973) – 258,000 pupils, 50,000 teachers and 10,000 schools in 19 countries were involved. We use preliminary results from a more wideranging study (IEA, 1988) conducted in the mid-1980s, which includes both Hungary and Poland in its sample.

The data refer to the scores of students of different ages on a standardized science test, which is designed to try to ensure that it is culture free and equally difficult for students studying different science curricula. Teachers are extensively involved in the preparation, testing, evaluation and interpretation of test results.

4.1.3. Two education systems.[10] Hungary has a long tradition of education which survived the socialist period largely unscathed. Compulsory schooling was introduced in 1777 and its role in social mobility and economic growth was recognized by the communists, with explicit

---

[10] This section draws heavily on *The International Encyclopedia of Education*, Jusen and Postlethwaite (1985).

emphasis on scientific and technological education. Equally clear was the preference for general education, which engenders flexibility, rather than vocational training; experts express high regard for Hungarian theoretical and formal schooling. In 1978, 89% of the relevant age cohort graduated from general schools (8th grade), 20% to academic secondary schools (gymnasia), 25% to vocational schools offering general and vocational education, and the remainder to trade schools. The last produce skilled workers, but the first two types of school offer access to tertiary education. In addition, adult education services are open to anyone who dropped out of school.

The Polish education system is much less well established. Its troubled history has left Poland with a fragmented and insecure school and college network. Just after World War I only 47% of children attended school and only one-third of teachers had been to teacher-training courses. Grammar schools existed but primarily to teach humanities, not science and technology. World War II saw the extermination or emigration of many intellectuals and the closure of the secondary schools, and even in 1948 only 55% of rural children had attended school. Primary education is now virtually universal and around 20% of students proceed from it to grammar schools. During the 1980s, however, both the number of students entering higher education and the number of school teachers holding university degrees declined. These trends stemmed from the low returns and few opportunities for the highly skilled in Poland, and probably also reflected a generally low assessment of the role of education.

4.1.4. Skill levels and IEA scores. The IEA studies generate data for three levels of schooling. We focus on 'level 2', roughly 14 to 15 year olds, and 'level 3', students at broadly the final stage of secondary school. We interpret level 2 as a measure of the level of scientific skill and awareness of the work force at large, and level 3 as indicative of what the upper echelons of the age cohort could achieve. The basic data, reported in Table 10, show clearly Hungary's very high levels of achievement in science education – ranked first at level 2, the broader indicator, and third at level 3. Poland is less spectacular but still in the same league as important western countries – on a par with Norway, and dominating Italy, Australia, Finland and Canada at level 3.

4.1.5. Comparative advantage. Can these measures of education explain any features of international trade? Our samples are too small to allow much formal analysis but we consider some simple correlations. The UN Economic Commission for Europe's *Economic Survey 1989/90* provides data on revealed comparative advantage in engineering exports (relative

Table 10. Educational levels and comparative advantage

Country	Mean science score		Revealed comparative advantage in engineering exports			
	Level 2	Level 3	Hi-tech	Adv-tech	Mid-tech	Lo-tech
Hungary	217	244				
Poland	181	210				
Australia	178	207				
Canada	186	193	55	79	250	52
England	167	246	120	121	59	107
Finland	185	200	34	64	38	123
Hong Kong	164	251	133	50	23	43
Italy	167	174	51	68	53	138
Japan	202	227	141	120	187	99
Norway	179	211	50	74	27	194
Singapore	165	231	267	107	64	75
Sweden	184	228	70	97	111	128
US	165	na	218	148	79	82

Source: IEA (1988), UN ECE (1990).

Table 11. Correlation between skill level and comparative advantage

	Average science score at	
	Level 2	Level 3
Hi-tech	−0.409	0.584*
Advanced-tech	0.002	0.371
Mid-tech	0.637*	−0.208
Lo-tech	0.183	−0.346

Note: Sample of countries shown in Table 10;
* denotes statistically significant at 5% level.

to all manufactured exports) disaggregated into hi-tech, advanced-tech, medium-tech and low-tech categories. Our hypothesis is that higher scientific skills in compulsory schooling (level 2) confers comparative advantage in medium-tech goods, which require a reasonably trained workforce. Better performance at the specialist level 3, on the other hand, would boost hi-tech and advanced-tech sectors.

Table 11 offers considerable support to our hypotheses even though not all the coefficients are statistically significant. In particular the level-2 scores are well correlated with mid-tech exports, and the level-3 cohort's skills relate well to hi-tech and advanced-tech trade. In all cases the inclusion of Singapore, with its exceptionally high comparative advantage in hi- and mid-tech engineering reduces the correlation coefficients significantly.

4.1.6. Hungary and Poland. Figures 1 and 2 plot, respectively the relationships between mid-tech industries and level-2 skills, and between hi-tech industries and level-3 skills. These figures also show skill levels in Poland and Hungary, and hence the industrial performance they might hope to enjoy. Clearly, Hungary is likely to be a significant exporter of engineering goods, both in hi-tech and mid-tech goods. Poland has less impressive qualifications and seems likely to operate at the lower end of the spectrum of sophistication.

These conclusions should not be taken too literally. There is more to comparative advantage than the performance of school children in standardized tests. However, these data are among the few really comparable between East and West, and their explanatory power for comparative advantage is, at least to us, surprisingly high. We certainly believe that the data refute the notion that Eastern Europe is doomed perpetually to produce simple labour-intensive goods. Hungary in particular appears to have the human infrastructure to become a formidable exporter of sophisticated goods.

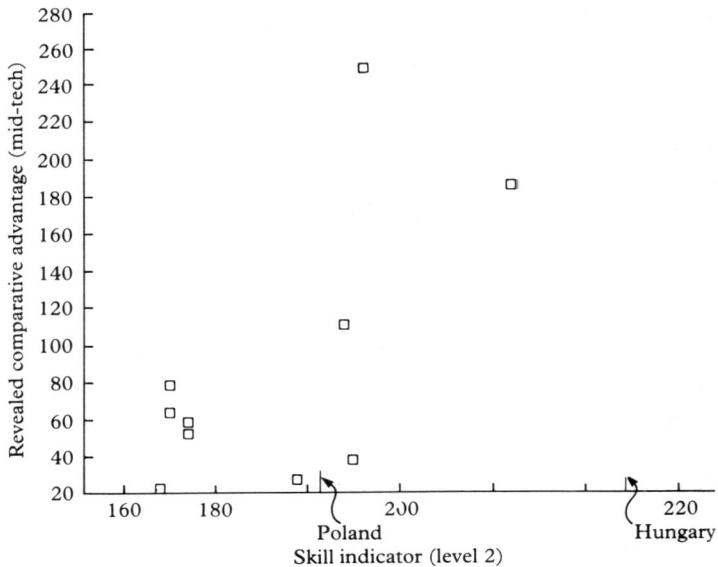

Figure 1. Level 2 skills and mid-tech goods

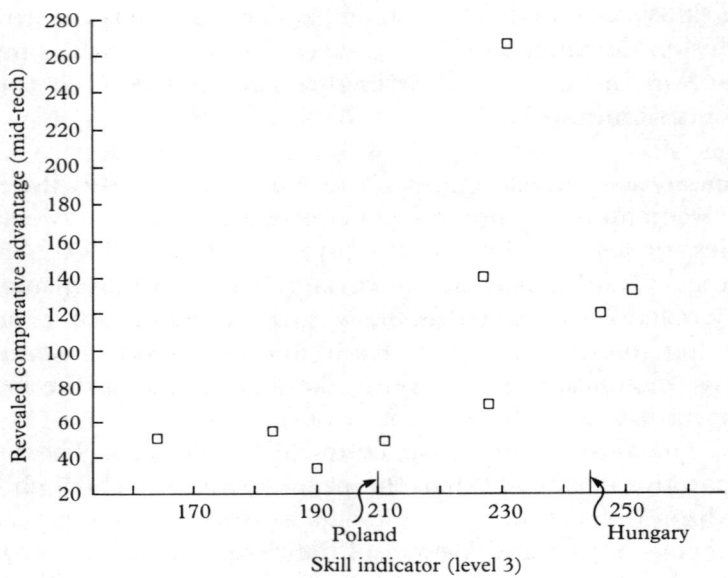

Figure 2. Level 3 skills and hi-tech goods

4.2. Secondary education and economic development

The importance of secondary education to economic development and hence indirectly to comparative advantage has been emphasized recently by Baumol *et al.* (1989). Working on a large sample of countries, they explore the ability of countries to catch up with the richest countries in per capita income. Catchup has been known as a statistical phenomenon for some time, (Baumol, 1986), but explanations for its patchy occurrence have taken longer to emerge. De Long (1988) found little role for religion (the protestant work-ethic) or political institutions. Recent research emphasizes catchup via technical spillover (broadly defined): richer countries generally have more to teach poorer ones than vice versa.[11]

There are two key conditions for effective spillover. First, the receptiveness to new ideas, and the ability to adapt them to local circumstances, may be related to an economy's stock of available skills: if skill levels lie below some minimum level, imitation and adaptation are

[11] Catchup is sometimes claimed to be a statistical artefact. Countries which initially have low incomes will *appear* to catch up either if all countries are converging to a single world mean income or if incomes are measured with error. In the latter case, an artificially low measured initial income suggests high growth if subsequent incomes are not subject to the same mismeasurement. Generally, the statistical analysis of Baumol *et al.* (1989) avoids such pitfalls.

too weak to permit catchup – hence the dismal performance among developing countries noted in Baumol *et al.* (1989). If the key to catchup is a *widespread* ability to imitate and adapt rather than to innovate *de novo*, the critical dimension of skill is likely to be broadly based rather than specialist. The second condition is that ideas are likely to flow more smoothly between countries that are similar, not least in the composition and level of their human capital.

Baumol *et al.* consider the role of education in these two dimensions, and with striking results. The inclusion of educational data restored 'orderly behaviour' in the catchup equations at nearly all levels of income. Specifically, 'countries with similar education levels were shown quite consistently to be converging among themselves (in real GDP per head), though not catching up with countries whose educational levels were higher'. Moreover, the statistical relationship was much stronger using enrolment in secondary education than using that in primary or tertiary education.

These results are corroborated in a slightly more formal analysis by Mankiw *et al.* (1990). They add human capital to a traditional Solovian growth model, and find that it improves the ability to explain cross-country differences in per capita growth rates and reveals catchup effects not evident in simpler models. The accumulation of human capital is measured by the ratio of enrolments in secondary education to total labour force. According to their estimates, based on market economies, a 1% increase in this ratio (not a 1 percentage point increase) raises steady-state income per head by 0.7%.

Figure 3 reports enrolments in secondary education around 1986, taken from World Bank: *World Development Indicators, 1989*. Within each of the six groups, countries are ranked GNP per head, except for the SUEE (group VI) for which those data are so doubtful; the groups are also conjoined broadly in income order. The figure gives a clear impression of the link between education and affluence. More significantly, it further suggests that the SUEE countries are more akin to the industrial countries than to any other group. The very low observation in group VI pertains to Czechoslovakia (39%), and may be erroneous. Otherwise, the bulk of SUEE countries rank with West Germany, Sweden and the UK in this critical aspect of economic potential.

Of course, SUEE incomes lag far behind those of the comparable group, and will probably take decades to catch up. Baumol *et al.* do not estimate speeds of convergence directly but, for given education levels, every $1,000 difference in two countries' initial incomes per head (in 1950) raised the poorer's growth rate over the period 1950–81 by 0.8% per annum above the richer's. In today's prices (four times higher than

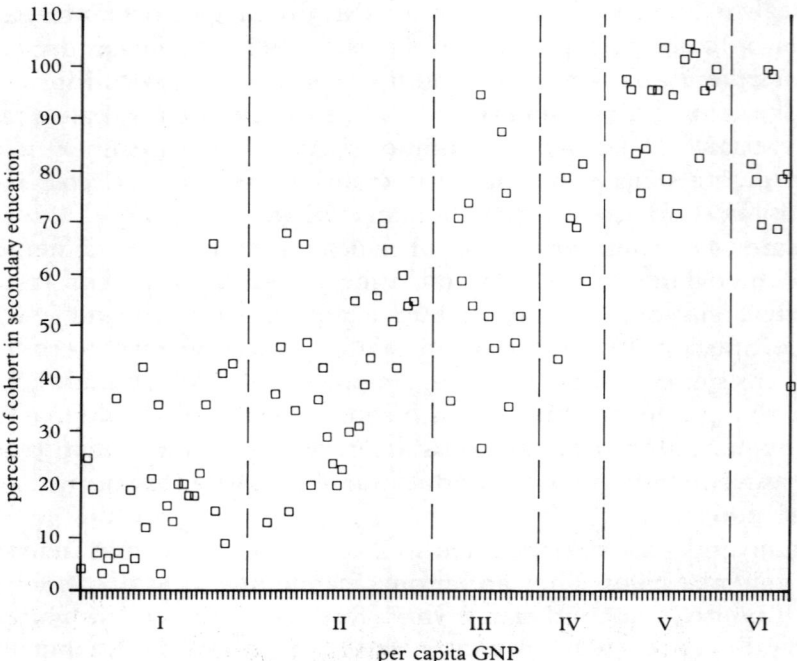

Figure 3. Secondary education enrolment and per capita GNP, 1986

Source: World Bank, *World Development Indicators*.
Notes: Countries grouped as follows: I = low-income, II = lower-middle income,
III = upper middle income, IV = high-income LDCs, V = industrial countries,
VI = Eastern Europe and the USSR.

1950s according to US wholesale price inflation) this implies about an extra 1% per annum on the growth rate for every $5,000 difference in income. Thus, the SUEE might grow at some 2% faster than the EC (average per capita incomes being roughly $6,500 and $16,500, respectively). At this rate it would make up half the income discrepancy in about 30 years.

Mankiw *et al.* (1990) approach catchup differently. They estimate that a country might make up slightly below 2% of the gap between its actual and its potential income in any year. (The latter depends on savings behaviour as well as on technology and education.) By including human capital, this approach suggests most economies have higher total capital (physical + human) than is usually presumed, and hence tends to support relatively slow convergence. A given savings rate must now support investment both in human and physical capital. However, if we believe the SUEE already has the human capital (essentially unused during communism), savings can be devoted solely to physical capital, and the SUEE would catch up faster than the average developing country. On the other hand, human capital depreciates, and investment is needed to update skill levels. Hence, net investment (savings less depreciation) will still be lower in this model than in a more traditional one.

Overall, catching up still looks likely to be long-lived. Yet the data reported here, coupled with the results of Baumol *et al.* and Mankiv *et al.*, offer an optimistic prognosis of the SUEE's fundamental ability to do so. This evidence further reinforces the view that SUEE comparative advantage will lie in relatively sophisticated goods.

5. Conclusions

It is widely accepted that international openness plays an important role in economic development. It will be even more important for the emergent SUEE economies as they try to throw off the yoke of (mis)managed trade and production. International trade has the potential to generate income, introduce new technologies and organizational skills, stimulate competition, inform tastes and broaden horizons. SUEE governments now show an appreciation of these benefits, but trade always involves two partners. The changes implicit in Eastern liberalization are dramatic, even for Western nations, which face increases in their trade of some 20%, and increased competition – in agriculture and labour-intensive goods at first but eventually in more sophisticated goods. Unfortunately, the impressive determination for change in the East is not matched by similar examples of determination and statesmanship in the West.

The association agreements to open EC markets to the East – the first of which was signed in November 1991 – are devalued considerably by EC prevarication over both agriculture, and textiles and clothing. The latter are subject to long transitional arrangements; the former remain subject to formal and informal controls. If agriculture and textiles remain blocked by quantitative restrictions, what are the prospects for other goods which Eastern countries might come to produce? The EC's armoury of anti-dumping duties and voluntary export restraints is quite sufficient to stifle the East's incentives to invest in the production of new goods. The EC bears a special responsibility in this regard: its interventionist stance on international trade may legitimize resistance to change and market forces in the eyes of the emergent Eastern economies. If pandering to special interest groups (producers) prevents the EC from opening its markets fully, EC countries will not only fail to reap benefits for themselves but also reap difficulties on consumers and producers in USSR and Eastern Europe.

Although attention is currently focused on the EC as the principal partner and closest neighbour of Eastern Europe, others, notably the US, also have opportunities and responsibilities. They too should respond positively and openly. Opening up international trade takes political courage, but the alternatives to giving the SUEE market access are likely to be more problematic in the long run. Closed Western markets increase pressure for (illegal) emigration from East to West and greater political tensions in the East; the latter in turn could engender a political hostility in the SUEE, and call forth authoritarian regimes hostile to the market economy and unable to tackle the pressing problems of efficiency, stability and equity. In that scenario we would all lose.

Discussion

Gordon Hughes
The World Bank, University of Warwick and CEPR

The fundamental point of this very interesting paper is that the transformation of the East European and USSR economies will make a profound difference to trading patterns within Europe and will thus require major adjustments in the economic policies followed by the OECD countries. This conclusion is strongest in agriculture, but we should be under no illusions that major shifts in trade in manufactured goods can occur without substantial conflict over market access in various industries.

The gravity model provides an interesting basis for thinking about how aggregate patterns of trade between Eastern Europe, the USSR and rest of the world might change as a result of liberalization. I am rather skeptical about its appropriateness for explaining the total volume of trade between pairs of countries. As the authors comment, it is most obviously relevant to intra-industry trade and the exclusion of the oil exporting countries gives a misleading impression of how well the model can cope with trade based on the exploitation of natural resources. This is especially important in applying the model to the USSR because fuels and electricity comprised 53% of total USSR exports in 1985 while other natural resource products accounted for at least a further 10% of total exports. It would be interesting to see the results of a similar analysis for trade in manufactured goods alone. I have no strong intuition about how the overall results would work out, but I am reasonably sure that it would modify the predictions about adjustments in trade volumes in four ways:

(a) The predictions for total trade between the former USSR and other East European countries are certainly too low. It is highly probable that, subject to reasonable management of the USSR's energy resources, the East European countries will continue to import most of their energy from the USSR.

(b) Since the USSR has to be classed along with the other oil-exporting countries, the magnitude of the coefficient associated with an oil-exporter dummy in any equation for trade in manufactured goods must be critical in making predictions for the USSR's trade. I would expect this coefficient to be negative and highly significant. That would imply that the existing equation is likely to over-estimate the potential volume of trade between the USSR and the rest of the world excluding Eastern Europe. In any case gravity equations tend to over-predict trade volumes for large countries such as China, India and the US.

(c) The USSR exports a relatively small fraction – 17.5% measured in terms of tonnes of oil equivalent (toe) – of its huge energy production. Once domestic fuel prices are increased to world or even European price levels, there is likely to be a large increase in the amount of energy available for export, even after allowing for the likely decline in production. I have carried out some modelling of the USSR's energy demand which suggests that by 1995 its energy exports could increase to three times their current level in toe. The impact of such an increase on European energy markets and on the balance of payments of Russia, Azerbaijan, Kazakhstan and Turkmenistan can only by guessed at, but it is clear that their exchange rates will be higher and their exports of non-energy items lower than is implied by the gravity model used by Hamilton and Winters.

(d) The rapidity of political and economic change in the Soviet (dis)Union has overtaken the analysis in this paper. There is an important question whether the separate republics of the former USSR will collectively trade with the outside world at the rate implied by the gravity model. Suppose we treat Russia as the inheritor of the main energy resources and of the 'big country' characteristic. The gravity model implies that most of the other republics would continue to trade with Russia as their major trading partner, but trade between the separate republics is likely to contract substantially since it was artificially boosted by planning arrangements for specialization in production. On the other hand, after controlling for income per head and the characteristics of trading partners, the gravity model implies that imports and exports absorb larger shares of GDP in small countries than in large countries. The likely result is that total trade volumes including trade with the other republics will decline but the share of non-Soviet trading partners in these totals will grow. Unfortunately, these predictions are greatly complicated by the large changes in the terms of trade for inter-republic trade due to the inevitable shift towards world prices for trade in energy, natural resources and agricultural products. The key republic is the Ukraine. Lacking substantial energy resources, it will have either to receive much higher average prices for its agricultural exports to the other republics or to expand its exports of manufactured goods to West European markets. The second option may prove difficult in the face of substantial competition from countries such as Czechoslovakia, Hungary and Poland.

Undoubtedly, there will be very large changes in both the level and the composition of the former USSR's trade with Western Europe, but the magnitude of the internal economic adjustments suggests that the gravity model may not provide a reliable guide to the extent of these changes.

I would be greatly encouraged by the authors' conclusions at the end of their discussion of agricultural trade if one could believe them. The demise of the CAP is something devoutly to be desired, but their conclusions do not, in fact, follow from the results presented in the tables. Compare Table 7 with Tables 8 and 9. Let us focus on EC dairy farmers, typical of the critical group of small farmers behind the political resistance to change in the CAP. In Table 7 such farmers' revenues increase when EC agricultural trade barriers are maintained; in Tables 8–9 their revenues fall when protection is withdrawn. The situation of wheat and pork producers worsens without changes in trade barriers but it is catastrophically bad if these trade barriers are eliminated.

Indeed, the model probably understates the threat to West European farmers from a liberalization in agricultural trade between Eastern and Western Europe (remember the likely increase in agricultural exports of the Ukraine). The changes in Eastern Europe might make reform of the CAP less rather than more likely in the short or medium term. What the authors should have said is that these changes increase the gains to the rest of the world from reform of the CAP, but the problem of arranging some kind of Pareto-improving trade deal over agriculture seems as intractable as ever.

The discussion of the link between education and income or economic growth touches on some hotly contested arguments in the UK, the US and elsewhere. The message seems to be that (a) some, maybe most, East European countries have effective education systems which cover most of the relevant age cohorts, and (b) the skills of their labour forces should allow the countries to compete in the production of relatively advanced goods and to catch up with income levels in the West, albeit over an extended period. This implies a causal link between education and comparative advantage which may not be warranted and is not necessary to arrive at the author's conclusions about the prospects for East European trade and growth.

The importance of education in boosting economic growth in developing countries is generally agreed and has been emphasized in the most recent *World Development Report* which suggests that the rate of growth over 1965–87 in countries with a 'high' average level of education of the labour forces was at least one-quarter higher than for countries with a 'low' education level. Equally, 'low distortion' policies have a similar effect on the average rate of growth and there is substantial positive interaction between the two factors. Since Eastern European countries have labour forces which are relatively well educated and are moving to 'low distortion' policies, we do not need to rely upon arguments of comparative advantage in sophisticated manufacturing activities to infer that the prospects for future East European growth after the recovery from the current shocks should be bright.

Further, the argument neglects crucial differences between Eastern Europe and other middle income countries. In most East European countries the share of industry in total GDP is well over 50% while in Brazil, Korea, Portugal and Turkey it lies in the range of 35–45%. East European countries have achieved almost as rapid rates of growth in industrial output over the last 30 years as those displayed by the most successful middle income countries. On a purchasing power parity basis their incomes per capita were between 25–35% of the US level. A very small number of countries – notably Japan, Hong Kong and Singapore – have sustained high rates of economic growth even after attaining this position relative to the rich countries. Others such as Greece, Israel, Portugal and Spain have found it hard to catch up despite reasonable or high educational levels. If we put aside the East Asian dragons and control for the initial size of the industrial sector, it is difficult to discern a clear relationship between education and economic growth among established middle income countries.

There is an alternative view to that put forward by the authors. The East European countries ought to be able to achieve relatively high rates of growth in industrial output measured at world prices over the next decade simply by transferring resources from inefficient and uncompetitive industries to more competitive industries. Simple calculations based on work which I have carried out with Paul Hare suggests that the resulting increase in industrial value-added in world prices might be of order of 30–40%, equivalent to a 3% per annum increment to their growth rate over a period of eight years. This is similar to the benefits derived by transferring under-utilized labour out of the agriculture sector in the standard story of post-war European growth. On the other hand, there is a large excess demand for services in these countries and historically the growth in total factor productivity in services is low. Thus, the gain in industrial productivity could be entirely absorbed by an expansion in the share of services in GDP, which would largely eliminate the potential for a rapid catchup towards West European standards of living.

These (admittedly rudimentary) calculations suggest the process of closing the gap between Eastern and Western Europe may be slower and more complicated than the authors envisage. Certainly, some East European countries may turn out to have a comparative advantage in relatively high technology industries. The work by Hare and myself referred to above supports this view for the engineering industry in Czechoslovakia but in the case of Hungary our calculations of current comparative advantage point to relatively unsophisticated industries such as clothing, footwear, leather and wood products as its most competitive industries. Since there is too little data to carry out any serious analysis of the likely pattern of comparative advantage that will emerge after the transition has occurred, my conclusion would be that it is the gains which may accrue from a rapid move towards a more efficient utilization of resources and the implications that such a shift has for trade patterns which ought to be the primary focus of analysis. The product which might be the source of the most serious trade conflict between the European Community and Eastern Europe on this basis would be steel, with potential problems in the paper and plastics industries. Here I fully agree with the authors' emphasis on the importance of avoiding reliance upon anti-dumping and other protectionist measures in Western Europe. This, of course, leads on to the crucial message of this paper, which I would fully endorse. Western Europe has a large stake in achieving a successful transition to market economies in Eastern Europe. Having willed the end, it should be prepared to bear the (relatively minor) costs of trade adjustment that may be involved.

Alasdair Smith
University of Sussex and CEPR

Carl Hamilton and Alan Winters address one of the central problems of current European economic policy-making. They are surely right to stress the historic role of the European Community in influencing the future economic, and therefore political, development of Eastern Europe. The experience of depression in the 1930s prepared the ground for communism in the 1940s. If the developed world now fails to support economic reform in Eastern Europe by offering market access to Eastern products, there are likely to be substantial and unwelcome political consequences.

The gravity model is an appealing approach to the prediction of the future levels of trade between the Eastern European economies and other countries, and the results presented here will probably command greater confidence than the historically-based estimates of Collins and Rodrik; though, of course, only the next two decades will show whether this confidence is well-founded. I had only one doubt concerning the results presented here. The measure of the distance between countries takes no account of whether the countries are in the same landmass (though a dummy variable is introduced for contiguous countries). Since the main conclusion of this section of the paper is that Eastern European trade with Japan and the US may increase more than trade with Western Europe, it would be good to find out whether this prediction of the model would be substantially changed if more differentiated measures of 'distance' were introduced.

The model suggests that there will be very considerable expansion of East–West trade as Eastern Europe reintegrates itself into the European and world economies. The likely commodity composition of this trade expansion implies quite sustainable consequences for the West, with the probable exception of agricultural trade. The innovative and exceptionally interesting use of data on the quality of the education system reinforces the rather tentative suggestion of CEPR (1990) that Poland, Hungary and Czechoslovakia, at least, should in the longer run be expected to display comparative advantage in medium-tech to high-tech products. The implication of this is that much East–West trade in Europe will have the same character as the West–West trade of the past 30 years. Rapidly growing intra-industry trade in relatively advanced industrial products engenders much less political opposition than inter-industry trade between more developed and less developed countries. Import competition destroys jobs, but with intra-industry trade, the jobs created by export opportunities are similar jobs, and the trade can be accommodated without the problems that arise when whole industries are destroyed by import competition.

But this optimistic picture is one of the long run, and the transition seems certain to be more problematic, as the European Community takes protective steps in the sensitive areas of steel, textiles and agriculture; and uses or threatens anti-dumping or 'safeguards' measures in other areas too. A full picture of the political economy of East–West trade in Europe requires study of the transitional path as well as of the long run.

The threat of migration, as Hamilton and Winters point out, is one of the main forces impelling the Community towards more liberal trade policies. Receiving the products of Eastern workers is assumed to be politically more palatable than receiving the workers themselves. Here too there is scope for further research. Is there evidence of strong migratory pressures? Are trade and migration really substitutes? (The theory on this subject is inconclusive.) To what extent will the development of the service sector absorb the less skilled part of the workforce and reduce the potential migration?

More serious even than the known curbs in areas such as textiles and steel is the prospect of anti-dumping and safeguards actions in areas of future development: the threat of a protectionist response by the EC to successful development in a particular area will inhibit to new investment, including foreign investment. The Community should be providing a framework for the development of market economies in Eastern Europe by offering unconditional market access, a stable policy environment, and clear and open rules of competition. Such a framework is of particular importance for economies with undeveloped domestic competition policies and high degrees of industrial concentration: trade, especially trade with the EC, can act as a substitute (albeit an imperfect one) for domestic competition policy. We can all agree that it is in the interests of Eastern Europe for the Community to show greater eagerness to accept its role in the reform process; Hamilton and Winters provide a convincing case both that the process will be in the Community's long-run interests and that its short-run costs will be easily containable.

General discussion

There was much discussion of the merits of the gravity model of international trade. Richard Baldwin said it was something of an embarrassment to trade theory that the gravity model explained as much as it did. Barry Eichengreen said that the model was really reflecting the determinants of intra-industry trade, but left out Ricardian considerations; it would be valuable to include factor endowments explicitly in the analysis. Jan Svejnar and Hans-Werner Sinn pointed to the effects of linguistic and cultural affinity on trade relations. Nick Crafts and Michael Mejstrik were both sceptical of the quality of the GDP data for Eastern Europe and would have liked to see some sensitivity analysis. Crafts was also doubtful about making inferences about catchup phenomena in the presence of evidently strong country and region effects. And he pointed out that nothing had been said about welfare effects; all the discussion was about trade volumes. The political economy of adjustment would require an explicit consideration of the distribution of welfare gains.

A number of discussants focused on difficulties of making inferences about comparative advantage. Richard Baldwin was particularly doubtful about the interpretation of revealed comparative advantage in the trade data, due to the high degree of distortion in the centrally planned economies. Attila Chikan said that the quality of higher education in Eastern Europe was comparatively less good than that of secondary education, which might qualify some of the optimism about a high-technology future. These considerations led on to a discussion of policy implications. Patrick Bolton pointed out that the Eastern European exporters would be joining a world economy that was well organized; conquering markets already occupied might be harder than growing into them gradually. Jan Svejnar asked whether the paper supported the case for an explicit industrial policy. After all, if one believed in the predicted outcome it might make sense to speed the process up rather than to wait 30 years for it to happen of its own accord. Alan Winters was doubtful that such strong conclusions could be drawn from what was essentially a fairly crude set of analytical tools. However, he was happy to endorse the view that protectionist policies which slowed down the necessary adjustments were greatly to be deplored.

Appendix

A.1. Price elasticities of supply in SUEE agriculture

Here we give details of the supply elasticities used in the simulation model in Section 3. As we explained in the next, we dampened the cross-elasticities in the original Tyers and Anderson model, which therefore modifies overall elasticities a little. Table A1 shows the individual elasticities we used, and the implication for overall supply elasticities.

A.2. Agricultural productivity in the USSR and Eastern Europe

We now discuss further our assumption that liberalization will induce large increases in agricultural productivity in SUEE countries.[12] Initial

---

[12] We are grateful to Jihe Song for assistance with this section.

Table A1. Price elasticities of supply for EE agriculture

Effect of 1% rise: in price of:	% change in quantity supplied						
	Rice	Corn	Wheat	Sugar	Milk	Beef	Pork
Rice	0.75	−0.01	0.00	−0.04	0.00	0.00	0.00
Corn	−0.06	0.80	−0.08	0.00	0.00	0.00	0.00
Wheat	0.00	−0.16	0.75	0.00	0.00	0.00	0.00
Sugar	−0.01	0.00	0.00	0.28	0.00	0.00	0.00
Milk	0.00	0.00	0.00	0.00	0.85	0.01	0.00
Beef	0.00	0.00	0.00	0.00	−0.06	0.72	−0.04
Pork	0.00	0.00	0.00	0.00	0.00	−0.05	1.12
aggregate supply elasticity:							
unmodified	0.52	0.27	0.47	0.24	0.65	0.53	0.99
modified	0.68	0.63	0.67	0.24	0.79	0.68	1.08

productivity levels are low, though for different reasons. Collectivized agriculture in the CSFR and the USSR undermined incentives, while in Poland, where land remained in private ownership, under-capitalization of peasant agriculture and inefficient distribution of both inputs and outputs kept yields very low. Within the SUEE, only Hungary, with quite a well-run state agricultural sector, came close to achieving its potential.

In CEPR (1990) we approached Eastern agricultural prospects in two ways: comparing factor inputs between East and West; and comparing the evolution of Eastern and Western agriculture since the (relatively undistorted) 1930s. We now explore the historical comparison in more detail. Table A2 presents data on the ratio of 1985 to 1938 levels both of crop yields and particular agricultural inputs. Soviet arable yields have fared especially poorly (even relative to the 1930s by which time collectivization had already taken some toll). Table A2 also highlights slow growth of mechanized inputs as likely source of slow output growth.

Elsewhere in Eastern Europe, the story is rather different; arable yields evolved almost in line with those in Western Europe, aided by a slightly faster increase in mechanization. Labour inputs have not declined as rapidly as in the West, however, so total factor productivity has not kept pace with Western levels. Since we shall go on to argue that in the 1930s the East was already substantially less efficient than the West, for social and economic rather than natural reasons, the data in Table A2 identify scope for a substantial catchup in agricultural productivity.

Table A2. Crop yields and inputs: ratio of 1985 to 1935 levels

	Yields				Inputs		
	Wheat	Barley	Maize	Rye	Tractors	Labour	Land
Albania	2.7	2.7	2.9	0.8			1.7
Bulgaria	3.0	2.2	4.6	1.7	12.7	0.2	0.9
CSFR	2.9	2.6	2.6	2.2	7.9	0.4	0.9
Hungary	3.5	2.8	3.2	1.7	4.8	0.4	0.9
Poland	2.4	2.1	3.0	1.9	68.4	0.5	0.9
Romania	2.9	4.7	4.4	0.0	16.1	0.3	1.1
Yugoslavia	3.2	2.8	2.3	2.1	93.2	0.5	0.9
GDR	2.1	2.1	1.5	2.1	5.5	0.5	0.9
All E. Europe	2.9	2.7	3.7	2.0	22.3	0.4	0.9
USSR	1.8	1.7	2.7	1.3	6.4	0.4	1.0
W. Europe	3.1	2.6	3.4	2.3	17.9	0.3	0.8
Canada	2.5	2.5	2.4	2.6	1.1	0.5	1.2
US	2.9	2.4	5.3	2.4	1.3	0.4	1.0

Notes: Data on tractor inputs is per unit of land, and the earlier date is the 1940–50 average. Data for Western Europe is the average for Austria, Benelux, France, UK, Italy, West Germany, Switzerland and Sweden.

Eastern Europe lagged the West in many respects during the 1930s, all of which help to explain its poor agricultural performance. At a broad level, per capita GNP was much lower in the East – everywhere below $112 a year in 1938 except for Czechoslovakia ($176), compared with France ($236) and $337 in (combined) Germany (Kaser and Radice, 1985). These differences were correlated with illiteracy rates – exceeding 25% except for Hungary (8.8%) and Czechoslovakia (4.1%), compared with Western Europe which ranged from 6% in France to 0.1% in Sweden (Kaser and Radice, 1985). As Schultz (1964) has shown, basic literacy offers very high rates of return in agriculture (as in other sectors), so these differences are very significant.

On a specifically agricultural level, both the quantity of arable land in use and the agricultural labour force were beginning to decline in the West during the 1930s, but were growing in the East, where agriculture was used as a sink for surplus labour. Several commentators have estimated that perhaps a quarter of the rural labour force was surplus to requirements (Kaser and Radice, 1985). This suggests serious undercapitalization but, given the dispossession of major landowners after World War I, there was little chance of developing the surpluses necessary to address the problem. Associated problems were the lack of mechanization (few tractors by Western standards) and low fertilizer

Table A3. Comparative cereal yields, 1985 (kg/hectare)

	Wheat	Barley	Maize	Rye
Eastern Europe	3,869	3,799	5,247	2,677
Western Europe	5,212	4,787	6,700	4,021
West/East	1.35	1.26	1.28	1.50
USSR	1,647	1,661	2,905	1,266
US	2,519	2,744	7,406	1,806
US/USSR	1.53	1.65	2.55	1.43

Source: *FAO Production Yearbook*, 1985.

use – 2 kg per hectare in Hungary and Poland in 1936–38 (the highest in Eastern Europe) compared with 100–300 kg in the West.

A more direct view of the costs of post-war mismanagement in East European agriculture comes from Czechoslovakia, easily the most advance and most Westernized of the SUEE countries in the 1930s, and in fact the fourth largest industrial producer in all Europe. It also enjoyed the highest crop yields in the region. Indeed, by the late 1930s there was little to choose between Czechoslovakian and Western European agriculture.

After the succession of the Communists, Czechoslovakian agriculture was collectivized and rapidly started to diverge from Western standards of performance. Its output stagnated between 1934–38 and 1956 while Western output increased by 25%. Part of the difference was explained by lower input use, but according to Lazarcik (1963) total factor productivity fell by 4% in Czechoslovakia but rose by 12% in the West. This example strongly suggests that recent changes in organization and incentives should have a powerful effect on agricultural productivity. Both because of its relatively good interwar starting point and the extreme degree of its subsequent centralization under state planning, Czechoslovakia may overstate the decline in agriculture throughout the region. Even so, some general productivity improvement is now likely.

Although circumstantial evidence is powerful, it remains hard to make any precise estimate of that improvement. Cochrane (1990) assumes that Poland could make up half the discrepancy between its yields and that of selected Western comparators. This generates increases of 0% for corn (a minor crop), but 15–30% for other crops. Liefert *et al.* (1990) apparently adopt a similar procedure for the USSR – generating 10% increases for grains, 15% for sugar and oil-seeds and 20–25% for meats. CEPR (1990) assumes that Eastern Europe and the USSR could make up two-thirds of the excess growth of western over eastern yields since the 1930s after allowing for the effects of western agricultural policy and acreage reductions. This suggests 30% increases.

Table A3 presents comparative yield data for the major grains. It suggests that catchups of 15% for Eastern Europe and 20% for the former USSR are reasonable and attainable. It is more difficult to assess productivity in meat production, but anecdotal evidence suggests that there is at least as much scope for improvement as in grains, so we adopt the same estimate.

References

Aitken, D. (1973). 'The Effect of the EEC and EFTA on European Trade: A Temporal Cross-Section Analysis', *American Economic Review*.

Barker, T. S. (1977). 'International Trade and Economic Growth: An Alternative to the Neoclassical Approach', *Cambridge Journal of Economics*.

Baumol, W. J. (1986). 'Productivity Growth, Convergence and Welfare: What the Long-run Data Show', *American Economic Review*.

Baumol, W. J., S. A. B. Blackman and E. N. Wolff (1989). *Productivity and American Leadership: The Long View*, MIT Press, Cambridge, Mass.

Bergstrand, J. H. (1985). 'The Gravity Equation in International Trade: Some Microeconomic Foundations and Empirical Evidence', *Review of Economics and Statistics*.

Brada, J. C. and J. A. Mendez (1985). 'Economic Integration Among Developed, Developing and Centrally Planned Economies: A Comparative Analysis', *Review of Economics and Statistics*.

Brenton, P. A. and L. A. Winters (1990). 'Non-tariff Barriers and Rationing: UK Footwear Imports', CEPR Discussion Paper No. 365.

CEPR (1990). *Monitoring European Integration: The Impact of Eastern Europe*, CEPR, London.

Cochrane, N. J. (1990). *Trade Liberalisation in Yugoslavia and Poland*, Staff Report AGES 9058, Economic Research Service, US Department of Agriculture.

Collins, S. M. and D. Rodrik (1991). *Eastern Europe and the Soviet Union in the World Economy*, Institute for International Economics, Washington DC.

Comber, L. C. and J. P. Keeves (1973). *Science Education in Nineteen Countries*, Almqvist & Wiksell, Stockholm.

De Long, J. B. (1988). 'Productivity, Growth and Welfare: Comment', *American Economic Review*.

Economic Commission for Europe (1990). *Economic Survey 1989/90*, UN ECE, Geneva.

GATT (1990). *International Trade, vols I and II*, GATT, Geneva.

Helpman, E. and P. Krugman (1985). *Market Structure and Foreign Trade*, MIT Press, Cambridge, Mass.

Hughes, G. and P. Hare (1991). 'Competitiveness and Industrial Restructuring in Czechoslovakia, Hungary and Poland', *The European Economy*, Special Edition No. 2.

IEA (1988). *Science Achievement in Seventeen Countries: A Preliminary Report*, Pergamon, Oxford.

Jusen, T. and T. N. Postlewaite (eds.) (1985). *International Encyclopedia of Education*, Pergamon Press, Oxford.

Kaser, M. C. and E. A. Radice (1985). *The Economic History of Eastern Europe 1919–1975*, Vol I, Oxford University Press, Oxford.

Krugman, P. R. (1989). 'Differences in Income Elasticities and Trends in Real Exchange Rates', *European Economic Review*.

Lazarcik, G. (1963). 'Factors Affecting Production and Productivity in Czechoslovak Agriculture, 1934–38 and 1946–60', *Journal of Farm Economics*.

Leamer, E. and R. M. Stern (1970). *Quantitative International Economics*, Allyn and Bacon, Boston.

Liefert, W. M., R. B. Koopman and E. C. Cook (1990). 'The Effect of Western and Soviet Trade Liberalisation on the USSR', mimeo, Centrally Planned Economies Branch, US Department of Agriculture.

Linneman, H. (1966). *An Economic Study of International Trade Flows*, North-Holland, Amsterdam.

Mankiw, N. G., D. Romer and D. N. Weil, (1990). 'A Contribution to the Empirics of Economic Growth', Discussion Paper 1532, Harvard Institute of Economic Research, Cambridge, Mass.

Schultz, T. W. (1964). *Transforming Traditional Agriculture*, Yale University Press, London.
Slama, J. (1983). 'Gravity Model and its Estimations for International Flows of Engineering
    Products, Chemicals and Patent Applications', *Acta Oeconomica.*
Summers R. and A. Heston (1988). 'A New Set of International Comparisons of Real Product
    and Price Levels: Estimates for 130 Countries 1950–85', *Review of Income and Wealth.*
Svedberg, D. (1981). 'Colonial Enforcement of Foreign Direct Investment', *The Manchester School.*
Tyers, R. and K. Anderson (1986). 'Distortions in World Food Markets: A Quantitative Assess-
    ment'. Background Paper for the *World Development Report 1986*, The World Bank, Washington
    DC.
—— (1988). 'Liberalising OECD Agricultural Policies in the Uruguay Round: Effects on Trade
    and Welfare', *Journal of Agricultural Economics.*
—— (1992). *Disarray and World Food Markets: A Quantitative Assessment*, Cambridge University
    Press, Sydney.
Wang, Z. K. and L. A. Winters (1991). 'Eastern Europe's Trading Potential', CEPR Discussion
    Paper No. 610.
Winters, L. A. (1984). 'Separability and the Specification of Foreign Trade Functions', *Journal of
    International Economics.*

Economic Policy April 1992 Printed in Great Britain

Poland

Andrew Berg and Jeffrey Sachs

Summary

The Polish economic programme is important not only in its own right, but as a key example of the benefits and possible costs of a rapid movement to convertibility. This paper proposes an analytical framework and new estimates of the costs and benefits. The framework shows that convertibility revolves around the relationship of two nominal variables, the money supply and the nominal exchange rate. Return to convertibility is achieved not mainly through a real depreciation, but through a nominal depreciation which helps to bring the overall price level back into line with nominal aggregate demand and particularly with the money supply. The new estimates show that the costs, a drop in living standards and output, are less than commonly believed. Given the extreme inflationary conditions in 1989 and the shock following the disintegration of CMEA trade, the loss of output was not caused in any important way by the rapid move to free trade.

Structural adjustment and international trade in Eastern Europe: the case of Poland

Andrew Berg and Jeffrey Sachs
Massachusetts Institute of Technology and WIDER,
Harvard University and WIDER

1. Introduction

Recent economic developments in Poland are widely viewed as a test case of rapid trade liberalization in Eastern Europe.[1] Starting on 1 January 1990, Poland moved to convertibility of the currency and substantial free trade with Western economies. The alleged successes and failures of these dramatic policy steps have been used as points of argument over currency and trade policies in other post-Communist countries in Eastern Europe, and in the (former) USSR as well. Therefore, the importance of an accurate assessment of the developments in Poland is paramount.

The need for an appropriate analytical framework is especially great, since Poland's economic experience in the past two years is anomalous when judged by the behaviour of normal market economies. Despite an alleged deep recession, growth of the service sector has been rapid, and both imports and exports of manufactures have boomed. Moreover, convertibility of the Polish zloty has been achieved *not* through a sharp real devaluation of the currency, as is widely believed, but *despite* a real appreciation of the currency.

As we will stress, one key to understanding these anomalies is that Poland began its radical liberalization from a position of significant macroeconomic disequilibrium. Three aspects were paramount. First, as the result of price controls combined with highly expansionary

---

[1] The rapid incorporation of the former GDR into the Federal Republic of Germany is sometimes considered another, and largely, negative example of rapid trade integration. Industrial production in the GDR plummeted in the year following economic union by an estimated 50%. But special circumstances in Germany – mainly the powerful drive towards wage equalization in the East and West – go far to explaining the collapse of East German industry, so that its general relevance for the other countries in Eastern Europe is doubtful. For evidence of the wage explosion in East Germany, and its negative consequences for GDR industry, see Akerlof *et al.* (1991).

macroeconomic policies, the overall price level was systematically below the level consistent with macroeconomic equilibrium. The result, of course, was a situation of chronic and generalized shortages. We will refer to this phenomenon as the pre-reform *monetary overhang*, even though the over-expansionary policies involved not just an excessive stock of money, but also large fiscal deficits and excessive real wage increases. Second, and consistent with the monetary overhang, there was a persistent and significant excess demand for foreign exchange at the official exchange rate. Foreign exchange was rationed, as the central bank lacked the means to make it automatically available to importers at the official exchange rate. This is a situation of *currency inconvertibility*, and more specifically, current-account inconvertibility.[2] Third, resources were systematically diverted from the service sector and into agriculture and manufacturing, the well-known phenomenon of *anti-service-sector bias* of the command economy. This was accomplished through a complex system of price controls, limitations on the right of individuals to start small businesses, the direct allocation of resources to the state sector and away from small private firms in the service sector, and extensive subsidies to industry.

The stabilization and liberalization programmes – which involved ending price controls, devaluing the currency, restricting the budget deficit and limiting the growth of new banking credits – succeeded in ending the chronic disequilibria in the economy. Shortages were ended; both exports and imports could grow as the result of the newly convertible currency; and the service sector could begin to expand at the expense of agriculture and manufacturing. However, the cost of these changes in terms of output declines and falling living standards remains in heated dispute and is a central topic of this paper. We have no doubt that the stabilization measures in Poland had a short-run cost in terms of lost output, although these costs have been significantly overestimated. In particular, official measures of consumption relying primarily on estimates of retail sales exaggerate the fall in consumption by missing much of the phenomenal growth in private sector trade. Moreover, the loss of output was caused mainly by the monetary contraction needed to choke off Poland's hyperinflation, and not in any important way by the rapid move to free trade. A special aspect of the macroeconomic costs was apparently an unloading of inventory stocks after the time of stabilization, in a reversal of the pre-reform tendency of households

---

[2] Convertibility refers to the automatic availability of foreign exchange in return for domestic money at the official exchange rate. When foreign exchange is freely available for current-account transactions, but not for capital transactions, we refer to current-account convertibility. When it is available at the official exchange rate for all transactions we refer to full convertibility.

and enterprises in Eastern Europe to hoard commodities extensively under the conditions of a shortage economy.

We should mention at the start that the response of the economy to stabilization and liberalization has been importantly conditioned by the nature of ownership rights in Poland. There is little doubt that the efficiency of the economic response has been reduced by the prevalence of socialized ownership, especially in the large industrial sector. Privatization, therefore, ranks together with stabilization and liberalization as a fundamental pillar of reform. Nonetheless, to limit the scope of the paper, we will not discuss the issue of privatization here.[3]

Section 2 introduces a simple theoretical framework for discussing stabilization and liberalization in the context of a monetary overhang, currency inconvertibility and a repressed service sector. In Section 3, we look empirically at the disequilibria in Poland on the eve of the 'big-bang', and in Section 4 we carefully assess the changes in consumption and production that followed the big-bang. In Section 5, we analyse the dynamics of trade and production on a disaggregated sectoral basis in response to the changes in trade policy. In the concluding section, we suggest some lessons for policy in Eastern Europe and the USSR.

2. Some theoretical aspects of stabilization and liberalization

We start with a simple framework (elaborated in the Appendix) which describes an economy that produces just two kinds of outputs, industrial goods and services. The economy consumes these two goods, and also a foreign-produced import. The domestic industrial good is also exported. The administratively set prices for the three goods are typically not the market-clearing prices, and most markets are characterized by excess demand. The market-clearing prices are established in unofficial parallel (or black) markets. While producers face the official prices, consumers may choose either to queue up for goods at the official prices, or to pay the higher parallel-market prices. On the margin, consumers are indifferent between joining the queue or buying the output immediately at the higher price.

For simplicity, we assume that all households pay the parallel-market price, in effect buying the goods from 'entrepreneurs' who wait in the queues and then resell the goods in the parallel market. As pointed out by many writers such as Kornai, and as recently modelled by Weitzman

---

[3] For detailed discussions of the privatization issue, and policy options in Poland, see Lipton and Sachs (1990b), Sachs (1991) and Berg (1992). For discussions of how ownership structures may have affected the dynamic response of Polish enterprises, see Frydman *et al.* (1990), and Berg and Blanchard (1992).

(1991) and Lipton and Sachs (1990a), such queuing activity represents a deadweight loss to society. As an approximation, we assume that aggregate demand is determined by the nominal money stock, M so that excess aggregate demand becomes the same thing as a 'monetary overhang'. (In fact, excess demand may result not only from an excessively large stock of money, but also from a large budget deficit, excess wages and so on.) Output by enterprises is a function of relative official prices, and resources assumed to remain fully employed. For most of the discussion relative official prices will remain unchanged, so that the division of output between industry and services is fixed. (Below, when the nominal price of industrial goods changes, for example because of a devaluation, we implicitly assume that the nominal price of services is adjusted proportionately, to keep intact the same real bias against the production of services.)

2.1. Basic mechanics of convertibility

2.1.1. The setup. When the country lacks foreign exchange reserves to run a trade deficit and capital flows are exogenously set, the quantity of imports depends on the fraction of the domestic production of the industrial good which is exported. Initially, the monetary and price structure is such that industry is a net exporter. More precisely, at the initial set of prices, the domestically produced industrial good is in excess supply on the domestic market, and this excess supply is exported. The exporter receives the world price for the export good multiplied by the official exchange rate. Similarly the official price of the importable good is the world price multiplied by the official exchange rate. When the currency is convertible, the parallel market price of the imported good will equal the official price. When the currency is inconvertible and there is an excess demand for foreign exchange (and for the imported good), the parallel market price of the imported good will exceed the official price. There may or may not be an excess demand for the imported good at the official price.

2.1.2. Money and inconvertibility. There is a unique level of money, M_c, that would just result in balanced foreign trade and currency convertibility, *for a given nominal exchange rate E.* If the money stock exceeds this amount ($M > M_c$), demand for the imported good (and the foreign exchange to buy it) exceeds supply (which is constrained by overall exports). A parallel market for imports develops. Foreign exchange must be rationed at the official exchange rate, and in the parallel market the domestic currency is depreciated relative to the official rate.

The ratio of the parallel-market exchange rate to the official exchange rate is increasing with the monetary overhang.

The domestic parallel-market price of the imported good is higher than the world price times the official exchange rate. The importers who are lucky enough to get rationed foreign exchange from the central bank at the official exchange rate can purchase imports at the official price and resell them in the parallel market at the higher price (alternatively, they may in fact simply sell the currency in the parallel market to other would-be importers, and earn the spread directly). This spread between official and parallel-market prices cannot, of course, be eliminated by arbitrage because other would-be importers do not have access to the rationed foreign exchange at the overvalued official rate.

Some of the higher demand resulting from an increase in M above M_c will fall on the exported good. Exports will thus fall, and through the trade balance constraint (imports equal exports plus exogenous net capital flows), imports will have to fall as well.[4] Since there is an initial excess supply of the exportable good on the domestic market, the increased aggregate demand leads to a reduced excess supply, but not to a situation of excess demand, unless of course the demand increase is so large as to choke off all exports. Assuming that some exports continue, the domestic price of the exportable good remains at the official price level (equal to the world price multiplied by the exchange rate), and does not rise. In the end, the increased nominal demand systematically raises the parallel-market price of importables relative to exportables. The money overhang lowers imports, lowers exports and raises the black market premium on the exchange rate and on services. Consumer welfare falls. The distortionary costs of the monetary overhang *vis-a-vis* international trade are the same as those of a tariff: both raise the relative price of the imported good relative to the exportable, and result in underconsumption of imports relative to exportables.

The cost of currency inconvertibility is illustrated in Figure 1. Consumption of the import good is shown on the x-axis and of the industrial good on the y-axis. The international trade line CC corresponds to the relative world price of the import good relative to the exportable good. When the currency is convertible, the consumption point is found at

---

[4] In the formal model presented in Appendix A we assume that the exported good is not in excess demand in the domestic market. What is needed for the argument we make here is less restrictive: simply that higher domestic demand causes more of the exported good to be diverted to domestic use. This is plausible, for two reasons. First, by the end of the 1980s, many firms were able to choose between the domestic and foreign market, and prices were roughly arbitraged between the markets. Second, where central planning persisted, there was a tendency by planners to view exports as a 'vent for surplus'. That is, planners encouraged exports mainly of goods whose 'needs' on the domestic market were already met.

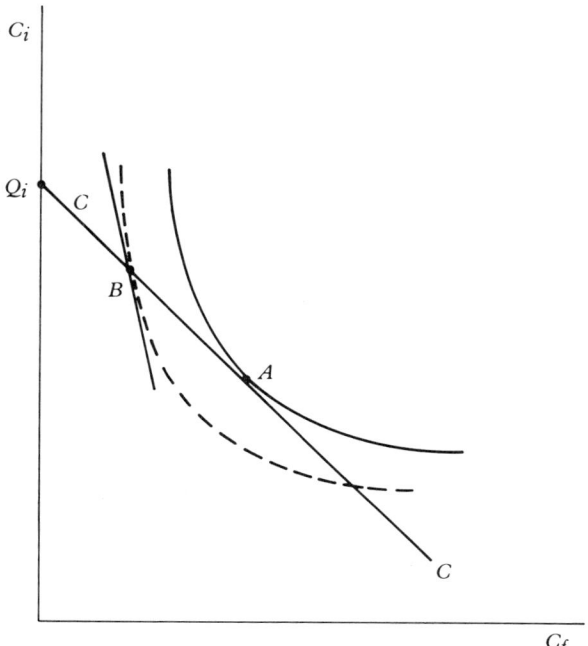

Figure 1. The utility costs of inconvertibility

the tangency of the indifference curve of a representative consumer and the international trade line at point A. When M rises above the level consistent with convertibility, the equilibrium moves northwest along the CC line to a point like B. At B, the steeper slope of the indifference curve is equal to the ratio of the parallel exchange rate to the official exchange rate. Obviously, the utility level at point B is less than at point A.

In the range of convertibility, for an unchanged exchange rate, a drop of M *below* M_c produces a trade surplus as spending on imports declines. (Although we are looking at a static framework, we should note that over time the trade surplus caused by $M < M_c$ would increase the money supply through the Hume mechanism: high-powered money would grow by the amount of the central bank's accumulation of foreign exchange reserves. This, in turn, would tend to eliminate the trade surplus.)

2.1.3. The exchange rate and convertibility. It is essential to realize that M_c depends on the nominal official exchange rate E. As E rises (the currency is devalued) domestic official prices of imports and exportables rise.

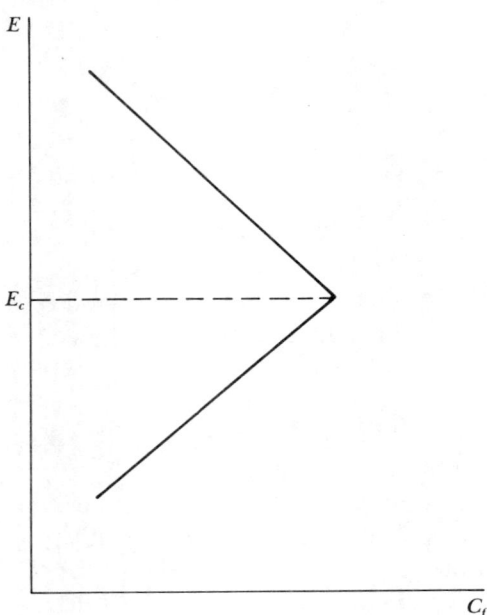

Figure 2. The relationship between the exchange rate and imports

The amount of money consistent with equilibrium of supply and demand at official prices, hence convertibility, rises as well. Thus, for a given level of nominal money stock, there is a nominal exchange rate consistent with convertibility, E_c. If E is higher (more devalued) than E_c, then the currency is convertible.

It is interesting in this light to examine how imports are differently affected by a devaluation in the cases of inconvertibility and convertibility. In Figure 2 the stock of money M is constant. When the *nominal* exchange rate E is less than E_c (the currency is inconvertible), a devaluation (higher E) is tantamount to a narrowing of the monetary overhang, so that both exports and imports tend to *rise*. On the other hand, when E is greater than E_c, an increase in E causes imports to *fall*. Starting with a monetary overhang, currency inconvertibility and a black market exchange-rate premium, monetary equilibrium can be restored by raising M_c or by lowering M, or both, until they are equal. Raising M_c is accomplished by a devaluation of the nominal exchange rate. Exports and imports will both increase. If M_c is raised *above* M, say by a large 'overshooting' devaluation, the result will be not only convertibility, but a trade surplus. Exports will rise, while imports may rise or fall, depending on the extent of the devaluation.

2.2. Queuing, inventories and shortages

A monetary overhang leads to underconsumption of imports and over-consumption of exportables. In a more general framework, in which there is an import-competing sector as well as an export sector, we would also find a distortion on the supply side, as resources are pulled out of the exportable sector and into the import-competing sector. There is another large category of real resource costs associated with the shortages caused by a monetary overhang: the waste of resources used up in queuing and in holding excessive inventories. Kornai pioneered the study of these costs, and Weitzman (1991) has recently provided an elegant model of these costs. Lipton and Sachs (1990a) applied the model in a simple setting, in which the real resources consumed in queues vary according to the spread between the official and black market prices of commodities.

Of most interest here is the tendency of households and firms to hoard inventories when shortages lead to queuing. Weitzman's argument (essentially that of the Tobin–Baumol framework for money demand) is that if each visit to the market is costly because of the need to wait in line for goods, and if real interest rates are low, then consumers will make large purchases on each visit to the market, and will, on average, hold large inventories between shopping trips. Producers, in turn, will hold large inventories of inputs to avoid running out of key supplies. Retail firms may also tend to hold large inventories to avoid 'stockouts' (an inability to meet customer demand), since they know that they cannot rely on quick shipments from the producer.

As soon as prices are liberalized, however, the hoarding motivation is ended. Firms will tend to dump existing stocks of inventories onto the market, while households will cut their new market purchases while they live off existing inventories. To the extent that the inventory stocks are easily exportable, the dishoarding should contribute to a bulge in exports. Table 1 confirms that the stock of inventories relative to sales was measurably higher than in the US and Canada, and that part of these inventories, those held in the trade sector (by domestic retail outlets and foreign-trade enterprises), fell sharply after the start of stabilization.

2.3. The service sector

Two aspects of the service sector require attention: the implications of price control (and liberalization), and the impact of the monetary overhang. We consider that service-sector production is artificially restricted by price controls. This is our shorthand way of describing

Table 1. Total inventories in months of turnover

	1989	1990
Poland		
All socialized enterprises	2.28	2.08
Industry	1.77	1.99
of which:		
Manufacturing	1.81	2.01
of which:		
Paper	1.10	1.49
Transportation equipment	2.49	3.44
Building	1.05	0.86
Consumer goods trade	2.22	1.32
US		
Manufacturing	1.48	
of which:		
Paper	1.31	
Transportation equipment	2.00	
Retail trade	1.56	
Canada		
Manufacturing	1.52	

Source: DRI, Own calculations based on GUS data (see Table 13 for methodological notes).
Note: For building and sub-sectors of industry data exclude firms with fewer than 50 employees. Inventory data for retail trade covers units engaged in trade in final goods. Sales data for retail trade covers retail sales in retail points (excluding direct sales by producers, etc.).

the bias of Soviet-type economies against services, and towards industry. Even when $M = M_c$, the market for services will not clear if the planners set the relative price at too low a level, the case we regard as empirically relevant. When the price control on services is eliminated, the relative price rises, causing an increase in service sector output and a fall in industrial good output. The effect of this shift of resources into the service sector and out of the industrial sector is to reduce consumption of all traded goods and to raise consumption of services. Both imports and exports will tend to fall as a result of the shrinkage of the industrial sector.

2.4. Summary: the effects of stabilization and liberalization

Initially, the economy is characterized by a monetary overhang and service-sector price controls. The overhang is eliminated by a sharp devaluation, and the price control on services is simultaneously eliminated. What are the overall effects? We should expect: (i) a rise in the overall price level, with service prices rising more than export prices; (ii) a rise in official import prices and export prices by the same amount (equal to the percentage devaluation of the exchange rate), but a rise in the parallel market price of imported goods that is less than the increase in export prices and service prices; (iii) an increase in service sector production and a decrease in industrial production; (iv) a fall in inventory stocks as hoarding is eliminated; (v) an indeterminate response of exports and imports. Both will tend to *rise* as the result of elimination of the monetary overhang and as the result of inventory dishoarding. But exports and imports could fall as a result of the shift of resources out of industry and into services. As a practical matter, though, the shift to services will probably be more gradual than the direct effects on excess demand and inventories resulting from the end of the monetary overhang. For this reason, we should expect to see imports and exports initially rise.

3. Application to the Polish liberalization and stabilization programme

3.1. Further Factors

The framework just outlined is only a crude basis for describing the structural adjustments in Poland. At least three important points need elaboration.

First, the 'monetary overhang' should not be thought of literally as relating only to the stock of money. A monetary overhang exists when *nominal aggregate demand exceeds nominal aggregate supply at the administratively controlled price level.* This excess demand can result from an excessive stock of money, but it can result from overly expansionary 'flow' conditions as well. In the case of Poland, Lipton and Sachs (1990a) have argued that the 'flow' factors (a large budget deficit in 1989, low real interest rates and a sharp rise in real wages during 1987–89) were probably more important than the money stock. There is an obvious, yet sometimes neglected implication. Unlike in the framework described above, macroeconomic equilibrium could not be restored simply by devaluing the exchange rate and raising prices. The large budget deficit meant that there was a risk of *ongoing* high inflation that had to be addressed through a sharp cutback in the budget deficit. Indeed, hyperinflation had already broken out in the fall of 1989. For this reason, macroeconomic stabilization also required sharp cuts in budget subsidies and a reversal of the real wage increases of the previous two years. It also meant that Poland had to pursue very restrictive monetary policies after the 'big-bang' to stop the momentum of earlier high inflation, and to prevent the one-time jump in prices from feeding through into higher nominal wages and continued high inflation.

Second, at a minimum, there is the need to take into account the effects of policy on the agricultural sector. Agriculture is important not only because of the scale of the sector (approximately 29% of employment and 13% of GDP in 1989), but also because the Communist regime had systematically supported the sector with large subsidies. Tiny, highly inefficient private farms were kept alive by producer and consumer subsidies that amounted to around 4.9% of GDP in 1989. (According to the IMF estimates, total subsidies in Poland amounted to 12.9% of GDP in 1989, of which 3.7% went to households for consumption of food, 1.0% went to the non-socialized agricultural sector and 0.2% went to the socialized agricultural sector.) Both to help close the budget deficit and to rationalize agricultural market, cuts in subsidies in 1990 amounted to roughly 0.9% of GDP.

Third, there is the crucial issue of Soviet trade. Until 1990, Poland and the USSR traded through barter-type protocols under CMEA agreements. The first year of the stabilization programme, 1990, was a transitional year for the CMEA. The scope of the trade protocols was reduced, and Poland set an appreciated exchange rate between the zloty and transferable ruble to try to cut back exports to the USSR. Starting in 1991, however, there was a watershed. The CMEA countries disbanded the barter arrangements with the intention to move to 'dollar-based trade at world prices'. In the event, the USSR fell into a debt crisis, and also failed to establish a market mechanism for allocating foreign exchange to enterprises. The monetary overhang in the USSR worsened considerably, exacerbating the anti-export bias of the Soviet economy.

3.2. Initial disequilibria

The macroeconomic situation on the eve of Poland's stabilization programme have been reviewed in Lipton and Sachs (1990a). The weakening of the Communist regime in the late 1980s, combined with partial reforms, let loose several inflationary trends, including sharp increases in real wages and a rise in the budget deficit. The real wage in June 1989 was 42.2% above the level two years before. The budget deficit in 1989 was around 7.3% of GDP according to IMF estimates, and probably topped 10% in the summer before being reined in the by the new Solidarity-led government in the fall. As of the first half of 1989, open inflation was running at around 8% per month. Table 2 shows

Table 2. Consumer price inflation, per month (%)

	1989	1990	1991
January	11.1	79.6	12.7
February	7.9	23.8	6.7
March	8.1	4.3	4.5
April	9.8	7.5	2.7
May	7.2	4.6	2.7
June	6.1	3.4	4.9
July	9.5	3.6	0.1
August	39.5	1.8	0.6
September	34.4	4.6	
October	54.8	5.7	
November	22.4	4.9	
December	17.7	5.9	

Source: GUS monthly statistical bulletin, various issues.

that it accelerated markedly in the second half of the year, following a partial liberalization of food prices, the widening of the budget deficit at mid-year and the initiation of formal wage indexation.

The expansion of aggregate demand and the continuation of administrative price controls led to an intensification of shortages in 1989, on the eve of the 'big-bang'. While there are no systematic measures of shortages and queues in the goods market, the widening of the gap between the black market exchange rate and the official exchange rate in 1989 is consistent with our view that the monetary imbalances – already bad in 1988 – worsened considerably the following year. The black market exchange spread was around 250% in early 1988, and rose to more than 500% by mid-1989, as seen in the final column of Table 3. Our framework holds that the spread should be increasing with the monetary overhang (M/M_c) which, in turn, increases with the dollar value of the country's money supply (M/E).[5] Between 1988 and 1989, the money supply measured in dollars increased considerably, at the same time that the black market exchange rate spread widened. This pattern in shown in Figure 3, where we graph both the black market spread and the dollar value of the money supply (measured as the reserve money of the central bank).

Long-standing restrictions on private economic activity in services had been liberalized only gradually in the 1980s, and the sector was

---

[5] According to Equation (A11), $P_f/E = (1-a-b)M/M_c/[1-b-a(M/M_c)]$. P_f/E is the same as the black market spread. Also, $M_c = EQ_i/[V(1-b)]$. Thus, according to the simple model, $E_b/E = (M/E)*[V(1-b)(1-a-b)/Q_i]/[1-b-a(M/E)*V(1-b)/Q_i]$. The spread therefore increases with the dollar value of the money supply, M/E.

Table 3. Real effective exchange rates and parallel-market spread

Date	Real effective rate[a,b]		Nominal rate (zloty/$)[a]		
	Official	Parallel	Official	Parallel	Spread
88M1	74	315	315.8	1,350	327.4
88M2	75	277	382.4	1,415	270.0
88M3	73	266	385.7	1,415	266.9
88M4	71	252	397.7	1,420	257.1
88M5	70	250	407.5	1,450	255.8
88M6	70	252	429.8	1,550	260.6
88M7	68	251	449.7	1,670	271.4
88M8	67	338	456.5	2,300	403.9
88M9	68	328	469.6	2,270	383.4
88M10	70	358	482.2	2,480	414.4
88M11	71	441	491.0	3,050	521.2
88M12	69	465	498.7	3,380	577.7
Average 1988	70.5	316	430.5	1,979	350.8
89M1	62	416	505.8	3,410	574.1
89M2	59	361	525.9	3,240	516.1
89M3	58	308	566.2	3,010	431.6
89M4	59	353	631.3	3,745	493.2
89M5	64	334	746.2	3,920	425.3
89M6	67	362	848.7	4,590	440.8
89M7	62	422	836.2	5,660	576.9
89M8	52	384	988.0	7,290	637.9
89M9	52	371	1,339.5	9,540	612.2
89M10	51	211	1,970.3	8,100	311.1
89M11	67	148	3,076.7	6,820	121.7
89M12	99	142	5,235.5	7,454	42.4
Average 1989	63	318	1,439.2	5,565	431.9
90M1	105	103	9,500.0	9,344	−1.6
90M2	92	92	9,500.0	9,460	−0.4
90M3	81	82	9,500.0	9,624	1.3
90M4	76	78	9,500.0	9,750	2.6
90M5	81	83	9,500.0	9,764	2.8
90M6	77	78	9,500.0	9,624	1.3
90M7	76	76	9,500.0	9,513	0.1
90M8	78	78	9,500.0	9,502	0.0
90M9	75	75	9,500.0	9,490	−0.1
90M10	73	73	9,500.0	9,489	−0.1
90M11	71	72	9,500.0	9,590	0.9
90M12	67	68	9,500.0	9,690	2.0
Average 1990	79	80	9,500.0	9,570	0.7
91M1	59	59	9,500.0	9,460	−0.4
91M2	57	57	9,500.0	9,499	−0.0
91M3	51	50	9,500.0	9,453	−0.5
91M4	47	47	9,500.0	9,438	−0.7
91M5	50	50	10,290.0	10,312	0.2
91M6	51	51	11,498.0	11,498	0.0

Sources: Official and parallel market exchange rate GUS monthly statistical bulletin, various issues. Trade shares and foreign price data from the IMF.
Notes: [a] A decline in the index signifies a real appreciation. [b] The real effective exchange rate is calculated as $\Sigma s_i E P_i^*/P_i$, where s_i is the share of country i's trade (exports plus imports) in Poland's total trade. Percentage shares are as follows: Austria, 7.5, Canada, 0.9; Denmark, 4.0; France, 8.6; Germany, 37.7; Japan, 3.5; Netherlands, 6.0; Norway, 1.8; Spain, 1.8; Sweden, 6.1; and Switzerland, 3.6. Australia, Italy and New Zealand were not included because of incomplete trade data.

Table 4. Sectoral allocation of employment, 1988
(percentage of total employment)

	Poland	Greece	Portugal	Spain	Costa Rica
Agriculture	29.0	27.0	22.2	16.1	28.1
Industry	28.7	21.6	26.0	24.3	18.8
Construction	7.8	6.5	8.6	7.6	5.9
Services	34.5	44.9	43.2	52.1	47.2
of which:					
Transport and					
communications	7.5	6.8	4.1	5.8	4.2
Trade	8.9	16.5	14.0	19.0	15.7
Finance	2.2	4.1	3.1	2.5	3.0
Other services	15.4	17.7	22.2	22.6	23.5
GDP per capita	1,719	5,244	4,017	8,668	1,638

Source: Economist (1990), 196–97.

chronically starved for resources. Price controls prevented adequate growth, administrative allocations of resources in shortage were targeted to industry rather than services and the tiny private service sector found itself unable to compete for scarce commodities and credits with the established state sector. Often, the private sector developed as an artificial appendage of the socialized sector, particularly as a way of avoiding controls that applied to state firms. (Rostowski, 1989, provides a discussion of the private sector in Poland in the 1980s.) The result was a service sector whose weight in employment and GDP was considerably smaller than that of other developing countries and the poorer countries of Western Europe. As seen in Tables 4 and 5, Poland's service

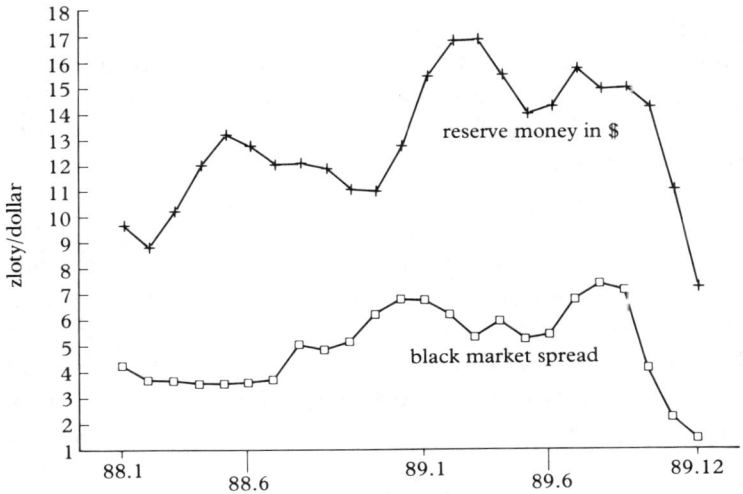

Figure 3. Monetary overhang and the black market spread

Table 5. Sectoral distribution of GDP, 1988 (% of total)

	Poland	Greece	Portugal	Spain	Costa Rica
Agriculture	13.1	13.2	9.1	5.1	17.6
Industry	58.0	30.3	39.6	37.4	30.1
Services	28.9	56.5	51.3	57.5	52.3

Source: Industry includes mining, manufacturing, construction, transport and communications. *Rocznik Statystyczny*, 1990, Table 3 (195), p. 112, for Poland; *Economist* (1990), pp. 36–38, for others.

sector was considerably smaller than in the three low-income countries of the European Community (Greece, Portugal and Spain), as well as in Costa Rica, which is the country ranked just below Poland in the World Bank's 1988 per capita income rankings. Long queues and poor customer service in pre-reform Poland resulted not only from the non-market-clearing prices for consumer goods, but also from the insufficient number of workers in the distribution network.

4. The effects of stabilization and trade liberalization

We now turn to the outcomes of the stabilization and liberalization measures undertaken since mid-1989. A partial liberalization of food prices was carried out in July 1989 as one of the final acts of the old regime. The new Solidarity government undertook some further partial liberalizing measures in the last half of 1989, and then implemented a full programme of liberalization and stabilization at the start of 1990. The general effects are well known. The hyperinflation quickly subsided, though monthly inflation still remains in the 1–5% per month range almost two years after the start of the stabilization programme. Shortages were eliminated: households and factories report in surveys that there has been a nearly total elimination of supply problems. Overt queues for consumer goods vanished in the first weeks of the programme. Inventories in the trade sector were extensively dishoarded. The currency was made convertible through a combination of price liberalization, exchange rate devaluation and tight credit policies. Convertibility was successfully maintained at a nearly constant nominal exchange rate linked to the dollar until May 1991, at which point it was devalued by 16.6% *vis-a-vis* the dollar in order to counteract the appreciation of the dollar *vis-a-vis* the European currencies. Since May 1991, the zloty has been stable in terms of a basket of currencies.

With regard to the real economy, there has been a decline in industrial production and an increase in services, mainly via new private firms. Real consumption has fallen, though apparently by far less than is generally believed. Unemployment has risen, to a rate of about 10% in the fall of 1991. And in 1991, the economy has been heavily hit by the fall of trade with the USSR, and the need to pay world prices in hard currency for energy imports.

These are the general trends, but the quantitative magnitudes involved are not known with much precision. How much did output actually fall? Has the standard of living plummeted, as many observers of the Polish reform programme assert? Did trade liberalization and strong import competition play a major role in the drop of industrial production? How significant is the Soviet trade collapse for real income and macroeconomic adjustment? These are the questions to which we now turn. We pay special attention to the weaknesses of the data used in assessing these issues.

4.1. Price trends since the big-bang

The economic reform had four major direct impacts on prices: a generalized end of price controls; a sharp cutback in subsidies; a rise of domestic energy prices; and the devaluation of the currency. While the overall effects of these changes are naturally complex, we can summarize the changes in the following broad terms, illustrated in Table 6. First, the dramatic cutback of food price subsidies led to a increase in the real price of food for consumers (that is, the price of food relative to the overall consumer price index), and a sharp fall in the real producer price of foodstuffs received by farmers (again, relative to the overall consumer price index). Second, energy prices rose in real terms. The main factors behind this increase are a cutback in subsidies, particularly to the coal sector, the shift from ruble trade in petroleum and natural gas to convertible currency trade, and the need to reverse a decline in relative prices of energy that had occurred during the high inflation of 1988 and 1989. Third, prices of the *service sector* rose more strongly than prices for non-food, non-energy commodities.

Most noteworthy is that convertibility has been sustained despite a real appreciation (Table 3). At the time of the 'big-bang', the government began with an 'overshooting devaluation', in which the nominal exchange rate was devalued to a level *above* the prevailing parallel market exchange rate. At the outset, the real exchange rate therefore depreciated sharply. Over time, however, as domestic prices increased during 1990, the real exchange rate appreciated. By the end of 1990, the zloty was actually more appreciated in real terms than the average for 1988 (when the currency was inconvertible). Note that the real exchange rate, calculated using the parallel market exchange rate, appreciated quite drastically after currency unification. This shows that the large undervaluation of the zloty on the parallel markets in 1988

Table 6. Relative prices, 1989–91, various indicators
(all prices relative to consumer price index)

A. Real food prices, consumer and producer[a]

	Cereals		Meat	
	Consumer	Producer	Consumer	Producer
1989M1–7	100	100[a]	100	100[b]
1990M1–7	408.7	67.9	159.1	74.9
1991M1–7	289.6	37.5	135.7	55.1

B. Consumer prices, main categories

	Foodstuffs	Nonfoodstuffs	Services
1989M1–7	100.0	100.0	100.0
1990M1–7	125.0	86.9	97.9
1991M1–7	110.5	89.5	132.3

C. Consumer prices, selected services

	Residential rent	Personal care	Culture and arts
1989M1–7	100.0	100.0	100.0
1990M1–7	83.2	95.4	78.6
1991M1–7	116.0	152.2	131.8

Source: *Biuletyn Statystyczny*, various issues.
Notes: [a] Producer grain price is thousand zloty per dt of wheat; producer meat price is zloty per kilogram of cattle for slaughter; consumer price of cereal is the index of bread prices. [b] First half of 1989.

and 1989 reflected the excess aggregate demand at the time, rather than the long-run purchasing power parity of the currency.

The fact that convertibility has been maintained despite a real appreciation is, of course, consistent with the above framework. It stresses that convertibility is achieved not mainly through a real depreciation, but through a nominal depreciation which helps to bring the overall price level back into line with nominal aggregate demand (and particularly, with the money supply).[6] Inconvertibility signals an overall price level and an official exchange rate that are too low compared with aggregate nominal demand. Either nominal aggregate demand must be cut (most

---

[6] This is a very important lesson today for the former USSR. The black market value of the ruble is approximately 40 rubles per dollar, while the commercial rate is around 1.8 rubles to the dollar. It is often claimed that convertibility cannot be achieved in the former USSR because at 40 rubles to the dollar, the average industrial wage would be around $8 per month. But this misses the point. If convertibility is achieved at 40 rubles to the dollar, it will be accompanied by a significant rise in the overall price and wage level. The sustainable real exchange rate, in view of today's wages and prices, might be around 8 rubles to the dollar, but the prevailing monetary overhang requires a much higher nominal exchange rate in order that monetary equilibrium can be reached.

drastically, through a monetary reform), or nominal prices must be allowed to rise (through a devaluation and end of price controls), as in fact occurred in Poland.

The real appreciation of the zloty after mid-1990 results partly from the increase in the price of services relative to industrial goods. Since the relative service prices were systematically too low in the pre-reform equilibrium, some rise in service-sector prices relative to export prices was to be expected and desired. But of course, this real appreciation could proceed too far if domestic prices and wages continue to grow rapidly while the nominal exchange rate remains stable. The result would be a weakening of the growth of manufacturing exports to Western markets and an excessive rise in overall unemployment. To protect the competitiveness of the export sector, the National Bank of Poland announced in October 1991 the policy of a gradual crawling peg.

4.2. Trade performance following the big-bang

The end of the monetary overhang and the move to currency convertibility was enormously successful in stimulating Poland's trade with the West. As shown in Table 7, the dollar value of Poland's exports to the convertible currency area (the non-CMEA area) rose from $8.5 bn. to $12.0 bn. in 1990, an increase of 41% in a single year. The dollar value of imports also rose, by an estimated 6%. Note that export earnings rose in every major category of output. With imports, on the other hand, total values increased for fuels and electrical machinery, but fell for the other categories of output. Both exports and imports from the West continued to rise rapidly in the first half of 1991. In truth, imports probably rose in 1990 by considerably more than is reported in the table. Comparing the imports from the West as reported by Poland with the exports to Poland reported by Western countries, we find evidence of significant *underreporting* of imports into Poland in 1990. (Poland's reported exports are also somewhat lower than Western reports of imports from Poland.) According to Table 8 Polish exports in convertible currencies increased by 51% and imports by 29% in dollar terms. (The rate of underreporting for exports is 0% in 1988, −1% in 1989 and 7% in 1990, while for imports it is 14% in 1988, 18% in 1989 and 43% in 1990.) The discrepancy probably originates in the liberalization of trade itself as considerable amounts of goods entered Poland in 1990 through small private traders in 1990 who escaped the statistical net.[7]

---

[7] The Polish Central Statistical Office instituted new measurement methods for foreign trade during 1990 which should begin to capture this activity starting in the end of 1990 and especially in 1991.

Table 7. Trade with the convertible currency area as reported by Poland (million US dollars)

	1987	1988	1989	1990	1991:6
Exports					
Total	7,079	8,311	8,533	12,020	5,841
Fuel and energy	987	977	1,028	1,277	683
Industrial goods					
Electrical machinery	1,761	2,000	2,042	2,764	1,314
Metallurgy	836	1,226	1,334	2,061	1,093
Chemicals	782	982	952	1,439	824
Wood/Paper	96	103	78	na	3
Light industry	560	654	558	842	335
Food	981	1,071	1,162	1,391	628
Agriculture	330	393	444	731	436
Imports					
Total	5,944	7,302	7,766	8,254	6,352
Fuel and energy	333	401	455	1,524	1,315
Industrial goods					
Electrical machinery	1,711	2,133	2,423	3,193	2,311
Metallurgy	496	633	685	567	327
Chemicals	1,329	1,576	1,453	1,034	865
Wood/Paper	199	192	210	na	13
Light industry	464	612	682	593	447
Food	746	960	980	716	423
Agriculture	468	603	704	188	206

Source: GUS annual trade yearbooks (GUS 1988, 1989, 1990d, 1991d), preliminary data for the first half of 1991.

Trade with the CMEA area, and mainly with the USSR, behaved quite differently from trade with the West. Table 9 shows that Poland's exports in transferable rubles fell by about 10% in 1990, while imports plunged by a reported 34%. Poland generated a huge trade surplus in transferable rubles, but was not allowed to use these rubles to purchase key items from the USSR, such as petroleum and natural gas. The breakdown of the CMEA trade arrangements started in 1990, but became precipitous in 1991, when the CMEA disbanded the barter trade arrangements and introduced hard-currency settlements for trade. In the first half of 1991, Poland's exports to the USSR fell by around 70%, while imports from the USSR fell by around two-thirds.

An index for overall changes in export and import volumes is presented in Table 10. (It weights the changes in the trade volumes with the convertible and non-convertible areas by the value shares, measured in zloty, of each kind of trade in Poland's total trade in 1989.) Aggregate

Table 8. Trade with the convertible currency area as reported by the IMF

	1986	1987	1988	1989	1990
Million US dollars					
Exports	6,716	7,072	8,297	8,446	12,183
Imports	6,567	7,005	8,351	9,161	11,806
Volumes (previous year = 1)					
Exports			1.10	0.99	1.51
Imports			1.13	1.10	1.20

Source: As reported by Poland's trading partners, from IMF *Direction of Trade Statistics*. Price indices from GUS trade annuals (GUS 1988, 1989, 1990d, 1991d).

Table 9. Trade in transferable rubles (millions)

	1987	1988	1989	1990	1991:6
Exports					
Total	10,950	11,938	12,217	11,014	1,612
Fuel and energy	814	944	870	782	628
Industrial goods					
Electrical machinery	6,672	7,285	7,501	6,694	493
Metallurgy	397	380	375	188	3
Chemicals	1,054	1,146	1,195	1,372	36
Wood/Paper	96	103	78		3
Light industry	594	578	448	228	173
Food	202	212	174	159	19
Agriculture	202	218	268	281	253
Imports					
Total	10,935	10,819	10,106	6,640	1,150
Fuel and energy	3,453	3,108	2,679	1,582	14
Industrial goods					
Electrical machinery	4,710	4,983	4,747	3,404	869
Metallurgy	835	790	742	404	12
Chemicals	809	777	721	427	76
Wood/Paper	199	192	210	na	13
Light industry	279	331	365	226	54
Food	260	235	241	177	74
Agriculture	55	54	23	73	28

Source: GUS annual trade yearbooks (GUS 1988, 1989, 1990d, 1991d), and GUS preliminary data for the first half of 1991.

real export volume rose by 29.4% in 1990, while aggregate real imports rose by a much smaller 3.3%. Poland had a significant trade surplus with both the convertible currency area and the non-convertible currency area in the year.

Table 10. Overall change in trade volumes, 1989–90

	Value share in 1989 trade (%)	Percent change 1990/89	Weighted average
Exports			
Convertible area	66.1	51.3	
CMEA area	33.9	−13.2	
Total	100		29.4
Imports			
Convertible area	68.5	20.4	
CMEA area	31.5	−34.0	
Total	100		3.3

Source: Value shares from GUS trade annual, various issues. Percent changes are from Table 8 for convertible currencies and Table 9 for the CMEA area.

4.3. Changes in living standards

4.3.1. The conventional evidence. Perhaps the most pressing question about the Polish reforms is whether they have been unnecessarily costly in real terms, either by causing an excessive decline in living standards, or an inordinate drop in real production. It is often asserted that living standards have been sharply reduced, with a frequent estimate of a drop of 'real incomes' of around one-third. It is also widely suspected that the economic reforms have created a depression in the country. Unduly rapid trade liberalization is commonly believed to be an important culprit, by subjecting Polish industry to intolerable international competition.

We present some quantitative evidence on these issues. On the first, we doubt that there was a significant drop of real living standards in 1990, at least not close to the magnitude commonly believed. We also suspect that the undoubted decline in real GDP has been significantly overestimated, though existing data cannot resolve this issue definitively. We also find no evidence that trade liberalization contributed significantly to the decline. In 1990, the production decline seems to be due to the tight macroeconomic measures used to end the hyperinflation, combined with a ngeative effect on aggregate demand caused by inventory dishoarding. In 1991, the decline is most importantly related to the collapse of Soviet trade, rather than to the economic reform programme.

4.3.2. A reappraisal. Early in Poland's stabilization programme it became a point of conventional wisdom that real living standards had declined precipitously as a result of the stabilization and liberalization measures.

Table 11. Average monthly wages in industry, 1987–91

	Nominal (zlotys)	Real[a]	Dollar[b] (market)	Dollar[c] (official)
June 1987	30,722	917	na	119.91
June 1988	50,661	969	32.68	118.37
June 1989	130,454	1,304	28.24	153.65
June 1990	946,822	822	98.38	99.67
June 1991	1,713,300	945	149.48	150.40

Source: Nominal wage index and consumer price index, from GUS monthly statistical bulletin, various issues. Exchange rate data from *International Financial Statistics* of the IMF.
Notes: [a] deflated using the CPI; [b] wage in dollars using the market (parallel) exchange rate; [c] wage in dollars using the official exchange rate.

This idea was largely based on a single, and misleading, datum, the measured decline in real wages between 1989 and 1990. Table 11 shows the basis of the calculation. From June 1989–June 1990, the average industrial wage deflated by the consumer price index fell by 37%. What this datum failed to reveal, however, was that the 1989 real wage level was itself anomalous. Real wages had risen explosively since 1987 in the course of the collapse of the Communist regime. Between June 1987 and June 1989, real wages measured on the same basis rose by 42.2%.

The high level of the real wage in 1989 hardly reflected an improvement of living standards from earlier years, much less a sustainable one. The expansion of nominal aggregate demand as a result of the wage increases and large budget deficits worsened the shortages considerably, so that goods were not available at the official prices. Not only could the 'real' wages not be turned into real purchasing power, but to get the limited amount of goods available required standing in longer queues or paying a higher premium on the black market. For this reason, a reversal of the real wage increase after 1989 is hardly definitive concerning the direction of change of real living standards. As part of its calculation of GDP, the Polish Central Statistical Office (*Glowny Urzad Statystyczny*, or GUS) has estimated that real private consumption fell in 1990 by 15.3%. This estimate is based mainly on data collection from state-owned retail establishments, supplemented with newly implemented surveys of private sector retail activity. It is not likely to capture well the overwhelming transformation from state to private retail trade during 1990. With the private sector share of retail rising dramatically, and with much of the trade going unmeasured

Table 12. Real consumption in 1990 compared to 1989

Budget expenditure category	Expenditure shares 1989	Effective weight	Real index 1990/89
Total	1.00	1.00	0.952
Food	0.44	0.45	0.98
Bread	0.02	0.03	1.02
Flour	0.00	0.00	0.97
Cereals	0.00	0.00	0.79
Pasta	0.00	0.00	1.00
Potatoes	0.01	0.02	1.03
Vegetables	0.03	0.04	1.02
Fruits	0.03	0.04	1.01
Meat	0.08	0.09	0.96
Meat products	0.08	0.10	1.01
Fish and products	0.01	0.01	0.83
Animal fat	0.01	0.01	0.92
Plant oils	0.01	0.01	1.10
Butter	0.03	0.03	1.00
Milk	0.01	0.01	0.93
Cream	0.01	0.01	0.82
Cheese	0.01	0.01	0.83
Eggs	0.02	0.02	0.91
Sugar	0.02	0.02	0.92
Sugar goods	0.02		na
Honey	0.00		na
Other food articles	0.03		na
Restaurants	0.01		na
Cakes	0.00		na
Other dairy	0.00		na
Rice	0.00		na
Alcohol	0.03		na
Cigarettes	0.01		na
Total other non-food	0.53	0.55	0.93
Clothes and shoes	0.16	0.24	0.80
of which textiles	0.01	0.02	0.52
Outerwear	0.02	0.09	0.90
Attire	0.06		na
Shoes	0.04	0.13	0.77
Other	0.04		na
Housing	0.10		na
Electro/mechan.	0.02	0.03	1.03
Rents and payments	0.02	0.03	1.00
Textiles and carpets	0.02		na
Other	0.05		na
Fuel, heating and hot water	0.02	0.02	1.07
Personal hygiene and health	0.03		na
Leisure	0.10	0.14	1.05
Cultural articles	0.06	0.09	1.17
Newspapers	0.00	0.01	1.17
Schoolbooks	0.00	0.00	0.91
Other published matter	0.00	0.01	0.79
Writing/painting material	0.00		na
Electronic equipment	0.03	0.07	1.22

Table 12—continued

Budget expenditure category	Expenditure shares 1989	Effective weight	Real index 1990/89
Other	0.02		na
Sports/tourist equipment	0.00		na
Services: education	0.01		na
Services: culture and art	0.01	0.02	0.88
Tourism/sport activities	0.02	0.04	0.72
Transport and communications	0.06	0.09	1.01
Travel and transport	0.01	0.02	0.85
Means of transport			
of which oil and gas	0.01		na
Other	0.03	0.06	1.08
Post, telephone and telegraph	0.00	0.00	0.93
Other	0.07		na
Balance	0.05		na

Source: Various GUS data. See text and appendix for explanation.

in very small firms, underestimation of the rapidly growing and elusive private sector is very likely.[8]

4.3.3. New evidence on consumption. A different way to measure consumption is to use evidence gleaned from household expenditure surveys and other sources, rather than from surveys of retail firms. This is obviously a imperfect approach as well, given the difficult of identifying an 'average' household, and distinguishing its real purchases from real consumption of items (particularly of durables), but we believe that enough direct evidence on consumption exists to make the effort interesting. In Table 12 we present estimates of physical volume changes for a detailed breakdown of the household consumption basket. Appendix B provides details on data sources and construction. For each item, we attempt to use survey data or other evidence to estimate the percent change in physical units of consumption, and then weight the volume changes by the consumption shares of each item in 1989 to come up with an aggregated change in real consumption between 1989 and 1990.

Aggregate food consumption is measured to fall by 2.2% between 1989 and 1990, while non-food items fall by around 7%. Taking a weighted average we find a real fall in consumption volume of about 4.8%. In fact, real consumption probably fell by less for several reasons.

---

[8] The GUS recognizes this problem and is improving its recently implemented surveys of private trade. We doubt, however, that GUS has successfully measured the extent of post-reform trade.

First, we put conservative estimates on the level of 1990 consumption in cases where there was conflicting evidence. Second, we are using fixed weights based on 1989, which tends to understate real consumption in 1990 by neglecting second-order effects due to substitution in response to relative price changes. Third, we are *not at all* reflecting the rise in the quality and variety of goods available on the consumer market due to the opening of trade with the West. This effect is probably of great significance. Fourth, we are not measuring the savings in real work time and leisure time made possible by the end of queuing and search for scarce commodities caused by the chronic shortages before 1990. Fifth, we cannot capture the new ability of consumers to choose the good they want among the varieties available. This is not the increase in overall variety already mentioned, but a question of matching between goods and consumers. Because goods were available when desired in the shops, it no longer became necessary to buy whatever was available whenever it was available, irrespective of whether it was exactly the right good (e.g. shoes of different sizes). In focus group interviews Polish consumers often mentioned a new ability to 'plan shopping' as one of the most important improvements.

4.3.4. Psychologically, however, we also neglect one heavy cost of the changes since 1989: the undoubted rise in anxiety and uncertainty in the Polish population as the result of the collapse of the old economic system. There are widespread fears of involuntary unemployment and job layoffs, a largely novel phenomenon, and even a sense of doom or despair among parts of the population. There may also be a loss of the hope that was held by some during the worst times of the 1980s, that getting rid of the Communists would quickly and painlessly give Poland a Western-European economy.[9] Economic inequality is widening, so parts of the population are surely worse off while other parts are better off. Many small farmers have suffered as the result of the end of a high level of agricultural subsidies, while many new businessmen in the private sector are earning several times the average wage in industry.

4.4. Changes in production and GDP

4.4.1. Hyperinflation and revolutionary conditions. In addition to the decline in living standards, the output costs of Poland's rapid liberalization of prices and trade cause widespread concern. Without doubt, physical

---

[9] We would like to thank Adam Biela for this point.

production in industry has declined significantly, though the size of this decline and of the overall decline of GDP remains in doubt. Moreover, the causes of the decline are also uncertain. It is crucial to remember that Poland has not merely undertaken a liberalization since 1990, but that the new Solidarity government that came to office in the fall of 1989 had to stabilize an economy that had just passed the threshold of hyperinflation. (Cagan's, 1956, classic definition of hyperinflation was a rate of price increase exceeding 50% *per month*. Poland passed that threshold in October 1989, when the consumer price index rose by 54%.) The stabilization programme could be expected to lead to a significant loss of output: most stabilization programmes to end high inflation do.

Moreover, in the context of a political revolution, with the virtual collapse of the old administrative order, and with an adverse ownership structure in industry, the institutional conditions for stabilization were extraordinarily problematic to say the least.[10]

4.4.2. New estimates from the demand side. GUS estimates a 12% decline of real GDP in 1990. An even greater drop, of 15%, has been widely reported, but this larger fall refers to the so-called 'gross output' concept which excludes most of the service sector, and therefore much of the fast-growing private sector. We find that while there is an important range of uncertainty, due particularly to the difficulty of measuring the change in inventory investment and the growth of the private sector,

---

[10] Just to mention a few of many factors: (i) the Solidarity-based government had only 35% of the seats in the Parliament, as a result of the political compromise in the Roundtable Agreement that had been reached between the Communist authorities and Solidarity earlier in the year; (ii) wage discipline at the enterprise level was almost non-existent, since enterprises were governed by Workers' Councils with the power to dismiss managers; (iii) the Roundtable Agreement dictated the introduction of backward-looking wage indexation, which could only be removed incompletely at the start of the stabilization programme; (iv) the new non-Communist government had, almost by definition, no trained and experienced team in monetary issues and stabilization policy, though the new Deputy Prime Minister Leszek Balcerowicz acted with extraordinary decisiveness and wisdom. Many key ministers had spent years of the 1980s in the underground movement or in internment camps, rather than in the study of stabilization programmes; (v) workers were socially mobilized after years of protests and demonstrations against the old regime. These energies created important demands on the new government, and led to wildcat strikes as well as organized protests; (vi) the formal trade union movement was itself deeply divided, with a weakened Solidarity trade union attempting to regain its plant-level influence after years of repression, and having to compete with the previously 'official' trade union, OPZZ, which had been given extensive resources (e.g. guest houses for worker vacations) by the previous regime. Moreover, OPZZ exercised considerable, and growing, populist appeals, as a way to try to win legitimacy in the new era; and (vii) the institutions of macroeconomic control had not yet been put into operation. The banking system remained almost entirely in state hands, and the 'commercial banks' were in fact recent spin-offs of the previously monolithic state bank. There was as yet no foreign exchange market for enterprises; no interbank lending market; no monetary programme for the central bank; and no bond market for Treasury issues.

the actual decline in real GDP is considerably smaller than the 12% estimate. Even conservatively, it is closer to 5%.

In attempting to measure the real output decline we make several key assumptions which differ from those of GUS. Throughout the estimates, we try to make conservative assumptions (that is, assuming a larger fall) when faced with a variety of plausible choices. In other words, we only differ with GUS where we feel the change is clearly warranted. The two most important such changes are, first, that we estimate the change in real consumption from consumer surveys, as described above, and, second, we place much greater reliance on employment data in measuring changes in value-added, especially in services. We do this in order to improve the measurement of private sector output, since the standard methods used by GUS tend to under-represent the production of the very small firms (and probably the larger firms as well, assuming that they underreport their income in order to lower tax payments).

The measurement of GDP change can be approached from the demand side, by adding up changes in real consumption (C), investment (I), government current expenditure on goods and services (G), and exports of goods and non-factor services (X), minus imports of goods and non-factor services (Z). Alternatively, changes in real value added by sector can be added, to get an estimate from the production side. Each method has its limitations. On the demand side, there are major gaps in estimates, especially regarding inventory investment, while on the production side, there are major limitations in measurement of private sector activity. We try both approaches, and compare the results.

We have already introduced our estimates for changes in real consumption (−4.8%), real exports (29.4%), and real imports (3.3%). It remains to estimate the changes in real government consumption, real fixed investment and real inventory investment. As described in Appendix B, we estimate real government consumption in part accord-ing to the inflation-adjusted value of government purchases, and in part according to the number of employees in public administration. (This last method is both universal and problematic: 'Comrade, how many people work in the Ministry of Industry?' 'Oh, about a third.'). On this basis, we calculate a slight increase in real government consump-tion, of about 1% between 1989 and 1990.

We take as given the official government estimate of a drop of 9% in real fixed investment spending, even though the sharp increase in imports of investment goods from Western Europe suggests that private-sector investment in new small enterprises in industry and construction might be undermeasured by the official data. The harder problem is

Table 13. Stocks of inventories

	1989	1990
All socialized enterprises + private sector trade		
Total inventories		
Change as percent of GDP	−2.1	−6.2
All non-trade socialized enterprises		
Total inventories		
Percent of GDP	20.1	18.4
Months of sales	1.70	1.81
Change as percent of GDP	−4.1	−3.0
of which:		
goods and finished products		
Percent of GDP	4.1	4.0
Months of sales	0.35	0.39
Change as percent of GDP	0.7	−0.4
Materials		
Percent of GDP	12.3	10.7
Months of sales	1.03	1.05
Change as percent of GDP	−4.1	−2.3
Socialized Trade		
Total inventories		
Percent of GDP	11.2	5.3
Months of sales	2.22	1.32
Change as percent of GDP	1.6	−6.3
Trade inventories in private sector		
Change as percent of GDP	0.3	3.1

Sources: Inventory and sales data for the socialized sector from GUS (1990c, 1991e). Employment and sales data for the private sector are from GUS (1991b).

Notes: GDP for 1989 is a GUS estimate, reduced by a downward re-estimation of inventory investment in 1989 (see Appendix, Section 5). Inventory change as a percent of GDP and months of sales are calculated by deflating the end-of-period stocks by a five-month backward moving average of the producer price index (where average prices in 1989 = 1), then comparing to 1989 GDP and current-year sales respectively. Private sector trade inventories are estimated by assuming that (1) the share of the private sector in trade at the end of the year is proportional to its share in employment, and (2) inventories per worker in the private sector are 50% of inventories per worker in the socialized sector. This is roughly equivalent to assuming that private sector inventory to sales ratios are the same as they are in the US. Because of data availability, the data we present for inventories in months of sales for socialized trade covers only retail sales of final goods.

to measure the change in inventory investment. Our procedure is explained in Appendix B. The evidence is reported in Table 13, and may be summarized as follows. In the *non-trade* socialized sector (mainly industry), inventories of materials tended to fall significantly while inventories of finished goods tended to fall slightly. This is consistent

Table 14. Real GDP growth in 1990 by category of demand

	1989 Shares (%)	Real change 1989–90 (%)	Contribution to total (%)
Total	1.00		−4.9
Private consumption	56	−4.8	−2.7
Investment	22		
Fixed	21	−9.0	−1.9
Inventories	1		−6.2
Government	18	1.0	0.2
Exports (merchandise)	21		6.1
Area 1	7	−13.2	
Area 2	14	51.3	
Imports (merchandise)	16		−0.5
Area 1	5	−34.0	
Area 2	11	20.4	

Note: See text and Appendix for explanation.

with the idea that industrial firms responded to a cutback in final demand by using up their accumulated stocks of materials. There is direct evidence marshalled by Schaffer (1991) that sales of industrial firms fell in advance of production, consistent with the idea that inventories of finished goods would tend to rise after the onset of the stabilization and liberalization programme, and then be reduced afterwards, following a cutback in production. The overall net change in non-trade inventories, taking into account both materials and finished goods, seems to be a fall of about 3% of GDP in 1990, following a fall of inventories of about 4% of GDP in 1989.

The situation in retail trade is more dramatic but more difficult to interpret. Using our assumptions on pricing, inventories of socialized firms in the trade sector seem to have declined by around 6% of GDP. Inventories in the foreign trade sector (i.e. stocks held by foreign trade organizations), dropped by about 1% of GDP. Part of the large drop of inventories is a reflection of the dishoarding phenomenon that we should expect when the shortages are eliminated. Another part certainly reflects the shift of trade to the private sector. Since we cannot make a precise estimate, but believe that the private sector rose to more than 40% of retail trade by the end of 1990, we estimate conservatively that the unmeasured rise in inventories in the private sector amounted to around 3% of GDP, in other words, less than half of the measured decline in trade-sector inventories. (Specifically, we assume that inventories per worker are 50% of those in the socialized trade sector. This leads to inventory/sales ratios about the same as those in the US, see Table 1.)

Based on these 'guesstimates', we end up with an estimated overall drop in inventories between end-1989 and end-1990 of 6.2% of GDP. This enormous (and perhaps overstated) drop in inventories should be added to the other changes in final demand. Using the methodology described in Appendix B, we come up with an overall drop in GDP of 4.9% for 1990, as shown in Table 14. This is obviously much less than the usual estimate, and it would be lower still if we accepted that more of the inventory decline is really a transfer to unmeasured private stocks, or used a less conservative assumption with regard to the pricing of inventory stocks.

4.4.3. New estimates from the supply side. The alternative approach to measuring GDP is to add up changes in real value added by sector. The main problem here is incorporating the important growth of the private sector in overall estimates of sectoral growth. We believe that the GUS methodology has probably understated the actual growth of the private sector, both by undermeasurement of very small businesses (including self-proprietorships) and the underreporting of private sector income. As seen in Table 15, there was a marked increase in the share of employment in the private sector (from around 34% of employment in 1989 to 38% of employment in 1990), particularly in private trade (where employment rose by 308%). The share of employment in industry (socialized and private) fell from 41% to 39%, while service sector employment grew from nearly 30% to nearly 32%.

Using the employment data, and assumptions described in Appendix B, our estimate of growth in the service sector in 1990 is 6%. We rely on Schaffer's (1991) index of industrial production in the socialized sector for our estimate of a 21.2% decline in that subsector. Conservatively, we stipulate a 5% increase in private industry (less than the 9% measured growth of employment). According to official data, in 1989 private industry accounted for 7.4% of the total production in the sector. Putting these estimates together, we arrive at a drop of 19% of industrial production. For the other sectors, we simply adopt GUS estimates of real changes.

Once again, we combine these individual estimates in order to arrive at an estimate of the change in GDP, shown in Table 16. Using the estimated shares of each sector in 1989 as weights, the weighted average of the estimated changes yields a drop of 8.7% of GDP. This is much higher than our demand-side estimate of 4.9%, though still much lower than the official estimate of 12%.

Table 15. Employment by sector and ownership

	1989		1990		
	Workers (000)	Shares (%)	Workers (000)	Shares (%)	Growth (1989 = 1)
Total	17,069.6	100	16,391.1	100	0.96
Socialized	11,222.4	66	9,988.1	61	0.89
Private	5,847.2	34	6,402.0	39	1.09
Industry	7,028.6	41	6,390.7	39	0.91
Socialized	5,743.0	34	4,988.8	30	0.87
Private	1,285.6	8	1,401.9	9	1.09
of which:					
Construction	1,224.5	7	1,091.1	7	0.89
Socialized	814.8	5	666.0	4	0.82
Private	409.7	2	425.1	3	1.04
Transportation	963.2	6	895.6	5	0.93
Socialized	911.9	5	821.0	5	0.90
Private	51.3	0	74.6	0	1.45
Agriculture	4,956.5	29	4,808.0	29	0.97
Socialized	874.9	5	734.1	4	0.84
Private	4,081.6	24	4,073.9	25	1.00
Services	5,084.5	30	5,191.4	32	1.02
Socialized	4,604.5	27	4,265.2	26	0.93
Private	480.0	3	926.2	6	1.93
of which:					
Trade	1,302.4	8	1,458.7	9	1.12
Socialized	1,161.8	7	884.9	5	0.76
Private	140.6	1	573.8	4	4.08

Source: GUS.
Notes: This table covers all workers ('pracujacy'), not just employees. (The difference is primarily the inclusion of sole proprietors etc.) 'Industry' is the sum of the GUS categories 'industry' ('przemysl'), construction, and transportation. The private sector is defined according to GUS 1990 definitions. Starting in 1991 certain types of organizations, in particular cooperatives, were reclassified as private. These are excluded from the private sector in this table.

4.4.4. Assessment. We have more confidence in our demand-side estimates. The consumer survey data is the least susceptible to the danger that it mismeasures private-sector activity, and we feel we have if anything overestimated the inventory decline. By using trading-partner data on trade we have measured an increase in imports much larger than that suggested by official data. On the supply side, we have had to rely much more on data coming from traditional methods of measurement which emphasize socialized sector production. This raises problems even beyond the probable undermeasurement of the private sector and 'grey-market' state sector activity. For example, a reduction in unnecessary cross-shipping of goods between factories, a commonly

Table 16. Real GDP growth, 1990 by category of value added

	1989 Shares (%)	Growth 1990/89 (%)	Contribution to 1990 growth (%)
Total	100		−8.7
Industry	57	−17	−9.8
of which:			
Manufacturing and mining			
Socialized	41	−21	−8.6
Private	3	5	0.2
Construction	8	−16	−1.3
Transportation	4	−14	−0.6
Agriculture	13	−2	−0.2
Services	31	6	1.7

Source: GUS data and own calculations. See text and Appendix for explanation.
Notes: Industry here includes construction and transportation, unlike usual GUS practice.

reported phenomenon in Soviet-style economies, would result in a fall in estimates of GDP in transportation.

While the drop of GDP was serious, it was probably much less than usually suggested. Negative inventory investment was probably a large component of this fall, and real consumption probably fell by considerably less than the overall GDP. 1991 is surely a year of additional GDP decline, perhaps of the same order of magnitude, but once again, real consumption almost surely declined by less than GDP, and may well have even increased. Indeed, household expenditures on major food products (meat, fish, fruit) rose in 1991, as did the statistical real wage. Imports also soared, with very large increases in consumer durable imports.

4.5. Macroeconomic evidence on the causes of the GDP decline

In our opinion, the simplest macroeconomic approach fits the facts in Poland in 1990. The anti-inflation programme, combined with the liberalization of prices and exchange rate devaluation, led to a sharp monetary squeeze, a partial selloff of inventories, and a drop in aggregate demand. This in turn caused an expansion of exports and imports, a restriction on domestic purchases of industrial goods, and a shift of resources from industry to services. There was probably some modest demand decline due to the initial contraction of exports to the USSR, but this effect was not pronounced until 1991.

Output declined largely because macroeconomic policy had to be tight enough to rein in the hyperinflation, under difficult circumstances. The initial freeing up of prices led to a near doubling of the price level in the month of January 1990, and follow-on effects from that shock in the form of monthly nominal wage increases and other administrative price changes (e.g. further cuts in subsidies, rent increases, energy price increases) imparted an inertia to the process. That tight money was needed to stem the high inflation was clear enough early in 1990, but was actually tested later in the year, when monetary policies were eased up in the second half of the year, and the inflation rate increased from the neighbourhood of 2–4% per month to the range of 4–6% per month. In particular, the rate of nominal wage growth appears to be very sensitive to the rate of domestic credit growth to socialized enterprises.

The idea that Poland suffered a supply shock rather than a demand shock, due to Calvo and Coricelli (1992), strikes us as seriously at variance with the facts. Evidence suggests, for example, that industrial demand fell ahead of industrial output (a fact found by Schaffer, 1991). Also the rise in exports seems to be only consistent with a view of demand, not supply restriction. The evidence suggests that inventory liquidation can by itself account for only about 20% of the export increase to the West in 1990, and in any event, the exports have remained strong in 1991, despite the winding down of the inventory selloff.

Another idea sometimes mooted, that import demand caused the damage to the state sector, also cannot be sustained on the evidence. First, it is clear that at the beginning of 1990, demand fell well before imports rose sharply. Poland in fact ran large trade surpluses for several months. Second, as we shall see below, there is no evidence on a sectoral basis that industries facing particularly large increases in imports are the same as those experiencing particularly large declines in real sales.

5. Sectoral evidence on production and trade in Poland

Another way to gain evidence on the effects of trade liberalization and on the nature of the production decline, is to study the evolution of sales by sub-sector of industry. We test three hypotheses: (i) that the output decline is related to import competition from the West; (ii) that the output decline is a supply shock, related to the rise in internal energy prices; and (iii) that the output decline is related to the collapse of trade with the USSR. The evidence on real sales for 20 broad sub-sectors of Polish industry (other than the energy sector) is presented in Table 17. The data measure the sales of domestic firms, for both the home and export markets. Real sales by domestic industry fell in every

Table 17. Change in real sales by industrial sub-sector (%)

	1991/90	1990/89	Share of total industry sales (%)
Basic metals	−12	−10	10.0
Non-ferrous metals	−13	−31	4.8
Metal products	−8	−27	3.7
Engineering	−21	−22	7.3
Precision instruments	−32	−25	1.0
Transport equipment	−33	−31	6.9
Electronics	−7	−35	4.1
Chemicals	−9	−28	9.8
Building materials	−12	−20	2.7
Glass	0	−25	0.8
Pottery and china	−12	−27	0.3
Wood	−2	−28	2.6
Paper	−4	−18	1.6
Textiles	−13	−39	0.4
Clothes	−9	−29	0.8
Leather products	−27	−27	1.5
Food	−5	−6	5.9
Fodder	9	−25	0.2
Printing and publishing	−15	−13	0.4
Other	−13	−27	0.5

Source: GUS.
Note: Data for 1991 is calculated as 12/5 the real sales for the first five months. Industry shares calculated for 1990. The sum does not add to 100, since in addition to the 20 sectors listed, there are three more sectors in Polish industry (coal, fuels and energy) which we have not included in the regressions. The three excluded sectors together account for 19.5% of industrial sales. Sales data exclude cooperatives.

sub-sector in 1990, suggesting a macroeconomic phenomenon such as a fall in aggregate demand, rather than a microeconomic phenomenon, such as increased import competition, which has varied widely across sectors. Indeed, the dollar value of imports from the convertible currency area actually dropped in 15 out of the 20 sectors.

In Appendix C, we present two simple cross-section regressions linking, sector by sector, total real sales to transferable ruble exports. The same regression was run to examine the evolution between 1990 and 1991. For the later period, the Soviet trade variable is significant, suggesting that a fall in Soviet exports of 1% of sales is associated with a fall of 0.44% of sales.[11] We also added as explanatory variables the

[11] The fact that a part of this decline in ruble exports was converted to dollars may explain why the coefficient is less than 1.

energy-intensity of production and the rise of imports from the convertible currency area. Neither of these variables was significant in either period. The coefficient on Soviet trade was not changed by the inclusion of the other variables, although it falls below traditional significance levels. We emphasize the complete lack of correlation between import penetration from the West and output decline, either in association with the other independent variables or in bivariate regression (not shown).

6. The Soviet trade shock

One way to measure the Soviet trade shock is in terms of lost demand for manufacturing. Table 18 shows the direct and indirect effects (as a percent of sales) for each sub-sector, and for the entire manufacturing sector. Appendix B explains the calculation. The largest effects by far are for the precision instruments sector and engineering sector. These two sectors produce machinery for Soviet industry, with a significant component linked to the military-industrial complex. With demand cut by half, far more than half of the precision machinery sector is in acute financial distress. Employment in engineering and precision machinery accounted for 12% of total industrial employment at the end of 1989. The total demand effect for *all* of the industrial sectors equals about 5% of total sales in industry.

Another way to measure the Soviet trade shock is to note that manufactured goods exports to the USSR used to pay for a large quantity of raw materials, mainly petroleum and natural gas, which must now be purchased on the world market, or at least with hard currency and at world prices from the USSR itself. The question is how much of *other* resources will now be needed to import the initial basket that used to be paid for by industrial products exported to the USSR. We will assume that the manufacturing capacity of the impacted sectors cannot be redirected, which is consistent with our finding that a drop of exports to the USSR created at least an equal drop in overall sales. A rough calculation suggests that Poland received in its barter trade from the USSR a volume of raw materials worth approximately $3.2 bn. at world prices.[12] If the old Soviet-directed industries must now be scrapped, Poland must devote $3.2 bn. of other resources to maintain the previous level of imports. With GDP estimated at around $70 bn., the collapse of Soviet trade represents a real income loss of about 4% of GDP, under the reasonable assumption that most of human and

---

[12] We have added the dollar values at world prices of the most important raw material imports from the CMEA zone, and subtracted the dollar value of raw material exports to the CMEA zone.

Table 18. Shock to demand from decline in exports to the CMEA (changes as percent of base-year sales)

	1990–91		1989–90	
	Exports to CMEA	Resulting demand shock	Exports to CMEA	Resulting demand shock
Coal	−4	−5	0	0
Fuel	−1	−3	−1	−1
Energy	0	−2	0	0
Basic Metals	0	−3	0	−1
Non-ferrous metals	0	−3	0	−1
Metal products	−4	−5	−1	−2
Engineering	−13	−15	−3	−3
Precision instruments	−48	−48	15	15
Transport equipment	−5	−6	−3	−4
Electronics	−8	−11	−1	−1
Chemicals	−5	−7	0	−1
Building materials	0	0	0	0
Glass	−1	−1	0	0
Pottery and china	−1	−1	0	0
Wood	−1	−1	0	−1
Paper	0	−1	0	0
Textiles	−1	1	−1	−2
Clothes	8	8	−3	−4
Leather products	2	2	−3	−3
Food	0	0	0	−1
Fodder	0	0	0	0
Printing and publishing	−2	−2	0	0
Other	3	3	−1	−1

Source: GUS.
Notes: See Appendix for explanation.

physical capital resources now devoted to production for the Soviet market cannot quickly be redeployed.

The social drama of the Soviet collapse should also be kept in mind. Dozens of large factories, often the only major employer in a town of several thousand, now stand to be scrapped. Entire towns are at risk, with enormous social and political consequences.

7. Some conclusions and policy implications

The Polish economic programme is important not only in its own right, but as a key example of the benefits and possible costs of a rapid movement to convertibility. As such, it has been closely scrutinized and the subject of controversy. It has been suggested that high costs favour

Table 19. Output changes in Eastern Europe, 1990 and forecasts for 1991 (%)

	GNP		Industrial output		CPI	
	1990	1991	1990	1991	1990	1991
Bulgaria	−15.0	−10.8	−14.1	−15.0	65	1,000
Czechoslovakia	−4.2	−5.2	−3.7	−4.5	15.7	70
Hungary	−5.3	−2.5	−5.0	0.0	29	27
Poland	−12.8	−3.8	−20.0	−4.0	684.3	80
Romania	−11.0	−4.8	−18.8	−9.0	75	150
USSR	−6.4	−17.7	−1.2	−12.0	10	250

Source: *Planecon*, reported by Reuters, 2 October 1991.

a more gradual approach. In this paper, we assess the costs and benefits of the Polish approach.

The costs are alleged to be the sharp drop in living standards and the steep fall in output but, on close analysis, these costs turn out to be less than commonly believed. Moreover, output has fallen everywhere in the region, even in countries that did not start like Poland in a financial crisis of very high inflation and intense shortages. The October 1991 forecast of *PlanEcon* reported in Table 19 shows that Poland is not such an outlier in output decline, especially if a more accurate (and *lower*) estimate for GDP decline is made for 1990. (Poland was, of course, an outlier in terms of the extreme inflationary conditions in 1989). In 1991, the GDP declines throughout the region are strongly related to the collapse of CMEA trade. That is why the only market economy heavily dependent on Soviet trade, Finland, is also expected to experience a decline of 6% of GDP in 1991. (For a useful survey of Finland's economy, describing a fall in output said to be 'the worst performance since 1920', see the *Financial Times*, 4 October 1991, pp. 29–32).

There is no evidence that the move to convertibility has hindered Poland's process of structural adjustment to market conditions. In fact, it seems to us that quick convertibility has been crucial in two respects. First, it has enabled domestic manufacturing firms to find new export markets in the West to compensate for the collapse of the Soviet market. Since Poland had a one-year head start in reacting to the Soviet shock by moving to convertibility in 1990, it might turn that Poland's output losses due to the Soviet shock have been a little bit cushioned. Similarly, the move to convertibility probably facilitated the export of some of the excess inventory stocks held by firms at the end of 1989.

We also examine one of the key questions about convertibility, the vulnerability of domestic firms to the rapid introduction of foreign competition. We find no evidence that the output decline in particular industrial sectors is importantly related to the rise in imports. Moreover, on the benefit side, Poland demonstrates that good exchange rate and monetary policies can generate a large increase in exports, even in a country that allegedly lacks 'quality of goods'. Despite all the pessimistic pronouncements about Poland's potential, exports to the convertible currency area have grown rapidly in the past two years, by around 65% in dollar terms. The main fallacy about quick convertibility is that a country must have an adequate level of technology before it is ready to compete internationally on the basis of free trade and convertibility. This ancient misconception confuses the real basis of free trade, comparative advantage, with the issue of absolute advantage. It also confuses the issue of convertibility, which revolves around the relationship of two nominal variables, the money supply and the nominal exchange rate, with the issue of real income levels.

The idea of moving slowly towards convertibility has been lent some credence because of the long time period in which Western Europe moved towards convertibility after World War II. It is certainly time to reassess that experience. In our view, there is no triumph in the European Payments Union and the gradual move to convertibility.[13] Rather, the European countries should simply have devalued their currencies more sharply at the end of the 1940s and through that means could have approached convertibility directly. There may be some truth to the proposition that no *individual* European country should have undertaken convertibility in the absence of such actions by the others, because a liberalization of trade when all other trade partners continue to maintain strong protection can have an adverse effect on the liberalizing country's terms of trade. Therefore, the case for a coordinated move to convertibility might have been present in post-war Europe. But the analogy to the current period is very weak, since each of the Eastern European countries has started with an inconvertible currency in a global economy in which almost the entire world economy now operates under convertibility.

---

[13] Even though the European Payments Union is frequently referred to as a policy success, there have been many important critics of the payments union since the early 1950s. One of the earliest, and perhaps the most influential, was Milton Friedman (1953). Friedman's advocacy of flexible over fixed exchange rates in that famous essay should in fact be understood as the advocacy of convertibility (which is guaranteed by a floating rate) over inconvertibility (which Friedman associated with a fixed rate system, where the rate has been set an overvalued rate).

Discussion

Richard E. Baldwin
Graduate School of International Economics, Geneva

This paper presents an assessment of the impact of the Polish 'big-bang' policy reform of 1990. The principal thesis is that the decline of Polish output resulted from a demand contraction that was driven by a sharp reduction in the budget deficit, price liberalization, credit restrictions and the 1991 collapse of CMEA trade.

In early 1990, Poland liberalized trade and sharply devalued its currency. To test the idea that trade liberalization was an important cause of this, we should look at the impact of trade opening on the prices domestic producers receive and then look at the response of producers to these price changes. Since the necessary producer price data are presumably not available, Berg and Sachs focus on correlations between imports and output. To fix ideas consider what such a liberalization would do to a well functioning market economy marked by sectors engaged in intra-industry trade. In a market economy the liberalization, if not entirely offset by the devaluation, would face domestic producers and consumers with lower prices in the net importing sectors, and higher prices in the net exporting sectors. Clearly in the net importing sectors, domestic production would fall while imports and domestic consumption would rise. The impact in net exporting sectors would be higher domestic output and lower domestic consumption of both local and imported goods. The important point is that trade liberalization should lead to output changes that are correlated with initial levels of net imports.

Suppose that Berg and Sachs had been wrong, and that trade had indeed been a leading cause of output drop: what should one have observed? It is true that the liberalization entailed the removal of administered prices, so consumer and producer prices need not have moved in the same direction. But price controls in exporting industries would have kept producer prices too low in net exporting sectors and too high in net importing sectors in an attempt to pursue socialist anti-Western trade goals. Thus, trade liberalization should still have boosted output of net exporting sectors and contracted output in net importing sectors. Again, the lack of a credible threat of bankruptcy, and the absence of well functioning factor markets, might have made it difficult for firms to adjust output to the price changes. But this simply dampens the magnitude of the expected effects rather than altering the sign of the expected output changes.

Appendix C shows the results from regressions of the change in imports from hard currency areas, the change in exports to the CMEA nations and a measure of energy-intensity on the change in the sectors' output. Although I think one should interpret the estimated parameters as multiple correlation coefficients rather than structural parameters, the fact that the change in hard currency imports had no explanatory power in either the 1990 or the 1991 regression suggests that something else was to blame. The regression for 1990 is odd in that none of the regressors is significantly correlated with the change in output. The 1991 regression shows that energy-intensity works as expected and the collapse of CMEA trade also had a large and statistically significant impact, however Western imports continue to be insignificant. I think this latter fact poses a bit of a puzzle since without further elaboration, I would have expected that if domestic output were sensitive to any trade flows, it would be sensitive to all trade flows. This leads me to wonder what would have happened if the regressions had included data on the export boom to the West suggested by Table 7. One explanation for the differential impact of Western and CMEA trade may have been that the import of Western goods was dampened by price cutting and loss-making while CMEA trade just stopped. Unless firms that were heavily dependent on CMEA exports allowed their inventories to rise without bound, the CMEA collapse would have a very direct impact on output. This is circumstantially supported by the fact that although CMEA trade fell in 1990, the variable is only significant in the year CMEA trade virtually evaporated. One could check this interpretation by looking at the correlation between sectoral plant closures and the output drops.

Finally, the Berg–Sachs argument that the Polish economy did not perform as badly as some claim can even be strengthened. GDP figures fail to capture the universe of productive activity even in nations with very sophisticated statistical agencies. A well known example of this is household services like cleaning and cooking. In so far as this unmeasured activity constitutes a relatively stable fraction of measured output, changes in GDP provide a reasonable gauge of changes in productive activity. However, for an economy in the throes of a radical transformation, it is unlikely that GDP drops accurately reflect drops in productive economic activity. To take just one example, in the modern world most markets are operated by a network of individuals or firms who all know each other repeatedly. The business of business is mostly a question of knowing your suppliers, knowing who wants your product and knowing how to sell it to them at a profitable price. The smooth operation of a market requires a great deal of information. Since this was not the case under a planned industrial sector, transition inevitably involves a substantial investment in information. Gaining this information may involve making mistakes that lower output and in any case will require resources. Although this is a productive investment, it will not show up directly in production numbers. Likewise learning-by-doing, development of labour markets and the retaining of workers may reduce measured output in the short run, but the creation of the intangible assets is unlikely to show up in GDP figures. Other intangible assets that are essential to the operation of a market economy but are impossible to measure are flexibility in production and consumption patterns and the entrepreneurial spirit. This all implies that the actual drop in Polish output may have been even lower than suggested by the Berg–Sachs revision of GDP data.

John Flemming
European Bank for Reconstruction and Development

The first quarter of this paper is devoted to the presentation of a simple model of a distorted economy with an overvalued and incovertible currency in which *all* suppliers face distorted official prices and *all* consumers face market-clearing black market prices. Except in the foreign exchange market, the spread represents queuing time – possibly that of professional intermediaries. In the case of foreign exchange, the spread accrues as rent to those given allocations at the official rate. A simple quantity equation relates excess demand and these spreads to a monetary overhang at the official exchange rate, but the authors stress the flow as well as the stock contributions to excess demand. These flows meant that to restore equilibrium in Poland required a sharp cutback in the budget deficit.

The model is explicitly simplified (indeed 'crude'). One of the odder assumptions is that while there are professional queuers there are no moonlighting hairdressers satisfying the excess demand for services generated by the anti-service bias of the command economy. In Section 3, a number of the features of the model are related to those of the pre-reform Polish economy. A rise in money wages relative to money prices had put the budget into deficit and contributed to a cumulative monetary overhang. Somewhat surprisingly, given the subsequent discussion, this is described as an increase in the real wage, although the model suggests that workers' welfare is likely to have fallen. The growing monetary overhang generated parallel movements in the black market exchange rate premium and the dollar value of the domestic money stock at the official rate – as predicted by the theory. Inventory levels exceeded those in North America and the service sector is shown to account for about half as much of GDP as in several Western countries with comparable income levels.

In the second half of the paper we come to the effects of Poland's 'big-bang' stabilization and liberalization on trade and activity. Shortages have disappeared, inventories in retailing were dishoarded, industrial output has fallen while service output has risen. Unemployment has also risen while exports to the USSR have fallen, largely independently. Detailed discussion of the magnitude of several of these developments leads to others' estimates of their magnitude being revised downwards, but the qualitative picture – much of which is consistent with the theoretical model – is unchanged. The model's only ambiguity relates to trade volumes, where the overall picture is confused by probable underreporting of imports as well as disruption of Soviet trade. The authors conclude that exports rose sharply and imports very slightly. They consider several possible causes of the fall in output and living standards whose reality, though often exaggerated, they accept. The candidates, not necessarily either mutually exclusive or clearly defined, are: fiscal stabilization, credit restrictions, international competition (coming through trade liberalization) and the fall in Soviet trade.

I have some difficulty with the import competition argument as typically presented, but the following related story is a distinct possibility. Abolition of subsidies and liberalization of trade change the relative prices of the value added of different sectors. Sector-specific capital and low *ex post* factor substitutability mean that this reduces the market-clearing real wage in all sectors and labour's share in value added at that equilibrium. Perhaps because of minimum wages and unemployment compensation, the real wage falls less and unemployment occurs instead. This story is difficult to describe as either a supply or a demand shock; it is a relative price shock – such as one to a country's terms of trade.

Though not described in these terms, the authors' evidence on the uniformity of output falls across industrial sub-sectors in 1990 (Table 17) reinforces their conclusion that stabilization, dishoarding and credit control, rather than liberalization, were to blame. In the first half of 1991, nearly half the growth rates were positive and, though the Soviet trade collapse was a crucial phenomenon, relative price effects may also have come into play. Their regression work is, however, open to question on the basis that both exports to the USSR and particularly imports from the convertible currency area are at least partially endogenous.

The authors defend Poland's rapid move to convertibility, although they admit that both rising unemployment and the loss of job security carry social costs. The relative price shock hypothesis is not refuted by noting that output falls are uncorrelated with import rises. If a subsidy is withdrawn, output and consumption may both fall without an import surge. The relative price hypothesis would, however, point to some possible advantages in a temporary wage subsidy redistributing quasi-rents between winners and losers. Such a measure (if feasible) might, by sustaining unprofitable production that nevertheless generates positive value added, increase the surplus available for investment in expanding sectors. It might thus be an alternative to the slow progress towards convertibility in Western Europe after World War II which is described as 'no triumph'. In the absence of either counter-factual study, the relative merits of gradual convertibility, transitional wage subsidy and big-bang market freedom cannot yet be assessed.

Berg and Sachs successfully show that the costs of their preferred alternative have been exaggerated. Their model implies that the black market exchange rate is a bad guide to the free equilibrium rate – a lesson that can be applied to the ruble. It is just as true, and hence as important, when the tourist ruble trades at 100 to the US dollar as at 40.

General discussion

A number of panellists took up the question whether conventional measures captured accurately the welfare impact of the fall in Polish output. Grzegorz Kolodko pointed out that a major redistribution of income was taking place, so that aggregate figures might disguise the fact that large numbers of people had suffered large falls in welfare. Miroslaw Gronicki pointed out that the end of queuing had significant welfare implications; in addition to the reduced deadweight loss from queuing activity there was also a loss of (unrecorded) rent to intermediaries. And he wondered to what extent the recorded surge in imports might be due to improved reporting as trade restrictions were removed.

The question whether there had been an excessive devaluation at the start of the reform programme was discussed by several panellists. Paul Seabright said that emphasis on the role of the exchange rate as a nominal anchor had prevented it from functioning as a relative price, sending signals about the relative profitability of tradeable production. This role was especially important given the misleading relative prices inherited from the command economy, but the need to establish credibility for the convertibility had led policy-makers to err on the side of undervaluation; many firms that had expanded exports during 1990 must be regretting their actions during 1991. Richard Portes agreed, and added that, among other odd features, the model of the paper misinterpreted the roles of both exports and the exchange rate under central planning. Exports should not be viewed as being determined purely as a residual. Hans-Werner Sinn doubted, however, whether the source of the undervaluation had anything to do with monetary phenomena: rather, he suggested, it might be an instance of a comparative advantage (common to many less developed countries) in non-traded products.

Richard Portes also pointed out that the initial reduction in inventories could not explain the persistence of the fall in ouput. Attila Chikan thought the fall in trade to the CMEA area was responsible for much of the decumulation of inventories.

Finally, there was discussion of investment. Paul Seabright pointed out that there were public good aspects to some labour market reforms, especially those improving coordination of access to health, education and training facilities along with employment, since many of these had been provided by enterprises under central planning. Jeffrey Sachs doubted that the State should stretch its scarce resources even further becoming involved in activities of this kind. In contrast, he pointed to considerable private sector investment in entrepreneurial activity; this might take many years to bear fruit, but was no less real an investment for its being under-recorded in national income statistics. In conclusion, he thought progress was still urgently needed in two main areas: the abolition of monthly wage indexation, and the commercialization of enterprises.

Appendix A. Some theoretical aspects of stabilization and liberalization

Consider an economy which produces just two kinds of outputs, industry and services, in the amounts Q_i and Q_s, respectively. The economy consumes these two goods, and also a foreign-produced import, in the amounts C_i, C_s and C_f, respectively. The domestic industrial good is also exported. The official exchange rate is E, in units of zloty per dollar.

The official prices for the three goods are p_i, p_s and p_f. As described in the text, we shall assume that the market-clearing prices are established in unofficial parallel (or black) markets, and designate the parallel-market prices as P_i, P_s and P_f.

Consider a very simple situation, in which nominal aggregate demand by households is given by Y^d, so that macroeconomic equilibrium requires:

$$Y^d = P_i Q_i + P_s Q_s + P_f Q_f \tag{A1}$$

In the simplest monetarist case, we can write:

$$Y^d = MV \qquad\qquad\qquad\qquad\qquad\qquad (A2)$$

where M is the money stock, and velocity V is a constant. More generally, of course, V is not constant, and Y^d is a function not only of M, but also of fiscal deficits, the real wage and so on. Consumption is governed by a Cobb-Douglas relationship, in which

$$P_i C_i = aY^d = aMV$$
$$P_s C_s = bY^d = bMV \qquad\qquad\qquad\qquad\qquad (A3)$$
$$P_f C_f = (1 - a - b)Y^d = (1 - a - b)MV$$

Output by enterprises is a function of relative prices, with:

$$Q_i = Q_i(p_s/p_i)$$
$$Q_s = Q_s(p_s/p_i) \qquad\qquad\qquad\qquad\qquad\qquad (A4)$$

Now, we will assume that the economy starts with a monetary and price structure such that industry is a net exporter. That is, $Q_i > C_i$. There is no excess demand for the industrial good on the domestic market, and the parallel market price equals the official price.[14] Moreover, the official price is simply the exchange rate multiplied by the world price index p_i^*:

$$p_i = Ep_i^* = P_i \qquad\qquad\qquad\qquad\qquad\qquad (A5)$$

The official domestic price of the foreign imported good is similarly given as the world price multiplied by the exchange rate:

$$p_f = Ep_f^* \qquad\qquad\qquad\qquad\qquad\qquad\qquad (A6)$$

Of course, for this good, we expect a situation of excess demand on the domestic market, so that $P_f > p_f$. For simplicity, we set $p_i^* = p_f^* = 1$, so that $p_i = p_f = E$.

Since the price of services is set exogenously at p_s, and $p_i = E$, the relative official price of services in terms of output is fixed, so that

---

[14] The crucial assumption here is that there is an excess supply of the exportable good in the domestic market. In a market economy, in which domestic prices are set according to supply and demand, and in which producers are free to choose between supplying the domestic market and exporting, the assumption is unexceptionable. Exports occur because there is an excess of supply over domestic demand at the domestic price, with the domestic price being set by the world price converted into domestic currency at the official exchange rate. In a non-market setting, however, it is possible that exporters are commanded or induced to export even in the face of intense domestic shortages. In our judgement, the model points in the right direction for Poland, even though surely some goods were exported that were also in excess demand. (See footnote 4).

output in the export sector is also fixed, at the level $Q_i(p_s/E)$. (Below, when we consider a devaluation, we assume that the price authorities maintain a fixed *relative* price between industry and services, so that p_s/E remains unchanged.) Similarly, output in the service sector is fixed at the level $Q_s(p_s/E)$. By our assumptions, these output levels will not be affected by the monetary equilibrium.

We assume that the country lacks foreign exchange reserves to run a trade deficit, so that international trade must be balanced or in surplus.

$$C_f = Q_i - C_i \tag{A7}$$

Let us now find the combination of the money supply and exchange rate that would just produce monetary equilibrium with balanced foreign trade and currency convertibility.

From (A3) and (A5) we know that $C_i = aMV/E$. Assuming currency convertibility, the parallel-market price of imports must equal the official price, so that $P_f = p_f = E$. Thus, $P_f C_f = E C_f$, so that from (A3), we have $C_f = (1 - a - b)MV/E$. Thus, from (A7), we find:

$$(1 - a - b)MV/E = Q_i - aMV/E \tag{A8}$$

By simply rearranging, we find the level of M that is consistent with balanced trade and currency convertibility at the exchange rate E, and we denote that level of M as M_c:

$$M_c = EQ_i/[V(1 - b)] \tag{A9}$$

When M is equal to M_c, the exchange rate E is convertible. When M rises above M_c, however, the exchange rate E becomes inconvertible, because it becomes impossible to satisfy the demand for imports out of export earnings. Specifically, exports fall since C_i rises (causing $Q_i - C_i$ to fall). This also causes a fall in the domestic availability of imports, according to the balanced trade condition (A7). At the same time, the nominal demand for imports rises, since $P_f C_f = (1 - a - b)MV$. Thus, at the initial domestic price $P_f = E$, there is an excess demand for the import good. Assuming that the monetary authorities leave the nominal exchange rate unchanged, foreign exchange would have to be rationed.

As a result of rationing, the domestic parallel-market price of the import god rises above the world price multiplied by the exchange rate, so that $P_f > E$. Specifically, the parallel market for the import good clears when $P_f C_f = (1 - a - b)MV$. Since $C_f = Q_i - C_i = Q_i - aMV/E$, we find:

$$P_f = (1 - a - b)MV/[Q_i - aMV/E] \tag{A10}$$

Note that Equation (A10) is derived under the assumption that exports are positive, which applies only for $aMV \le EQ_i$. This is equivalent to the condition that $aM \le (1-b)M_c$. For M higher than this amount, imports are zero, C_i equals Q_i, and P_i is equal to aMV/Q_i, which would be greater than E.[15] Henceforward, we will always assume that we are in the range in which exports are positive.

Using (A9) and rearranging, we find the following interesting relationship:

$$P_f/E = (1-a-b)(M/M_c)/[1-b-a(M/M_c)] \qquad M > M_c \qquad (A11)$$

Equation (A11) can be interpreted as follows. The expression M/M_c is a measure of the monetary overhang, since it is the ratio of the actual money supply to the level consistent with balanced trade and convertibility. When a monetary overhang exists, the domestic parallel-market price of the imported good is higher than $p_f = E$, because foreign exchange must be rationed at the official exchange rate. The importers which are lucky enough to get the rationed foreign exchange can purchase imports at the price P_f and resell them in the parallel market at the price P_f.

Under certain assumptions (mainly that the imported good can be costlessly imported and exported on the parallel market, using parallel, or black, market dollars), P_f/E is not only the premium on the imported good, but is also the *premium on foreign exchange in the parallel (or black) foreign currency market*. That is, the ratio of the parallel (or black) market exchange rate E_b to the official exchange rate E, is equal to P_f/p_f, which in turn is an increasing function of the monetary overhang:

$$E_b/E = P_f/p_f = (1-a-b)(M/M_c)/[1-b-a(M/M_c)] \qquad (A12)$$

Consider the real trade consequences of the monetary overhang. The higher is the money overhang, the smaller is the level of exports and imports, and the lower is consumer welfare. This can be seen as follows. Exports X_i are equal to $Q_i - C_i$, and the proportion of output that is exported, X_i/Q_i, can be calculated as follows:

$$X_i/Q_i = 1 - [a/(1-b)](M/M_c) = C_f/Q_i \qquad (A13)$$

The equation also reflects the fact that when the currency is inconvertible, the rate of import equals the rate of export. When $M < M_c$, the currency remains convertible and the trade balance moves into surplus. In particular, we have $P_f = p_f = E$, and $C_f = (1-a-b)MV/E$. At the same time, $Q_i - C_i = Q_i - AMV/E$. Combining these two expressions, we find

---

[15] The domestic price rises above the world price multiplied the exchange rate. International price arbitrage no longer holds since domestic firms no longer export to the world market.

an expression for the trade balance, which is equal to $TB = Q_i - C_i - C_f$. In particular, we find:

$$TB = [(1 - b)V/E]*(M_c - M) \qquad M < M_c \qquad \text{(A14)}$$

This expression is the counterpart of (A13) for the case in which the money supply is *less than* the level consistent with convertibility and balanced trade. For an unchanged exchange rate, a drop of M below M_c produces a trade surplus. In effect, the low level of the money supply evaluated at world prices, M/E, restricts imports and produces the surplus.

As described in the text, our maintained assumption for the service sector is that service-sector production is artificially restricted by price controls. Specifically, when nominal demand for services, bMV, is greater than the nominal supply, $p_sQ_s(p_s/E)$, a parallel market for services will develop. The parallel market equilibrium is reached when nominal consumer demand bMV, is equal to the value of output measured at the black market price: $bMV = P_sQ_s$. Thus,

$$P_s/p_s = bMV/(p_sQ_s) = (M/M_c)(bQ_i/[(1 - b)p_sQ_s]) \qquad \text{(A15)}$$

As with the imported good, the black market premium in the service sector is an increasing function of the monetary overhang.[16]

Appendix B. Data and methodology

B1. Estimation of the change in real consumption, 1989–90

B1.1. Sources. Our most important source of data is the GUS household budgetary survey (GUS 1990a, 1991a). This survey consists of a rotating random sample of over 8,000 households in Poland. Through 1990 it excluded the self-employed as well as households of persons involved in military or police service, hence a source of underreporting since the self-employed sector experienced a boom in 1990.

B1.2. Methology. Poland's household surveys use a four-way population breakdown, among workers' households, farmers' households, agricultural workers' households and pensioners' households. Rather than weighting up each of these categories, we simply take the workers' household category as our base for measurement. For easily identifiable consumption items, mainly the food category, this simplification does

---

[16] It is obviously possible that the money supply could be so low that P_s would fall below p_s. That would in fact be a situation of excess supply in services at the official price, a situation which we take to be outside of the relevant range of our analysis.

not appear to introduce a systematic bias.[17] As explained below, we try to identify quantity measures for as many categories of items as possible. In the end, we are left without any direct evidence for about 40% of the basket, and some 'guesstimates' for another part. We simply drop the items we cannot identify, and raise the weights proportionately on the included items, so that the new effective weights sum to 1.0.

We were tempted, for some categories of non-food consumption (such as textiles, furniture and carpets), to use what is called 'supply' (domestic production + imports − exports) as an indicator of domestic consumption. We suspect, however, that consumer imports of these items probably went up, even substantially. Unfortunately, direct official measurements of imports of these items is also likely to be of little avail, since these items were imported heavily by individuals and small private firms, whose import levels are almost surely underreported. Where it is possible to compare supply data directly with consumption from the household budget surveys, it seems clear that supply is underreported. For example, butter supply in 1990 is reported to have fallen by 16% of 1989, while consumption of butter is reported to have *increased* by 4%. The number of pairs of leather shoes supplied is supposedly down 42%, while consumers report a 30% fall in purchases. Finally, we observe a 22% decline in bread supply and a 5% decline in bread consumption.

B1.3. Weights. The weights are based on the results from the budgetary survey for 1989 (GUS 1990a). We then looked for indicators of change in real consumption for each category. One of the principal problems with this approach is that the base-year weights are unsatisfactory. First, by ignoring substitution in consumption, which is likely to have been important, this method tends to *overstate* the real consumption decline. Second, it essentially ignores the services from housing, since rents and payments for housing were highly subsidized in 1989 and hence had a very small weight. Since housing services fell only slightly if at all, again the real consumption decline is overstated.

B1.4. Consumption Categories and Sources

(1) *Food and clothing/shoes.* Consumption of physical quantities is taken directly from the survey.
(2) *Housing and related expenditures.* The most important sub-category for which we have data is electrical/mechanical goods for the

---

[17] Workers represent about 55% of the groups covered by the survey. Retirees and farmers represent about 20% each. The income of retirees relative to workers *rose* by 25% in 1990, while that of farmers fell by 5%.

home. We use data from the GUS survey information on consumer durable stocks. Services derived from these goods are assumed proportional to stocks, and the indices for the relevant types of durables (washing machines, vacuum cleaners, sewing machines, refrigerators and freezers) are weighted by retail sales in 1989, with weights covering 40% of total retail sales in this category.

(3) *Rents and payments.* These are assumed to be constant (in real terms). This should in principle represent services from housing, which has presumably remained roughly unchanged. Note that housing is an exception to the procedure of using the available information from subcategories to calculate an index for the category, then aggregating the categories using the full weights. Because of the size of the missing categories and because the sub-categories we have covered have been perhaps unusually positive, we reduce the effective weight of 'housing' to the weight of the covered sub-categories only.

(4) *Fuel, heating and hot water.* Data on tons of gas, watts of electricity and gallons of hot water used by households comes from GUS (1991b). Separate indices for each are averaged.

(5) *Personal hygiene and health.* Nothing is available.

(6) *Leisure.* Newspapers are measured as the number of titles published. The number of school-books and other books published ('other published matter') are found in GUS (1991b).

(7) *General electronic equipment.* Consumption is derived from household budgetary survey data on stocks of durables, with consumption assumed proportional to the stock. (Of course, no allowance is made for the quality improvements which must have taken place.) Indices for radios, stereo radios, black-and-white and colour televisions and tape recorders were combined with weights derived from retail sales data for 1989. The goods used cover 70% of retail sales reported for this category for 1989.

(8) *Services.* Culture and art are measured as the number of concerts and performances given. Tourism and sport activity corresponds to data from the household budgetary survey.

(9) *Transport and communication.* Travel and transport indices come from total passenger miles. PTT derives from a simple average of intercity telephone conversations (with an index of 1.00) and number of ordinary letters sent (with an index of 0.86).

B2. Inventories (Table 13)

B2.1. Sources. From GUS (1990c, 1991e), we get nominal end-of-year stocks of inventories as well as sales. 1989 GDP, used to calculate changes as a share of GDP, comes from GUS estimates, except for inventory investment itself (see Section B5 below).

B2.2. Methodology. Inventory change as a percent of GDP and months of sales are calculated by deflating the end-of-period stocks by a five-month backward moving average of the producer price index (where average prices in 1989 = 1), then comparing to 1989 GDP and current year sales, respectively. Trade inventories in the private sector result from assuming that the share of the private sector in trade at the end of the year is equal to the end-of-year share of the private sector in employment in trade. The private sector is assumed to hold 50% of the inventories per worker of the state sector.

There are two major problems in meaasuring inventory investment. First, there are no clear ground rules in Poland for cost accounting for inventories, so it is unclear (not only to us, but also to the official statistical agency) how to measure *real* inventories based on the nominal inventory figures reported by enterprises. The contribution of inventory investment to GDP in 1989 was measured by GUS as the change in nominal stocks of inventories from the beginning to the end of the year. This greatly overstates real inventory investment in a hyperinflationary environment, as increases in the value of inventories due to inflation appear as positive real investment. We use the overall producer price index for industry as the price index for inventories, and assume that firms use FIFO accounting. We also assume that inventories are held for five months, and that at any time, the age of the inventory stock is uniformly distributed between one and five months. Based on these assumptions, we take as the inventory deflator a backward-looking five-month moving average of producer prices, with uniform weights on past months.[18]

The second problem is that there is virtually no information on inventory stocks held by small private firms. This is particularly distressing, since the big drop in *measured* inventories is in the trade sector, which is exactly the sector in which private firms are developing most rapidly. As of early 1989, it is estimated that the private sector accounted

---

[18] It may seem excessive to assume five months' of inventories, either *a priori* or because our own estimated inventory/sales ratios are much smaller. Indeed, we emphasize the sensitivity of our estimates of inventory investment to this assumption. For example, if we use a four-month ,lagged average of prices to deflate inventories, we find a fall in inventories of 3.2% and not 6.2% as reported in the text. Instead of the 2.1% fall in inventories as a percent of GDP in 1989, we get a fall of 5.0%. We believe it plausible to assume that the decline in inventories took place in 1990 and not 1989. Assuming a lower lag length does not change much the overall decline in inventory investment from 1988 to 1991, but does result in more of the inventory decline taking place in 1989 and less in 1990.

for less than 10% of retail outlets. As of mid-1991, the official government estimate is the private sector accounts for 80–85% of retail outlets! In view of the fact that tens of thousands of small shops in retail trade were privatized together with their inventory stocks, and in view of the fact that official inventory statistics cover the socialized sector, much of the drop in measured inventories might simply represent a transfer of inventory stocks to private firms. But it was not possible for us to find data to measure this effect. Certainly, new private establishments had inventory holdings not measured by the GUS statistics.

B3. Change in real government expenditure

We used OECD preliminary data for nominal expenditures on wages and salaries, goods and services, and defence, for 1990 and 1991. Goods and services and defence were deflated by the CPI (which rose more than the PPI or the real wage), while the change in total government employment (from the *Maly Rocznik*, 1991) was used to measure the change in the component of government expenditure represented by wages and salaries.

B4. Calculation of change in real GDP by components of demand (Table 14)

The 1989 shares come directly from the GUS (1991b) except for one difference: inventory investment in 1989 is recalculated using methods as described in Section B2 above. GUS estimates inventory investment at some 26.1 tn. zloty, or some 23% of GDP, by considering the (nominal) difference between end-of-year and beginning-of-year stocks as the contribution of inventory investment to (nominal) GDP for the year. We attempt to calculate real inventory stocks using a lagged weighted average of past prices in order to measure inventories and GDP in comparable real terms. We estimate 1989 real inventory investment to have been 1 tn. zloty in average 1989 prices, or 1.1% of GDP. This reduces our estimate of 1989 GDP from 113.8 tn. zloty to 93.3 tn. zloty.

B5. Calculation of change in real GDP from the supply side (Table 16)

B5.1. Shares. 1989 levels and shares are from GUS (1991e) according to the SNA system, except for the breakdown of industry into private and socialized sectors. This is inconsistent with the shares used for the demand-side estimation of change in real GDP, where we adjusted 1989 inventory investment as described in Section 5. This is unavoidable because we did not have enough information to make the adjustment by sector. Shares for the private and socialized sector in industry are GUS data on levels of sold production by sector (GUS 1991b).

B5.2. Growth rates

(1) *Industry*. Estimates for the socialized sector are from the index of industrial production in Schaffer (1991). The growth of real private sector industry is simply assumed to be 5%, a conservative estimate given corresponding employment growth of 9% according to GUS.

(2) *Construction, transportation and agriculture*. GUS estimates of change in value-added in constant prices are used.

(3) *Services*. Real growth indices are taken directly from employment. The difference between overall growth in employment in services (from Table 15) and the contribution to GDP here is due to the fact that the shares used to aggregate the growth rates are different. Employment in trade grows much more than employment in the non-material sphere, and the share of the non-material sphere in GDP as given by GUS (1991b) is much less than that implied by employment shares.

B6. Calculation of CMEA shock

We used two methods to estimate the size of this shock. To produce a sectoral breakdown of the demand shock to firms, we started with the change in ruble values of exports to the CMEA zone for each period (1989–90 and 1990–91). For 1991 we simply multiplied the value for the first five months by 12/5, for reasons of data availability. We multiplied this by the base-year average ruble/zloty exchange rate and divided by base-year sales. This represents our measure of the final demand shock.

To calculate the total shock we made use of an input–output table of the Polish economy from 1987 used by the Polish Ministry of Finance. This table contains 38 sectors, including the 20 we use in our regressions. Using standard techniques, we calculate the total shock as

$$dY = (I - A)^{-1} * dE, \tag{B1}$$

where dE is the change in export demand described above and A is the input–output matrix.

The second method involved calculating the dollar value of imports of raw materials and energy from the CMEA area.

Appendix C. Regression analysis: cross-section of industry

The regressions examine whether the decline in the home industry's real sales during the 1989–90 and during 1990–91 is linked to: (1) the fall of ruble-denominated exports to the CMEA area, *DXTR*; (2) the rise in imports into the sector from the convertible currency area, *DMCA*: and (3) the energy-intensity of production in the sector, *EI*. Each of these variables requires a brief explanation.

The fall of ruble exports, *DXTR* is measured as a percent of total sales of the sector, using an input–output model to calculate both the direct and indirect effects of CMEA demand on the sector in question. For example, if output of the metal sector is both exported directly for rubles, and is sold as an input to the precision machinery sector, whose output is in turn exported for rubles, then we aim to capture both effects. The rise in imports from the convertible currency area, *DMCA*, is the change in real imports of goods in the sector, measured as a percent of total sales of the domestic industry. The sectoral energy-intensity is measured as the percentage share of energy-sector inputs (coal, fuels and energy) in total material input costs, based on the 1988 input–output table.

Definitions of variables:

$DSALES$ = percent change in real sales, year to year.

$DXTR$ = the total effect on demand of the change in final demand for exports to CMEA areas (measured using base-year ruble/zloty exchange rate) as a percent of base-year sales.

$DMCA$ = the change in the dollar value of imports from the convertible currency area, as a percent of base-year sales.

EI = energy-intensity of production, measured as the percentage of total material costs accounted for by coal, fuels and energy.

C1. Change, 1989–90, 20 sectors

$$DSALES = -0.25 + 0.16 * DXTR$$
$$(15.4) \quad (0.4)$$

$R^2 = 0.01 \qquad R^2\text{-adj} = -0.05$

t-statistics in parentheses

C2. Change, 1990–91, 20 sectors

$$DSALES = -0.10 + 0.44 * DXTR$$
$$(4.8) \quad (2.5)$$

$R^2 = 0.25 \qquad R^2\text{-adj} = 0.21$

t-statistics in parentheses

C3. Change, 1989–90, 20 sectors

$$DSALES = -0.28 + 0.20 * DXTR + 0.26 * EI + 0.04 * DMCA$$
$$\quad\quad\quad (1.03)\,(0.5)\quad\quad\quad (1.3)\quad\quad (0.1)$$

$$R^2 = 0.11 \quad\quad\quad R^2\text{-adj} = -0.06$$

t-statistics in parentheses

C4. Change, 1990–91, 20 sectors

$$DSALES = -0.11 + 0.41 * DXTR + 0.12 * EI - 0.01 * DMCA$$
$$\quad\quad\quad (3.0)\quad (1.7)\quad\quad\quad (0.4)\quad\quad (0.1)$$

$$R^2 = 0.26 \quad\quad\quad R^2\text{-adj} = 0.12$$

t-statistics in parentheses

Source: Appendix B, based on 20 sub-sectors of industry.

References

Akerlof, G., A. Rose, J. Yellen and J. Hessenius (1991). 'East Germany In From the Cold: The Economic Aftermath of Currency Union', *Brookings Papers on Economic Activity*.

Berg, A. (1992). 'The Logistics of Privatization in Poland', mimeo, National Bureau of Economic Research.

Berg, A. and O. J. Blanchard (1992). 'Stabilization and Transition: Poland 1990–1991', mimeo, National Bureau of Economic Research.

Cagan, P. (1956). 'The Monetary Dynamics of Hyperinflation', in M. Friedman (ed.) *Studies in the Quantity Theory of Money*, University of Chicago Press, Chicago.

Calvo, G. and F. Coricelli (1992). 'Stabilizing a Previously Centrally Planned Economy: Poland 1990', *Economic Policy*.

Friedman, M. (1953). 'The Case for Floating Exchange Rates', in M. Friedman (ed.) *Studies in the Quantity Theory of Money*, University of Chicago Press, Chicago.

Frydman, R., S. Wellisz and G. Kolodko (1990). 'Stabilization in Poland: A Progress Report', in E. M. Classen and R. Mundell (eds.) *Exchange Rate Policies in Developing and Socialist Countries*, International Center for Economic Growth, San Francisco.

Glowny Urzad Statystyczny (GUS). Warsaw:
   (1988) *Handel Zagraniczny: Stychen-Grudzien 1987.*
   (1989) *Handel Zagraniczny: Stychen-Grudzien 1988.*
   (1990a) *Budzety Gospodarstw Domowych W 1989 Rok.*
   (1990b) *Rocznik Statystyczny.*
   (1990c) *Wyniki Finansowe Przedsiebiorstw Uspolecznionych I–IV kwartal 1989.*
   (1990d) *Handel Zagraniczny: Stychen-Grudzien 1989.*
   (1991a) *Informacja o Wybranych Elementach Warunkow Zycia Ludnosci w 1990 Rok.*
   (1991b) *Maly Rocznik Statystyczny.*
   (1991c) *Wyniki Finansowe Przedsiebiorstw Uspolecznionych I–IV kwartal 1990.*
   (1991d) *Handel Zagraniczny: Stychen-Grudzien 1990.*
   (1991e) *Rocznik Statystyczny*
   Statistical Bulletin and *Biuletyn Statystyczny* (monthly, various issues).

Lipton, D. and J. Sachs (1990a). 'Creating a Market Economy in Eastern Europe: The Case of Poland', *Brookings Papers on Economic Activity*.

Lipton, D. and J. Sachs (1990b). 'Privatization in Eastern Europe: the Case of Poland', *Brookings Papers on Economic Activity*.

Rostowski, J. (1989). 'The Decay of Socialism and the Growth of the Private Economy in Poland', *Soviet Studies*.

Sachs, J. (1992). 'Accelerating Privatization in Eastern Europe: The Case of Poland', World Bank Annual Conference on Development Economics, World Bank, Washington D.C.

Schaffer, P. (1991). 'A Note on the Polish State-Owned Enterprise Sector in 1990', Centre for Economic Performance, Working Paper No. 106.

Weitzman, M. (1991). 'Price Distortion and Shortage Deformation or What Happened to the Soap?' *American Economic Review.*

Economic Policy April 1992 Printed in Great Britain

Stabilization in Poland

Guillermo A. Calvo and Fabrizio Coricelli

Summary

We examine the dynamics of the January 1990 stabilization programme in Poland, focusing on the substantial and sudden collapse in industrial output, and inflation persistence. We discuss three, non-mutually exclusive, explanations of these phenomena: (1) excessive initial stocks of inventories, (2) an exogenous fall in household demand and (3) tight credit. We conjecture that tight credit was at centre stage: it helped to magnify the fall in output, and to coordinate such a fall across sectors.

We base such a conjecture on the existence of substantial credit segmentation, and on the underdevelopment of private credit markets. The latter may explain the substantial shrinkage of interenterprise credit, compounding the initial contraction of bank credit. They argue that credit tightness is reflected in firms offering wages below the programme's ceilings, especially given that firms are controlled by Workers' Councils. This conjecture is further strengthened by the fact that wages increased, and even went beyond the programme's ceilings, as credit expanded during the year. We argue that the wage hike may be the reason why credit expansion did not result in a major output recovery, and inflation persisted during the year.

Stabilizing a previously centrally planned economy: Poland 1990

Guillermo A. Calvo and Fabrizio Coricelli
International Monetary Fund and The World Bank

1. Introduction

In January 1990 Poland started a radical stabilization programme involving practically full liberalization of prices and removal of subsidies on primary inputs like coal. The official exchange rate against the US dollar was devalued by 31.6%, unifying *de facto* official and parallel markets. Additional nominal anchors were provided: guidelines on bank interest rates, and ceilings on bank credit and wages. As expected, after the initial price jump, the effect on inflation was swift and effective. Inflation fell from 17% in December 1989 to 4% in March 1990. However, output suffered a significant fall of about 12% during 1990, and inflation remained at much higher levels than programmed.

Several explanations have been proposed to account for the decline in output: (i) excessive initial stocks of inventories held by both firms and households, (ii) tight credit and (iii) household demand connected with liquidity constraints. All of these factors may have played a role at different points of the process. However, we argue that tight credit conditions (high interest rates at the beginning of the programme, and binding credit ceilings afterwards) should be high on the list of suspects. Because firms still depend very strongly on its cost and availability, bank credit tightening had a direct negative effect on production and magnified the effects of the other two factors. The credit view is particularly helpful to explain the puzzling fact that wages were set below the programme's norm. The credit view also sheds light on inflation

We are grateful to John Black, Peter Bofinger, Michael Burda, David Burton, Grzegorz Kolodko, Manmohan Kumar, Timothy Lane, Stanislaw Wellisz, Charles Wyplosz, the Economic Policy Panel and the participants in the International Economics Seminar at Princeton University for useful comments on a previous version of the paper. The views expressed in the paper are exclusively those of the authors, and do not reflect the opinion of the International Monetary Fund or the World Bank.

persistence. The relaxation of *bank* credit during the year allowed for higher wages which raised aggregate demand for non-tradables. Output was little affected by credit relaxation because the additional bank credit was used to repay involuntary interenterprise credit and to increase wages toward the programme's ceiling. Alternatively, if firms continued to use simple markup pricing rules, the increase in wages could directly explain inflation persistence.

The paper includes two complementary parts: the main text, which is self-contained, and the appendices which expand on theoretical and methodological issues. Section 2 presents a summary of developments since 1980, while Section 3 overviews the main features of the Polish programme and singles out the main issues. Supply-side explanations, relying on technological factors and drastic changes in prices and interest rates, are presented in Section 4. Section 5 discusses household demand factors. Section 6 subsumes some of the previous supply and demand-side factors in a more general framework which highlights the role of credit and the possible existence of a 'credit squeeze'. Finally, Section 7 closes the main text with some lessons from the Polish experience. Appendices offer additional support for points made in the main text. Appendix A provides some alternative measures of the credit stance. Appendix B offers the theoretical background. Appendix C discusses measurement problems.

2. Background

The programme of January 1990 was certainly the most radical programme attempted in Poland in recent times, although there had been several incomplete reform attempts during the Communist regime (IMF, 1989). An acceleration in the reform process took place during the 1980s, particularly after 1986 with the so called 'second stage' of reforms aimed at improving the efficiency of the system by decentralizing economic decisions. From 1981 to 1989 the price system was gradually liberalized, the central allocation of inputs was sharply reduced, and the exchange rate system and the allocation of foreign exchange were modified to ensure access to foreign exchange and to maintain the competitiveness of Polish exporters. Trade directed to the convertible currency area increased substantially (Table 1).

These reforms significantly increased the autonomy of decisions of enterprises. Nevertheless, key elements of the socialist economy were maintained: state ownership of enterprises, *de facto* commitment to full employment, and the absence of effective bankruptcy procedures. (Agriculture remained in private hands throughout the socialist regime.) Despite a significant increase, at the end of 1989, the private

Table 1. Poland: background information

Population (end-1989)	38 mn.			
GDP per capita (1988)	1,850 US$			
External debt at end-1990				
in billions of US$	49.0			
in percent of GDP	80.4			
National accounts	1980	1988		
GDP (%)	100	100		
Agriculture	13	13		
Industry and construction	54	52		
Services	33	35		
Structure of external trade	1980	1989	1990	1991Q1
Exports (fob) (%)				
In convertible currencies	52	64	72	96
In nonconvertible currencies	48	36	28	4
Imports (fob) (%)				
In convertible currencies	52	64	79	96
In nonconvertible currencies	48	36	21	4
Socialized and private sectors	1970	1989	1990	
Share in total employment (%)				
Socialized	68	67	62	
Private	32	33	38	
Private non-agriculture	3	12	16	

Source: Central Statistical Office (GUS).

non-agricultural sector accounted for slightly more than 10% of total employment (Table 1). The financial sector remained largely segmented; only in 1989 were nine commercial banks established to perform operations previously carried out by branches of the Central Bank. It is doubtful whether by the beginning of 1990 commercial banks had acquired the skills to operate efficiently. Rigidities in the labour market at the end of 1989 were still very substantial. Non-wage income and other benefits as well as the lack of a housing market were still impairing labour mobility.

Another important phenomenon, which resulted from increased autonomy of enterprises combined with absence of bankruptcy threat, was the flourishing of interfirm credit. By 1989 it was apparent that the attempt by the Central Bank to reduce credit available to enterprises was largely counterbalanced by the expansion of interfirm credit. Abstracting from the issue of efficiency, the growth of interfirm credit increased systemic risk by making the system vulnerable to domino effects arising from the transmission of financial difficulties from one enterprise to another. The presence of a large stock of interfirm credit, of which a large component represents capitalization of arrears, complicates the assessment of the financial conditions of enterprises.

Reforms enacted during the 1980s attributed an important role to Workers' Councils in the control and decision-making process of enterprises. Until 1989 the power of the Workers' Councils was somewhat limited due to political interference with enterprise decisions. Yet, the system inherited in 1989 by the new democratic government incorporated control of the enterprises by Workers' Councils. Somewhat paradoxically, the shift to a market-oriented government resulted in a transformation of the *de jure* power of Workers' councils into *de facto* power (Schaffer, 1991).

Finally, a legacy of the old regime was the large – albeit declining – share of trade with the USSR and other countries belonging to the CMEA area, and a large stock of foreign debt (Table 1).[1] Although crucial for the medium-term prospects of the Polish economy, these legacies did not play an important role in 1990: the demise of CMEA trade took place in January 1991, while rescheduling agreements exempted Poland from servicing her external debt in 1990.[2]

3. The stabilization programme: central issues

3.1. The situation in 1989

Table 2 summarizes some key aspects of the macroeconomic situation in 1989. High inflation rates throughout the 1980s, in particular the hyperinflation of the second half of 1989, probably eliminated most of the monetary overhang. The premium of the parallel market exchange rate over the official exchange rate was drastically lower at the end of 1989. There remained important flow imbalances, such as the budget deficit and real wages (Lipton and Sachs, 1990). The reduction of subsidies through increases in administered prices (of energy and public utilities) was one of the main instruments for reducing the budget deficit, while the wage policy was set to achieve a targeted reduction of (statistical) real wages of about 30%.

Microeconomic distortions and inefficiencies were also a main target of the transformation process, including drastic liberalization of the

---

[1] CMEA trade implied for Poland large subsidies on imports of oil and gas, and provided a demand for Polish goods that, to all accounts, hardly exists in the convertible-currency area.

[2] While the decline in demand from the USSR and the former East Germany affected some Polish industrial sectors in 1990, CMEA trade did not exert a significant contractionary pressure on output. The 'CMEA shock' played a fundamental role in the recession of 1991.

Table 2. Initial conditions: macroeconomic variables in 1989

Inflation	640% (December to December)
Output growth	1.4% in the 1980s, 0% in 1989
Rate of unemployment	0% in the 1980s, 0% in 1989
Current account	US$1.8 bn. deficit
Gross external debt	US$40.6 bn. (end of 1989)
International reserves	US$2.5 bn. (end of 1989)
Black market exchange rate premium	400% on average in 1989, 40% before the plan
Fiscal Deficit	7.2% of GDP
Ratio of M2 to GDP	47.8% (average 1989)
Share of foreign currency deposits in M2	69.3% (December 1989)
Seigniorage (change in M1 divided by GDP)	13.5%

Source: Authors' calculation on data from the Central Statistical Office (GUS) and the National Bank of Poland.

price, exchange rate and trade systems. The government announced plans to restructure and privatize enterprises and banks, although progress in those areas has been somehow slower than planned. Box 1 summarizes the main stabilization and liberalization measures (for a more detailed discussion see Coricelli and Rocha, 1991; Frydman *et al.*, 1990; Lipton and Sachs, 1990).

3.2. The stabilization plan and the 1990 outcome

The Polish plan can be classified as an *exchange rate-based heterodox* programme (see Kiguel and Liviatan, 1989) which relies on the use of nominal anchors – e.g. the exchange rate and wages/prices – to achieve a rapid decline in the rate of inflation. (Bruno, 1990 and Calvo and Vegh, 1990, discuss the rationale for multiple anchors.)[3] A key characteristic is that large increases of administered price were taking place at the same time that nominal anchors and monetary targets were established.

3.2.1. Successes. During the first half of 1990 there were no policy slippages. Actually, most of the targets were overfulfilled. Net domestic

---

[3] The wage anchor was not designed as a pure anchor, as there was no predetermined nominal path for wages. Instead a low coefficient of indexation on prices should have eliminated wage inflation pressures. The coefficient of indexation determined the ceilings for wage increases. The indexation scheme was contemporaneous, and therefore firms needed to form expectations on price increases when setting monthly wages. The ceilings – the so-called norms – applied to the total *wage bill* of a firm, with high and steeply progressive tax penalties on wages in excess of the ceilings. Unused norms could be carried forward.

Box 1. The Polish stabilization programme for 1990

The programme was based on 'orthodox' measures of fiscal and monetary tightening and 'unorthodox' measures establishing three nominal anchors: the exchange rate, nominal wages and credit ceilings.

Stabilization measures

1. **Fiscal policy:** The programme provided for a tightening of fiscal policy to restore a balance in the general government accounts for 1990 (in 1989 the deficit was 7.5% of GDP). The goal was to cut subsidies to reduce expenditures by 8% of GDP, and eliminate income tax reliefs yielding additional revenues equal to 4% of GDP.
2. **Credit and monetary policy:** Ceilings on Net Domestic Assets (NDA) of the banking system were imposed, allowing for a nominal growth of 22% in 1990Q1 and a growth of about 50% for the year as a whole. Ceilings on lending by each commercial bank were imposed only beginning in September 1990. On January 1st the National Bank of Poland increased its interest rate for refinancing from 7% to 36% per month. The authorities planned to adjust this rate at least monthly in order to maintain it positive in real terms and higher than the return on deposits in foreign currency.
3. **Nominal anchors:** On 1 January, the market for foreign exchange for current transactions was unified at a rate of 9,500 Zl/US$, a 31.6% devaluation of the official rate. This rate was frozen from January 1990, and an active interest rate policy used to defend the peg was announced. The exchange rate was maintained constant until May 1991. The permitted increase in the wage bill was set at 30% of the rate of inflation in January, 20% in February, March and April, and 60% for the rest of the year, except July when it was set to unity. Enterprises were subject to tax penalties of 200–500% on any increase above these ceilings.

Liberalization measures

1. **Price system:** In January most remaining price controls were removed. No more than 3–5% of retail prices continued to be set by the state, as compared to 50% in the latter part of 1989.
2. **Exchange and trade system:** Foreign exchange could be provided without restrictions for most current transactions, as opposed to the previous system of rationing. Also, enterprises were required to surrender all foreign exchange receipts to the Central Bank. The authorities eliminated all quantitative restrictions on imports from the convertible currency area and introduced a unified, and low at around 4%, customs tariff for commercial and personal imports.

Table 3. Initial results of the programme during 1990

Inflation (December–December)	1989: 640%
	1990: 250%
Output growth	Industry: −23%
	GDP: −12.5%
Rate of unemployment	1989: 0%
	1990 (December): 6.1%
Fiscal balance	3.8% of GDP
(general government)	
Trade in convertible currency	
(change in %)	
Exports	
Volume	48.9
Price	−0.4
Imports	
Volume	10.5
Price	6.5
Current account balance	1989: US$1.8 bn. deficit
	1990: US$0.7 bn. surplus
Increase in net international	US$4.4 bn
reserves	
Monetary aggregates	Cumulative real percentage changes:

	M1	M2
December–June:	−15	−42
December–December:	41	−38

Share of foreign exchange	December 1989: 69%
deposits in M2:	June 1990: 42%
	December 1990: 31%
Foreign exchange deposits	(US$ bn.)
December 1989–December 1990	

Households	4.8	5.9
Enterprises	1.5	0.4

Source: Authors' calculations on data from the Central Statistical Office and the National Bank of Poland.

assets grew well below their targets, lending interest rates were positive in real terms from February to June, a large budget surplus was generated in the face of a programmed deficit, international reserves increased sharply and wage increases were below the ceiling. Under strong political pressures for a 'reflation' of the economy, which mounted during the presidential election campaign, both fiscal and monetary policies were relaxed during the second half of the year. Interest rates were reduced and became slighly negative in real terms, budgetary expenditures increased, and the wage policy was slightly modified by reducing tax penalties on wage increases in excess of the ceilings. Concerns with continuing high inflation prompted a tightening of credit policy in the last quarter of 1990. Tight credit conditions for the non-budgetary sectors continued during 1991. However, a second deep

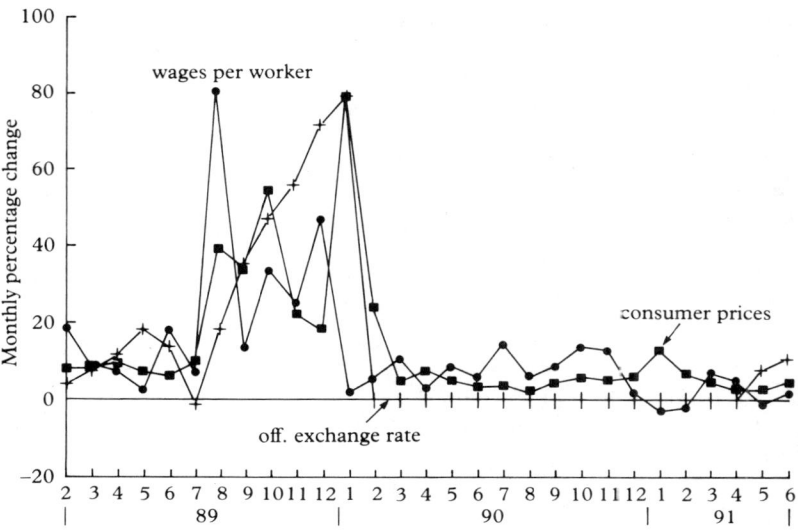

Figure 1. Prices, wages and the exchange rate
Source: Central Statistical Office.

recession at the beginning of 1991, partly due to the demise of the CMEA, resulted in a collapse of government revenues and in large budget deficits, mostly financed through money creation. Overall credit ceilings were overshot. A summary of the initial results of the programme during 1990 is contained in Table 3. The programme had succeeded in halting hyperinflation, and the nominal anchors were maintained without serious problems until the end of 1990 (Figure 1). The elimination of shortages and the maintenance of convertibility were also remarkable achievements. However, the programme also yielded several surprises.

3.2.2. GDP declined in 1990 by 12% (Table 4). Consumption was more affected than fixed investment. The fall in inventories explains 5% of the decline in GDP. On the other hand, foreign trade contributed 5% to GDP growth. The official figures have been criticized for underestimating the contribution of the private sector to GDP and for a significant measurement error in the estimate of inventories. As a result, consumption, calculated as a residual, would also be mismeasured. Alternative estimates by Berg and Sachs (1992) find a decline in GDP about 4 percentage points lower and a much smaller fall in household consumption, offset by a larger decline in inventories. Berg and Sachs' estimates attribute a much less significant role to final demand. Their estimates suggest that the sharp decline in inventories is the main factor

**Table 4. Poland: GDP in 1990. Contribution to
GDP growth (%)**

	Official	Berg–Sachs
GDP[1]	−12.0	−7.7
Consumption	−10.0	−3.7
Private	−10.0	−4.1
Public	0.0	0.4
Investment	−7.0	−9.6
Fixed	−2.0	−1.9
Inventories	−5.0	−7.7
Foreign balance	5.0	5.6

Source: GUS; Berg and Sachs (in this volume).
Note: [1] Public sector GDP fell by 19.6%, while private sector
GDP increased by 7.4%.

behind the decline in GDP, since the fall in domestic consumption is
more than compensated by the increase in net exports. Overall, the
recession affected mainly the public sector. The private sector GDP
increased by about 7%, mainly in the trade sector, since private sector
industrial output remained practically flat.

3.3. Eight outstanding issues

3.3.1. The fall in output has been drastic and sustained. The 12% decline
of GDP in 1990 (7.7% according to Berg and Sachs) exceeded an official
expectation of 3%. Industrial value added fell by about 23%, while
production of socialized industry fell by almost 30%. All industrial
sectors were hit by the recession. Agriculture was not affected, showing
an increase of 2.5%. Private sector sales are estimated to have grown
by about 17%, part of which is due to a mere reclassification of previous
socialized sector activities. The bulk of the increase in private sector
activities seems to have occurred in trade, services, construction and
transport. (Data on the first quarter of 1991 show a significant fall in
private sector production, especially in industry.)

The decline was highly synchronized across sectors and concentrated
at the beginning of the programme, without a significant number of
bankruptcies. Production stagnated in the following months, showing
a mild recovery in the last quarter of 1990. In the first quarter of 1991
production recorded a new large decline (Figure 2).

The stock of inventories declined sharply at the beginning of the
programme (Figure 3). In the first two months of 1990 the real stock
of inventories dropped by about 30%. In January 1990 inventories of

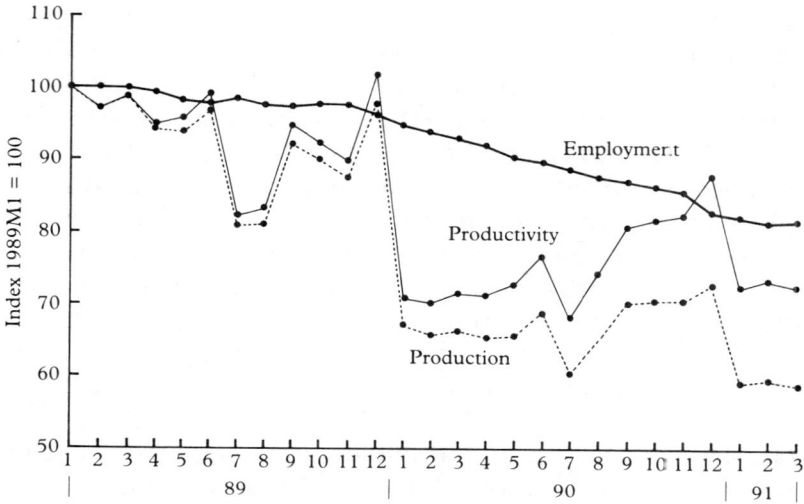

Figure 2. Production, employment and productivity

Source: Central Statistical Office.
Note: Production is sold production in real terms and in comparable work-time.

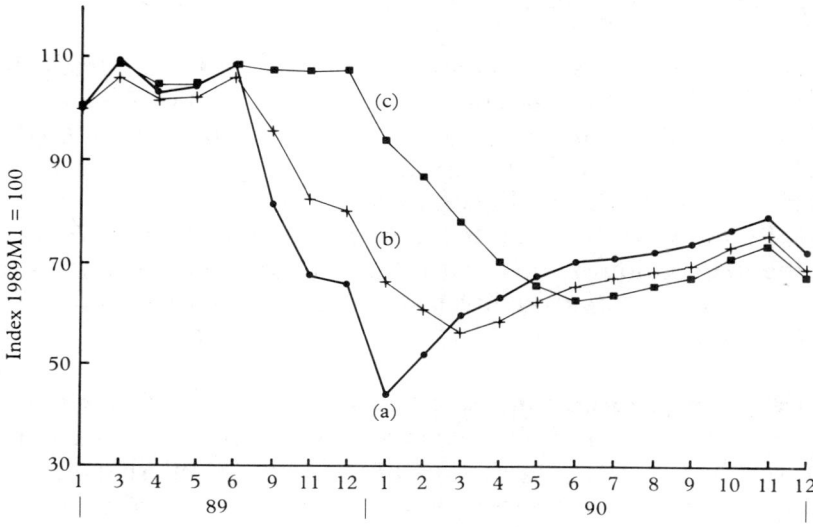

Figure 3. Real inventories

Source: Central Statistical Office.
Note: (a) Nominal stocks deflated by producer price index; (b) nominal stocks deflated by three-month moving average of producer prices; (c) nominal stocks deflated by six-month moving average of producer prices.

every category of goods – raw materials, finished and unfinished goods – declined in real terms. Thereafter inventories of finished products increased in the industrial sector and declined in the trade sector.

Employment fell across-the-board in the socialized sector, though less than output. As a result, productivity dropped, by about 20% for the year. Institutional barriers to firing may account for some sluggishness in the adjustment of employment (for instance a 45-days advance notification to employees that are about to be fired, and notification to the Labour Ministry prior to mass layoffs). However, given the pervasive overmanning characterizing the Polish economy before 1990, the relatively small adjustment of employment with respect to the decline in output is somewhat puzzling.

3.3.2. Inflation. The magnitude of the initial price jump and the subsequent persistence of inflation constituted another surprise. In January 1990 actual (CPI) inflation was 80%, compared with an official projection of 45%. (The Ministry of Finance forecasts monthly inflation.) Cumulative inflation in 1990 was 250%, compared with an expected 90%. With the exception of August 1990, when inflation was low due to the seasonal decline in food prices, monthly inflation oscillated around 3–5% throughout the period March–December 1990. Interestingly, consumer price inflation was persistent, but not producer price inflation. For instance, producer price inflation was negative in March.

3.3.3. The budget surplus constitutes another unexpected result. The balance of the consolidated non-financial public sector showed a surplus of about 4% of GDP, against expectations of a deficit of 0.1% of GDP. This surplus, entirely accumulated in the first half of the year when a deficit of about 2% of GDP had been expected, is mostly due to taxes on profits. Profits were boosted at the beginning of 1990 by capital gains on the revaluation of inventories and on sales of dollars. This amounts to a one-time tax on inventories and enterprises' foreign-denominated deposits.

3.3.4. The balance of payments improved markedly, mainly through the trade balance. Export volume increased sharply, in particular exports to the convertible currency area (Table 3). Imports fell sharply, in particular imports of intermediate products. The improvement in the current account led to a sizable increase in international reserves, since firms were forced to surrender their entire foreign exchange earnings to the Central Bank. However, when the bulk of the drop in output occurred in January, the trade balance showed a small deficit. In the first quarter of 1991 the trade balance turned into deficit.

3.3.5. Interest rates in domestic currency-denominated deposits were very high in relation to interest rates in foreign currency-denominated deposits. The spread between lending and deposit rates was very high, particularly at the beginning of the programme (Table 5). Yet households did not shift their savings from foreign currency to zloty deposits for the whole of 1990. Actually, US dollar deposits of households increased during 1990 (Table 3), although a shift away from US dollar deposits into zloty deposits began in the first quarter of 1991. In contrast, enterprises depleted their foreign exchange deposits almost entirely, due mainly, but not entirely, to new regulations requiring the surrendering of foreign exchange receipts.

The fact that the share of foreign exchange deposits in total deposits declined (Table 3) may be misleading. Given the very high interest rate differentials in favour of zloty deposits, capitalization of interest payments would have produced a significant increase in domestic relative to foreign exchange deposits. Subtracting capitalization, the ratio of foreign exchange to zloty deposits did not decline significantly.

3.3.6. Profit rates (ratios of profits to sales or to total costs) were higher in 1990 than in 1989, except for December 1989 (Figure 4). This is puzzling given the large negative shocks of 1990. The revaluation of inventories and the capital gains on sales of dollars, together with the

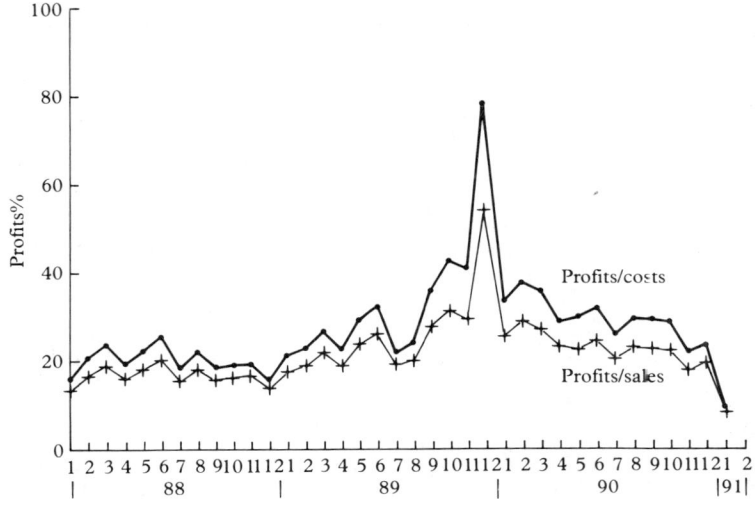

Figure 4. Profitability in socialized industry

Source: Polish National Bank.

Note: Profits defined as sales – costs + subsidy – turnover taxes.

Table 5. Interest rates in 1990 (% per month)

	1989	1990											
	XII	I	II	III	IV	V	VI	VII	VIII	IX	X	XI	XII
Refinancing rate	7.0	36.0	20.0	10.0	8.0	5.5	4.0	2.8	2.8	2.8	3.6	4.6	4.6
Lending rate (average prime rate)	14.1	46.5	22.0	10.5	8.5	6.3	4.5	2.9	2.9	2.9	3.4	4.2	5.1
Deposit rates (weighted average)	13.3	30.5	17.3	7.5	6.7	4.7	3.7	2.6	2.6	2.7	3.3	4.2	4.6
Rate on US$ deposits	na	0.8	0.8	0.8	0.8	0.8	0.8	0.8	0.8	0.8	0.8	0.8	0.8
Real interest rates: *(ex post)*													
Refinancing[1]	-22.4	-35.1	9.5	10.0	5.8	4.9	2.5	-0.5	-0.1	0.1	-1.3	0.9	1.2
Lending[1]	-17.3	-30.1	11.3	10.5	6.3	5.6	3.0	-0.4	0.0	0.2	-1.4	0.6	1.7
Deposits[2]	-3.1	-27.3	-5.3	3.1	-0.7	0.1	0.3	-0.9	0.8	-1.9	-2.3	-0.6	-1.3
Refinancing[3] *(ex ante)*	na	-6.2	-2.4	3.8	1.9	2.9	1.0	-2.5	-0.2	-1.6	-0.4	1.5	4.6
Interest rates spreads (in percentage points):													
Lending/deposits	0.8	16.0	4.7	3.0	1.8	1.5	0.8	0.3	0.3	0.3	0.2	0.0	0.5
Zloty deposits/US$ deposits	na	29.7	16.5	6.7	5.9	3.9	2.9	1.8	1.8	1.8	2.4	3.3	3.7
Inflation rate													
CPI	37.0	79.6	23.8	4.3	7.5	4.6	3.4	3.6	1.8	4.6	5.7	4.8	5.9
PPI	37.9	109.6	9.6	-0.02	2.1	0.6	1.5	3.3	2.9	2.7	4.9	3.6	3.3
CPI-forecast	na	45	23	6	6	2.5	3	5.5	3	4.5	4	3	3

Source: Authors' calculations on data from the National Bank of Poland.
Notes: 1 in terms of producer price inflation; 2 in terms of consumer price inflation; 3 in terms of forecast CPI.

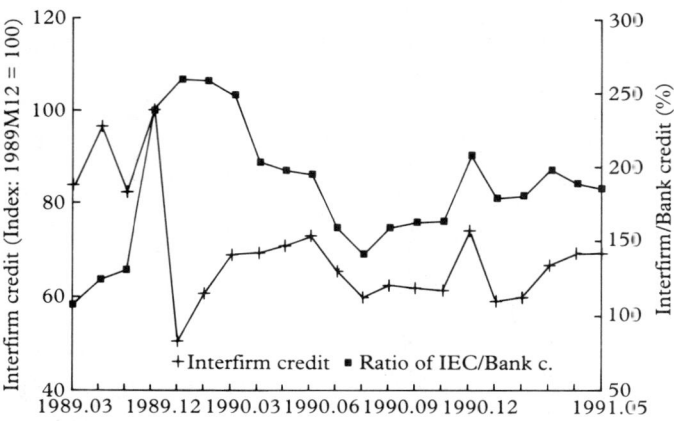

Figure 5. Interfirm credit

Source: Polish National Bank.

decline in real wages, partly account for such a phenomenon. Interestingly, profit ratios were high at the beginning of the programme when credit policy was tight and declined in the second half when credit policy was relaxed.

3.3.7. The stock of interenterprise credit, which in the past had compensated reductions in bank credit for working capital, declined significantly in real terms during 1990 (Figure 5). In July and August the Central Bank made an attempt to earmark commercial bank lending to payments of interenterprise debts. This resulted in a nominal decline in interenterprise credit. However, in the following months, the tightening of bank credit left no room for such operations, and the ratio of interenterprise to bank credit increased again, suggesting the presence of payment arrears among enterprises.

3.3.8. Wages. While for the year as a whole real wages behaved in accordance with the programme's targets (declining by 31% during the year), their behaviour over the year was not anticipated (Table 6).[4] In the first

---

[4] That real wages declined as planned, despite much higher inflation than anticipated, is somewhat puzzling. *Ceteris paribus*, the higher inflation rate would have induced a reduction in real wages of 53%. In addition to forecast errors, two main factors explain the smaller decline in real wages. First, the much larger than anticipated fall in employment made room for increases in the wage per worker during the year. This effect explains more than 10% of the smaller decline in real wages. Second, in the last two months of 1990 the ceilings were overshot substantially (see Table 6).

Table 6. Poland: wage policy in 1990

	Jan	Feb	Mar	Apr	May	Jun	Jul	Aug	Sep	Oct	Nov	Dec
						(Percentage changes)						
1. Indexation coefficient	0.3	0.2	0.2	0.2	0.6	0.6	1.0	0.6	0.6	0.6	0.6	0.6
2. CPI – forecast	45.0	23.0	6.0	6.0	2.5	3.0	5.5	3.0	4.5	4.0	4.3	3.0
– actual	79.6	23.8	4.3	7.5	4.6	3.4	3.6	1.8	4.6	5.7	4.9	5.9
3. Actual wage increase (without bonuses)	4.6	5.4	10.5	2.5	8.7	5.6	14.4	5.9	8.7	13.7	12.8	1.6
4. Max rate of growth of wage per worker												
Acc. to CPI forecast	13.7	4.7	1.2	1.2	1.5	1.8	5.6	1.8	2.7	2.4	2.6	1.9
Acc. to actual CPI	24.1	4.8	0.9	1.5	2.8	2.1	3.7	1.1	2.8	3.5	3.0	3.7
						(In thousands of zlotys per worker)						
5. Actual wage (without bonuses)												
Monthly	618	652	720	738	802	847	969	1,026	1,116	1,269	1,431	1,454
Cumulative	618	1,270	1,990	2,729	3,531	4,377	5,347	6,373	7,489	8,758	10,189	11,643
6. Maximum wage (wage norm)												
Monthly	740	784	801	824	863	891	938	963	1,004	1,052	1,098	1,175
Cumulative	740	1,524	2,326	3,150	4,013	4,903	5,841	6,804	7,808	8,860	9,958	11,133
7. Forecast norm	678	783	802	822	847	896	950	970	1,005	1,043	1,093	1,134

8. Unused actual norm end of period	122	254	335	421	482	526	494	431	319	102	−231	−511
As share of cumulative wage norm	16	17	14	13	12	11	8	6	4	1	−2	−5
As share of monthly wage	20	39	47	57	60	62	51	42	29	8	−16	−35
9. Previous month wage plus unused cumulative norm in previous month	607	740	906	1,056	1,159	1,284	1,373	1,464	1,458	1,435	1,371	1,200
As share of actual wages	98.2	113.6	125.8	143.0	144.5	151.7	141.6	142.6	130.7	113.1	95.8	82.5

Source: Authors' calculations on data from Ministry of Finance.

two months nominal wages increased well below the ceilings imposed by the wage policy. Beginning in March, the rate of growth of wages consistently exceeded the rate of inflation (Figure 1). Only after June did firms begin to use up some of the reserves accumulated in previous months. Beginning in October 1990 average wages exceeded the ceilings, and enterprises paid large excessive-wage taxes. At the end of 1990 this type of tax accounted for almost one-half of income taxes.

These eight issues need to be explained. Some observers have linked the recession to macroeconomic policies and/or to price and trade liberalization measures (Kolodko, 1991, Rosati, 1990, Gomulka, 1991, Blanchard *et al.*, 1991), while others have emphasized the behaviour of worker-controlled firms (Schaffer, 1991). Some have attempted to link macroeconomic and microeconomic considerations (Frydman and Wellisz, 1991), highlighting the role of domestic credit distortions (Calvo and Coricelli, 1990). Finally, it has been argued that official figures on the decline of output largely overstates the actual decline (Lipton and Sachs, 1990 and Berg and Sachs, 1992). Our interpretation is organized around three complementary approaches. The first one focuses on supply or technological factors. The second approach emphasizes household demand factors, and the third one brings up the role of credit.

4. Supply shock: technological factors

4.1. Two supply-side effects

January 1990 marks the beginning of a partial, but significant, removal of subsidies on critical production inputs like coal and petroleum, and a liberalization of most other prices and quantitative trade barriers.[5] At that time interest rates (the Central Bank's refinancing rate) were raised to *ex ante* positive real levels. The price of coal increased by 400% in January 1990, while the consumer price level and wages increased by only 79% and 2%, respectively. Monthly interest rate on bank loans increased by more than 30 percentage points between December 1989 and January 1990, and never fell below 3% per month. The exchange rate remained at the January 1990 level until May 1991. Facing a sharp increase in their production costs and distinctively higher real interest

---

[5] The almost complete dismantling of CMEA trade in January 1991 represents another major structural change, with the elimination of subsidies on imports of raw materials from the USSR. Its effects became evident in the first quarter of 1991 through the sharp fall of enterprises' profitability and production. Because these effects were not operative in 1990, they are not taken into account in the present paper.

rates, firms should have reacted by (i) minimizing costs by economizing on the consumption of fuel and electricity and (ii) unloading (or trying to unload) a large portion of their inventories.

4.1.1. Cost minimization. There is a tendency to liken the Polish experience with the oil shocks of the 1970s (Bruno and Sachs, 1985) and their stagflationary effects. However, Poland's shock is not imported, but rather 'self-induced', and it is not clear why it should yield a decline in value added for the economy as a whole. The economy as a whole does not become poorer because of an increase in domestic input prices. If firms could adjust and minimize cost very quickly, a new equilibrium would be reached with different factor intensities, without an overall output contraction and unemployment. Of course, output contraction and unemployment could reflect significant adjustment costs. Such effects, however, should be gradual and unevenly distributed across sectors. They were in fact drastic, sudden and across-the-board. Furthermore, given that real wages fell sharply, a cost-minimizing reaction would imply the substitution of labour for other inputs and a rise in employment, or at least not a fall. On the contrary, unemployment increased sharply. Thus the decline in energy consumption (by about 18% in 1990) probably *followed* the fall in output, rather than causing it.

4.1.2. Unloading of inventories is likely to be of much greater significance. Until the reforms of 1990, the Polish economy was accustomed to operate under significantly negative real interest rates. Furthermore, with the exception of export-oriented enterprises which could hold foreign-currency deposits, firms could only accumulate 'liquid' wealth in the form of bank deposits, yielding sharply negative real interest rates, or in the form of inventories of raw materials or final goods. Consequently, enterprises had strong incentives to accumulate inventories at levels that would be considered 'excessive' in market-oriented economies. The January 1990 reforms induced firms to sell a sizable share of their inventories. In addition, the sizable trade surplus could reflect the enterprises' effort to unload inventories abroad, given that the domestic market was unlikely to be able to absorb them. The unloading of inventories also explains output contraction in sectors producing inventory goods which could not be placed abroad. Depletion of inventories also accounts for the *persistence* of low output, since output of inventory goods will have to be low until enterprises reach their desired new (and lower) inventory levels.

4.2. Unexplained features

However, some facts contradict the technological explanation.

4.2.1. Inventories. Depending on how stocks of inventories are measured, at the end of 1989 they amounted to between 1.4 months and 2 months of turnover.[6] This is not a clear-cut case of excessive inventories. In the US and Canada, inventories stand at 1.5 months of turnover (Berg and Sachs, 1992).

4.2.2. Inflation persistence. While the technological view cannot *per se* explain the *persistence* of high inflation, a number of additional factors might fill the gap. They do not. Explanations based on staggered wage setting, or backward indexation of wages, are contradicted by the mechanism of the wage indexation scheme. This scheme implies contemporaneous wage adjustment in all enterprises each month. Inertia could only occur if firms formed their expectations on price changes in an adaptive manner.

Firms were allowed to carry forward the unused wage norms. In the first half of the year wages increased well below the monthly ceilings, while in the second half they went well above the ceilings. Thus one could argue that exogenous price shocks explain inflation in the first half, while wage pressure accounts for its continuation in the second half (Blanchard and Layard, 1991). But what about the unusual wage behaviour during the year? The technological view does not explain this.

Staggering of price-setting decisions did not play an important role in 1990. Given the high rates of inflation prevailing since 1989, prices were most likely revised at short intervals. Moreover, the large aggregate price shock at the beginning of 1990 suggests a substantial bunching, not a staggering, of price-change decisions (probably triggered by the stabilization programme itself). Frydman and Wellisz (1991) present evidence at both the sectoral and enterprise levels that every enterprise changed its prices in January 1990.

Monetary factors also fail to explain inflation persistence. Under current-account convertibility, as was the case in Poland, excess supply of money will tend to give rise to current-account deficits. However, Poland enjoyed a sizable current-account surplus during most of 1990.

Finally, administered energy prices constitute independent inflationary factors. The price of coal, for instance, increased by 100% from

---

[6] To adjust for the upward bias due to the high inflation rates of the second half of 1989, we have adjusted the nominal stocks of inventories following three different methods. The first simply deflates the nominal stock of inventories and the flow of sales by the producer price index of December 1989. The second, uses a three-month moving average of producer prices, while the third uses a six-month moving average. While the real flow of sales is the same in the three cases, the real stock of inventories increases as an average price index is used.

January to December 1990, while large increases in electricity, rents and public transport prices took place in the second half of 1990. However, as shown in Coricelli *et al.* (1990), administered prices explain only a fraction of observed inflation.

4.2.3. The fall in labour productivity documented in Figure 2 is another phenomenon not accounted for by the technological view. The standard interpretation is labour hoarding. However, if labour hoarding is easy to rationalize in a demand-constrained situation (with training/hiring costs, for example), it does not fit supply-side shocks. As a general rule, no competitive firm should be seen employing its workers only part-time. The most convincing interpretation emphasizes the heterogeneity of workers in terms of quality. New job opportunities in the private sector may attract the best qualified workers from the socialized sector. Such loss of the best qualified workers could reflect the existence of pre-reform misallocation of resources with the socialized sector employing an inefficiently high share of skilled workers. Then indeed output in the socialized sector would fall more than in proportion to the decline in employment, bringing about a fall in labour productivity.

4.3. The role of credit

According to technological explanations, the output contraction is a temporary phenomenon because of (possibly unavoidable) adjustment costs. In order to succeed, however, the transformation process requires that firms and individuals have access to credit. Credit is the *sine qua non* for investment in new sectors and technologies, and even, occasionally, for enabling firms to 'ride out the storm'. Credit becomes even more necessary if the transformation process requires a transitory fall in incomes, like in Poland. Without sufficient access to credit, the contraction of inventory-producing firms, for example, could lead to non-optimal depreciation of installed capacity. Thus, without access to credit, the initial adjustment process may leave a lasting negative imprint on the economy, delaying the resumption of growth and enhancing social tension.

In sum, technological explanations of the output loss and its persistence, although highly plausible, fail to account for the eight features previously documented. At any rate, technological explanations highlight the important role of credit during the transition to prevent the economy from sliding into a 'bad equilibrium'. (For a further elaboration of this point, see Calvo and Frenkel, 1991a, b.)

5. Household demand factors

5.1. Analytical framework

Another popular interpretation stresses demand-side factors (Blanchard *et al.*, 1991, Rosati, 1990, Kolodko, 1991, Frydman and Wellisz, 1991). It highlights two factors: (i) the fall in real wages and households' real wealth; and (ii) the dramatic increase in interest rates. Factor (i) is quantitatively impressive because real wages fell in January by about 40% and real money (M2) in the hands of households also fell by about 40%. However, it should be recalled that price liberalization was a key feature of the Polish programme. Under price flexibility, real wages and wealth are endogenous and, thus, cannot be taken as exogenous determinants of the adjustment process. The same argument applies to the interest-rate channel. The Polish programme set the refinancing rate at which the Central Bank charges banks but, in principle, allowed full freedom for banks to set deposit and lending interest rates. Hence, interest rates are also endogenous variables. The demand-side view has to rely on additional factors.

5.1.1. Price rigidity. High among those factors is the monopolistic structure of the Polish industrial sector (Blanchard *et al.*, 1991). Evidence on monopolistic behaviour is inconclusive because markups did not increase after price liberalization (Frydman and Wellisz, 1991; Blanchard and Layard, 1991; Schaffer, 1991). Anachronistic behaviour on the part of managers, following a somewhat rigid cost-plus formula independently of new market demand conditions, remains the best argument in favour of the typical Keynesian assumption of nominal price rigidity.

5.1.2. Fixed exchange rate. The stabilization programme relied very heavily on the stability of the exchange rate against the US dollar, which remained fixed until 17 May 1991 (when the zloty was devalued by about 17% against the US currency, and fixed against a basket of currencies). At the start of the programme foreign exchange deposits held by households amounted to about $5 bn., the equivalent of two-thirds of M2 held by households (Table 2). The interest rate on those deposits has followed closely international levels. Thus, as a first approximation, the economy was operating under perfect international capital mobility. With well-functioning *domestic* credit markets, and abstracting from wealth effects and income distribution considerations, the picture that emerges resembles the well-known Mundell–Fleming model under fixed exchange rates and perfect international capital mobility (for a recent exposition of the Mundell–Fleming model, see Frenkel and Razin, 1987).

5.2. The demand-side channels

5.2.1. A liquidity squeeze? With *credibly* fixed exchange rates, the money supply becomes endogenous. Any attempt to control domestic interest rates through monetary policy will be nullified by capital movements. In particular, if in December 1989 there was no significant stock 'monetary overhang', the price jump in January 1990 should have been immediately accommodated by an equiproportional increase in the supply of money. The Mundell–Fleming model offers little support for the view that the fall in output stems from a demand-side contraction due to a liquidity squeeze.

Consequently, the household demand view must rely on income distribution and wealth effects, and on credit market segmentation. For example, Blanchard *et al.* (1991) claim that the initial price jump distributed income against wage earners and in favour of profits which, in a typical Kaldorian manner (but without capitalists!) depressed aggregate demand. Frydman and Wellisz (1991), on the other hand, claim that the fall in aggregate demand is due to the negative wealth effect associated with the initial price increase. A possible objection is that, given widespread shortages prior to January 1990, prices did not reflect the effective cost of goods. Hence, the initial 'statistical' price rise overestimates the actual rise in the cost of living.

Less controversial is the possibility that imperfect *domestic* credit markets sever the close link between international and domestic interest rates. Then the initial price increase is not necessarily accommodated by a proportionate increase in the money stock and negative output effects may follow. The next section discusses credit market risk after the Central Bank reduced its role as 'lender of last resort' (or as Maurice Obstfeld suggested to us, 'lender of first resort'). The resulting higher credit market risk induces households to require large risk premia to lend to enterprises. In the limit, households may simply refuse to lend to enterprises. Contrary to the view of perfect *international* capital mobility a la Mundell–Fleming, even if households were flush with foreign assets, those funds would not have been transferred to enterprises. The initial price rise may have resulted in stringent liquidity conditions for enterprises. This type of effect, however, corresponds more closely to a credit-driven supply shock, rather than to a demand shock.

5.2.2. Intertemporal substitution. A more solid argument in favour of the household demand view, is that the price increase of the big-bang programme was widely anticipated. Households found it optimal to accumulate inventories of durable goods before January 1990, and purchased less for a few months afterwards. We have no strong evidence on this.

5.2.3. Interest rate effect. Finally, the rise in interest rates on zloty-denominated bank deposits may be the reason of the contraction of household demand. However, the empirical relevance of this effect is questionable because, as indicated in Section 3.3.5, there was no massive switch from dollar to zloty-denominated bank deposits. Thus, households may not have perceived *ex ante* the increase in interest rates.

5.3. The behaviour of inventories

The fact that inventories fell after December 1989 (Figure 3) casts a serious doubt on the household demand explanation. Faced with a decline in demand, enterprises are expected to smooth out production, hoarding labour and accumulating inventories.[7] The fact that inventories in enterprises of finished products increased in 1990, while inventories of materials dropped sharply, is often interpreted as a confirmation of a demand-led recession (Blanchard *et al.*, 1991, Allen, 1991). However, in January 1990, when output fell most, finished goods inventories in industry declined. The statement that 'industrial demand fell ahead of industrial output' (Berg and Sachs, 1992) is factually incorrect.

Emphasis on inventories of finished goods in the industrial sector can be misleading because most of the finished goods inventories were held in the trade sector where the January decline was even sharper. Over the whole of 1990 inventories in the trade sector actually dropped. (Table 7). Also the shift from a shortage to a market economy implies an increase in inventories of finished goods held by enterprises and retailers. Such an increase should not be mistaken for a sign of standard Keynesian recession.

Summing up, without denying some role for household demand, this interpretation of the 1990 output decline is not convincing. In

---

[7] Empirical evidence, largely based on US data, shows that inventory movements are procyclical and that production is more volatile than sales. These phenomena do not accord with a simple production-smoothing theory of inventory accumulation (see Blanchard and Fischer, 1989 and literature cited therein). It has been argued that cost or productivity shocks, rather than demand shocks, explain inventory behaviour (West, 1986).

Table 7. Inventories of finished goods

		December 1989	January 1990	December 1990
(End-period nominal stocks, in '000 bn. zlotys)				
Total		20.8	28.4	51.4
of which	Industry	4.1	6.9	18.0
	Trade	16.2	20.8	31.5
(End-period real stocks, December 1989 = 100)				
Total		100.0	65.1	84.4
of which	Industry	100.0	80.3	149.9
	Trade	100.0	61.3	66.4
Producer price index		100.0	209.6	292.8

Source: Polish Central Statistical Office (GUS)
Note: Real stocks are obtained by deflating nominal stocks by the producer price index. Data are for socialized sectors.

particular, the initial lag of wages behind the wage norm remains unexplained. At the minimum, other factors must be added to complement the household demand view.[8]

6. Credit market factors

Three puzzles remain: (i) the large, sudden and synchronized drop in output across all sectors; (ii) the growth of wages below the norm over the first six months of 1990; and (iii) the decline of inventories in January 1990. This section elaborates on previous hints that credit markets have played a crucial role in transmitting supply and demand shocks to the economy. The conclusion is that credit markets have magnified the recessionary impact of supply and demand shocks.

6.1. The role of credit

Partial economic liberalization measures give enterprises greater command over their profits and wages, but do not make them responsible for remaining solvent. The outcome is high inflation or recalcitrant shortages of consumer goods. Without accommodating credit, liquidity would not have expanded and, instead of inflation/shortage (or shortage-flation as it was called by Kolodko and McMahon, 1987), the enterprise sector would have experienced massive bankruptcies (which were

---

[8] Although we are somewhat skeptical about the relevance of household demand interpretations, Section 6 will show that household liquidity constraints play an important role in explaining inflation persistence.

ruled out by the previous regime). In the absence of bankruptcy and with greater enterprise autonomy, claims came to exceed endowments, an inconsistency that could only be (temporarily) resolved by a passive or accommodating expansion of Central Bank credit. This is why the 1990 stabilization programme in Poland has relied on setting interest rates at *ex-ante* positive real levels and credit ceilings for the entire banking system and – after September 1990 – individual banks.

The credit market view stresses the productive role of credit. Firms need liquidity or credit for their daily operations, for example to pay wages or acquire substantial inventories of coal and other raw materials before output sales take place. Insufficient liquidity/credit levels prevent firms from operating at full capacity and output is lost. The credit and the technological views both explain the fall of output by the induced depletion of inventories. In addition, the credit view suggests that output falls *directly* in response to the (forced or induced by high interest rates) contraction of credit/liquidity, because the latter lowers firms' *working capital* and prevents them from operating at 'full' capacity. (Appendix B develops a formal model bearing out the flavour of the discussion.)

6.2. Enterprise credit conditions

Bank credit in terms of production costs shrank by about 30% at the beginning of the programme. For the year as a whole, the average stock of bank credit – calculated as the ratio of the average stock of working capital credit (geometric average of beginning and end of the year) to the average value of sales and costs – was more than 50% below its 1989 level. Deflated by producer prices, the stock of working capital credit fell by 51% in January 1990 (see Figure 6).[9] Credit conditions prevailing at the beginning of the programme were indeed stringent.

A possible flaw in this interpretation is that firms made capital gains when the January 1990 price increase reduced their real indebtedness. The answer is that before January 1990 banks' real interest rates were set at substantially negative levels, while real interest rates were expected to be positive afterwards. Thus, firms switched from a situation in which they received a positive flow transfer from banks (in real terms), to one in which the transfer was eliminated. In fact, firms are now supposed to make positive real transfers to banks: even if the 'base' of the transfer has shrunk, the transfer now goes in the opposite 'direction'!

It is true that, during the first months of the programme, credit ceilings were not binding. However, this occurred when interest rates

---

[9] A more detailed discussion of credit conditions in Poland is contained in Appendix A, where we examine different definitions of credit/liquidity available to enterprises for working capital.

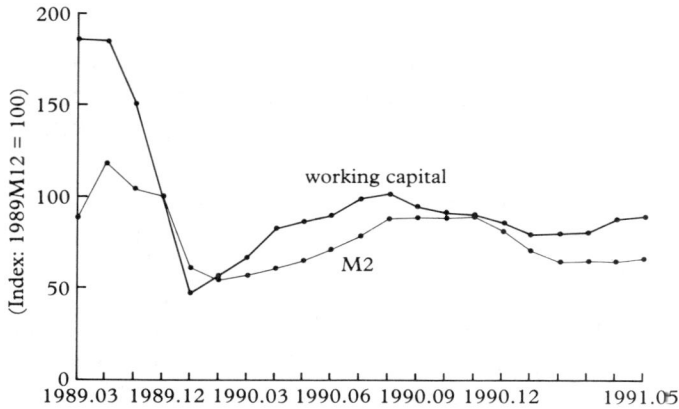

Figure 6. Working capital and money

Source: Polish National Bank.

were extremely high, which may have induced firms to borrow less than the credit ceilings. Given the lack of direct credit flows between households and firms, high bank interest rates on loans generated 'virtual' credit ceilings which turned out to be even more stringent than those implied by the programme's explicit credit ceilings.

It may still be argued that it is the stock of real money carried from the previous period, not credit, which is relevant for production as it determines the purchasing power of firms. Figure 6 shows that real M2 holdings of enterprises exhibit the same pattern as working capital.[10] This contraction is not merely a reflection of the elimination of a monetary overhang in the enterprise sector. Real monetary balances had already been reduced by high inflation in the second half of 1989 (Lane, 1991). Furthermore, because of an extremely high spread between lending and deposits in 1989 (average lending rates were about 180% while sight deposit rates were about 20%, and sight deposits accounted for about 95% of enterprise deposits in domestic currency), it was not in the interest of enterprises to hold excess liquidity. The taxation of profits seems to have played a crucial role in this process. Indeed, the enterprises' attempt to reconstitute their liquidity by unloading inventories was largely frustrated by taxation, which absorbed more than 50% of the profits (more than 4% of GDP for 1990) mostly generated by capital gains.

---

[10] There is no presumption of a positive correlation between credit and M2 for a subset of the whole economy (i.e. the enterprise sector). In response to credit tightening, enterprises could sell inventories to the household sector or abroad and their money balances might even increase. Some of this happened in early 1990.

6.3. Inventories, liquidity and output

Because enterprises held a supposedly large stock of inventories of inputs at the end of 1989, they could still have operated at full capacity (Lane, 1991). Excessive inventories have been traditionally identified as one key feature of centrally planned and even partially reformed economies (see Kornai, 1980). The 18 tn. zlotys stock of input inventories in socialized sectors at the end of 1989, revalued by applying the increase in producer prices in January 1990, would have reduced their credit needs by 36 tn. zlotys. If a more restrictive definition of credit requirements is used – defined in Appendix A as bank credit for working capital – the shortage of credit is quite small (4 tn. zlotys). However, the reduction of inventories could have a contractionary effect as it leads to a fall in demand to firms producing inventory, unless firms can export the *ex ante* excess supply. The fall in output, in turn, reduces households' income and leads to lower demand for consumer goods. This line of reasoning makes it difficult to distinguish between the 'technological view' and the 'credit view'.

But, were inventories at end-1989 really excessive? As noted in Section 4, the ratio of inventories to turnover at the end of 1989 was not particularly high by the standards of market economies. In addition, it is worth recalling that the phenomenon of excessive hoarding of inputs in socialist economies is typically associated with a very uneven and inefficient distribution of inventories across firms. As pointed out by Kornai (1980), a typical feature of shortage economies is a wrong mix and excessive input inventories in each firm. Production is still subject to serious input bottlenecks because enterprises are typically constrained on the supply side by shortage of complementary inputs. To maintain production firms need to purchase inputs from other firms, which requires monetary exchanges or credit among enterprises.

6.4. The credit view

6.4.1. Interenterprise credit.
The 'Big-Bang' of January 1990 was accompanied by a more radical, and distinctively more credible, commitment to market-oriented economic transformation than those in the past. An essential ingredient of this commitment is the risk of bankruptcy. The Central Bank has relinquished its previously unconditional role of 'lender of last resort', thus making the whole credit network more vulnerable.[11] As a consequence, the supply of credit to enterprises is

---

[11] There is fast growing literature applied to market economies which stresses the role of credit markets – as opposed to, for instance, price rigidities – in affecting real economic activity through the supply side. A comprehensive survey is in Gertler (1988). Examples of applications to historical episodes like the Great Depression or to business cycles are in Bernanke (1983), Calomiris and Hubbard (1989).

likely to shrink, even when the Central Bank continues extending credit to enterprises at the same levels as before. Interenterprise credit has played a prominent role in the 1980s. For example, Figure 5 shows that in December 1989 (gross) interenterprise credit was twice as large as bank credit for working capital. Interenterprise credit fell by about 40% in January, and at the end of 1990 was roughly at the same level as in January 1990.

6.4.2. Borrowing from workers. The credit view helps explain developments in the labour market that would be hard to rationalize under the purely technological perspective. Socialized enterprises in Poland are heavily dominated by Workers' Councils to which managers are accountable. As a first approximation, enterprises operate so as to maximize the welfare of their own workers. Then survival of the firm must stand as one of the highest priorities, since the firm's disappearance leaves its workers at the mercy of other firms that are basically concerned about the welfare of their own workers (see Commander *et al.*, 1991). Under these circumstances, the January 1990 reduction in credit to enterprises (in terms of production cost) must have sent them scurrying for credit/liquidity to meet their payroll and the purchase of new raw materials. In addition to liquidating inventories, firms must have tried to borrow from other firms (interenterprise credit) and from their own workers. Although these developments cannot be fully documented, the increase in the ratio of interenterprise credit to bank credit in the first few months of the programme suggests the presence of *forced* interenterprise lending caused by firms falling into arrears with one another (this is confirmed by anecdotal evidence). Furthermore, during the first few months of the programme, wages in socialized enterprises stood below the ceilings imposed by the stabilization programme which, in turn, suggests that firms also 'borrowed' from their own workers.

Arrears with other enterprises and borrowing from workers are particularly costly ways of obtaining liquidity. Arrears interfere with supplier–customer relationships, and could impair a firm's operations in the future if it is 'black listed' by other firms. Offering lower than permissible wages is likely to be either the reflection of prediction errors (e.g. the price level rises more than expected), or a desperate attempt to build up working capital. This is why one would expect firms to raise wages to the programme's ceiling and to pay back arrears as soon as their liquidity position improved.

If lower than permissible wages reflected prediction errors one would expect wages to reach their ceilings in an even shorter period of time, irrespective of the liquidity position of enterprises. Prediction errors do not account for the gap between permissible and actual wages. Risk-averse firms trying to avoid penalties could have followed a very simple rule after the first month, namely, offer in month t the wage specified by the programme's wage norm for month $t-1$. This rule would have shielded firms completely from any excess-wage penalties risk (unless the consumer price fell). In Table 6 (line 9) we show how this simple rule would have implied higher than actual wages for the entire period from January to October 1990.

Interestingly, after June firms started to raise wages towards the wage norm (Table 6), while interenterprise credit *fell* in nominal terms, and bank credit for working capital increased in the third quarter of 1990. Firms obviously used part of the additional official credit to pay arrears to other enterprises and to raise wages. The rise in wages and the reduction of previously non-performing interenterprise loans increased disposable and permanent income of households and, in turn, stimulated aggregate demand. (As in Section 5, inflation persistence does not follow from supply-side considerations exclusively.) Since, according to the credit-market view, output was credit-constrained (particularly if interenterprise credit is included in the notion of credit/liquidity at enterprises, see Appendix A), such a view would predict that the rise in aggregate demand was likely to be associated with higher domestic prices (particularly, prices of non-traded goods). This provides a rationale for the persistence of inflation throughout 1990 (the model in Appendix B exhibits all of the above features).

6.4.3. The decline in output. An important implication of the credit-market view is that the expansion of bank credit during 1990 may not have been enough to stimulate production, because enterprises used official credit to repay 'forced' loans from other enterprises and from their own employees. A reactivation of the economy may, therefore, have required a bigger infusion of bank credit. However, under the worker-control system prevailing in Polish enterprises, and the system of free (from the firms' viewpoint) unemployment insurance, a stronger credit expansion could very well have just meant higher wages.[12] Thus, expansion should have been accompanied by strong and unyielding wage ceilings. Tight wage ceilings have not been easy to enforce. Indeed,

---

[12] An individual in Poland is entitled to unemployment benefits if he has been employed or self-employed for at least six months in the previous year. However, there are numerous exceptions under which these conditions do not apply. For example, the eligibility restrictions are waived for individuals who become unemployed through a mass layoff, are school leavers or under 18, or sole breadwinners. Benefits levels are tied to past earnings with a declining replacement rate (70% initially, falling to 40% after nine months). The minimum benefit is 95% of the minimum wage (defined as 35% of the projected average wage). At present, duration is not limited, but an amendment under consideration would limit the maximum duration of unemployment compensation to one year.

some observers feel that a credit crunch was actually needed to ensure compliance with the programme's wage ceilings.

The credit-market view also explains the decline in productivity. A cut in credit lowers working capital available to firms. Thus, given employment, output and, hence, labour productivity fall. This fall may occur even though no employed worker remains idle (the technological explanation needs the existence of idle employed workers). Labour productivity may fall also if employment falls, because the lower stock of working capital interferes with normal operations.

7. What have we learned?

7.1. The three views summarized

The Polish programme demonstrates, once again, that strong nominal anchors are capable of dramatically lowering inflation from levels verging on hyperinflation to rates in the range of 2–5% per month. However, the monetary surgery has caused some damage to the real part of the economy in the form of sizable output and employment losses. How much welfare was lost is a debatable issue, because output statistics are shaky (e.g. it is very hard to adjust for quality changes), and because the statistical measure of output loss may not represent welfare losses (e.g. when the loss is due to previous overaccumulation of inventories).

One interpretation (Section 4) is that the new economic conditions, chiefly the change in interest rates, have led firms to engage in a massive running down of inventories. This giant tide of goods looking for a commercial outlet is partly responsible for the sizable trade surplus exhibited during 1990, and for output contraction in sectors where excessive stocks could not be exported. However plausible, the technological explanation cannot account for inflation persistence, the fall in labour productivity and the initial lag of wages behind the wage norm.

The credit view argues that the contraction of bank credit to enterprises after December 1989 had a direct depressive effect on production (Section 6). Like the technological view, the credit view implies that firms will decumulate inventories to increase liquidity. Unlike the technological view, however, the credit view gives straightforward explanations for the existence of non-binding wage ceilings and the fall in labour productivity. However, neither of these two views accounts for inflation persistence.

The household demand view fails to account for stagflation and the running down of inventories, unless it is appended with supply side considerations (like the role of Workers' Councils in the process of wage determination). While it has been important in the whole process, household demand cannot explain the output loss *without contractionary enterprise-side factors, possibly based on simple markup pricing.* Household demand considerations are important because when coupled with credit tightness, they explain inflation persistence.

The puzzles listed in Section 3 can be explained by the enterprise-side view, a combination of the technological or credit-market views coupled with demand side credit/liquidity constraints. At centre stage is the role of credit markets. The rudimentary nature of credit markets in Poland explains output contraction directly and emerges as a key ingredient for recovery, even in the happy case in which output contraction reflects the costs of efficient economic transformation.

7.2. Implications for credit markets

Reallocation of resources is a costly process in which idle capacity and labour unemployment are just the tip of the iceberg. It is useful to distinguish between *temporary* and *permanent* efficient reallocation of resources. Temporary reallocations are called for by the earlier over-accumulation of inventories. This phenomenon is likely to be relevant in several other Eastern European countries and the former USSR, where inventories are one of the most attractive assets that enterprises were allowed to hold in the pre-reform period. To prevent this type of resource reallocation from snowballing into a permanent destruction of installed capacity, credit markets must develop.

A major deterrent of fluid credit markets is the transformation process itself, since it is very difficult for the 'private sector' to pick out winners from losers. Activities which are going through a temporary slump are easily mistaken for activities in which the country has no comparative advantage. In addition, this state of turmoil is likely to lower the market value of firms and reduce the collateral against which firms – whose managers have presumably better information than the market about its future – could borrow to ride out the storm. Another road-block for the development of credit markets is uncertainty about property rights. When private ownership is still in its infancy, workers are also managers and capitalists, but their rights to future profits are not clearly defined. This provides incentives for running down capital and inventories below their socially optimal levels (Hinds, 1990; Commander *et al.*, 1991). By the same token, credit is likely to be misused, since responsibility for debt repayment may fall on somebody else's shoulders.

A workable credit system requires solving two major difficulties: poor information and incentives. An early development of private ownership is the best way of providing the right incentives. Poland is moving in that direction, but the process has proved to be slow relative to the stabilization programme. In contrast, improving information – or rather, not destroying information – looks more promising. One measure is the 'cleaning of the books' of enterprises from debts incurred in the pre-reform period. This offers a way of disentangling the prospects of individual firms from the prospects of the rest of the productive system. Moral hazard problems are minimized if it is clearly understood that 'cleaning of the books' is an operation that just wipes away memories of the old regime, and there is no chance that it will be repeated in the future. One possible procedure is *debt cancellation.* Momentarily leaving aside liquidity considerations, debt cancellation does not interfere with efficient resource allocation, because a firm's social desirability is independent of its stock of debts or credits.

Liquidity considerations make debt cancellation considerably more complex. Losers may find themselves unable to operate due to lack of sufficient working capital. The solution is to complement debt cancellation with *debt socialization,* in which the central government 'capitalizes' certain key sectors of the economy (like banks).[13]

7.3. Monetary policy

The Central Bank's role used to be to provide the necessary credit to ensure the implementation of centrally-determined output targets and, on occasion, to bail out firms experiencing financial distress. The entire financial system was, therefore, tied to an accommodative Central Bank. Under these circumstances a stabilization plan relying on stringent bank credit ceilings or high bank interest rates may lead firms to cut down on output, employment and wages, below the levels that 'technological' supply-side considerations would call for. This is an instance in which macroeconomic policy could make a difference.

Were, then, interest rates set too high, or credit ceilings too tight at the beginning of the Polish stabilization programme? Based on the limited evidence available, the answer is affirmative. A more lax policy could have accommodated the initial maxi-devaluation and the removal of sizable energy subsidies. Against this view, two objections can be raised. First, an accommodative credit policy was precisely the nemesis of past semi-liberalized regimes which led to inefficiency and inflation. Adopting it is to repeat old mistakes. Second, in the absence of tight credit conditions, wage ceilings would not have been honoured and the stabilization programme would have 'fallen on its face' a few months after implementation. The first objection confuses stock with flow

---

[13] This is apparently the motivation behind the decision to capitalize the banking sector in Poland for losses connected with foreign exchange-denominated deposits. For further conceptual discussion of these issues, see Calvo and Frenkel (1991b).

accommodative monetary policy. The credit policy suggested above consists of adjusting the *stock* of credit at the beginning of the programme to compensate, partially, for the exogenous rise in input prices. In contrast, the policy followed by past regimes consisted of *continually* adjusting credit for any increase in wage/price that affected firms' production cost. The second objection is much harder to refute. It is claimed that, were it not for the existence of tight credit conditions, firms would have overshot the wage norm early in the programme. Penalties for exceeding the wage norm would not have mattered because workers are not owners of the firm and, hence, workers/managers would be scarcely swayed by the associated loss of net revenue. Indeed, as credit conditions improved towards the end of 1990, firms stopped honouring the wage norm and paid steep penalties for having done so.

We are not in a position to judge at this point if tight credit was an adequate way to discipline Polish firms run by non-owners. However, even if it was adequate in the short run, we have serious doubts about the *durability* of tight credit policy as a disciplinary device. For, after a few months, firms realize that they are not the only ones undergoing financial problems. They may start raising wages despite tight financial constraints in the expectation that the government will not let a large section of the productive system go bankrupt. As a matter of fact, this observation suggests that the relaxation of bank credit during 1990 may not be the only reason for firms to have overshot the wage norm. *Wages may have overshot when firms found out that they were not much worse-off financially than their peers* (the elections of November 1990 may also have contributed to the loss of wage discipline).

The main lesson is that policy-makers should try to devise ways to make the wage targets stick other than through a sustained tight credit policy. Israel and Mexico (and their corresponding 'social pacts') are successful examples to keep in mind. In the mid-1980s Mexico and Israel generated only a slight real credit contraction compared to Poland. (It should be admitted, however, that in January 1990 it was difficult to persuade policy-makers of the virtues of a wage/price compact given that a major objective of the big-bang programme was to generate the 'right' set of relative prices for which, *prima facie*, price liberalization looked like an ideal instrument.)

To summarize, the sudden drop in production that followed the Polish stabilization programme appears to be rooted in typical characteristics of previously centrally planned economies: the existence of initially excessive inventories and the strong segmentation of the credit market. Inflation persistence, in turn, appears to be rooted in the gradual easing of credit/liquidity constraints and, possibly, in the programme's diminished credibility towards the end of 1990.

Discussion

Michael Burda
INSEAD and CEPR

This paper delivers an unusual and controversial interpretation of the 1990 Polish stabilization. It tells an interesting story about interactions between financial conditions (especially credit availability) and the supply side as an explanation of the persistent output loss in Poland, as well as of the curious behaviour of the measured real wage and inflation. But in doing so it downplays the role of demand to such an extent that I am skeptical of the authors' case. My comments amplify this concern.

First of all, it is common to observe sharp declines in economic activity in the course of stabilization programs; the authors do not satisfactorily establish that the Polish case is remarkable by international standards (especially in light of data problems). In fact, the Polish experience seems little different from that of other centrally planned East European economies which produced vast quantities of unsaleable output. The restructuring of Polish industry was also accelerated by the collapse of CMEA and especially Soviet trade (see Collins and Rodrik, 1991 for estimates of the massive redirection of trade that will ensue). The fact that East Germany experienced a similar output decline and restructuring after monetary union, without having experienced either hyperinflation or heterodox stabilization and with credit freely available, does not offer much support to the credit availability story.

Second, is the taxonomy of sources of output decline proposed by authors a useful one? The simple supply and demand paradigm offers a much less strained interpretation of the data. Before 1990 Poland was in an excess demand regime; this was eliminated by the collapse of demand resulting from the liberalization. Inventory reductions due to positive interest rates on financial assets led to a decline in the demand for durable goods and inventories (a component of investment). Add to this the collapse of CMEA trade (the GDR shock for Poland occurred in 1990), and reduced consumption demand (increased precautionary savings). Although we may be at times unwilling to admit it, the IS–LM model that some of us teach in our macro classes gives a quick answer which is largely correct: real aggregate demand at any real interest rate declined exogenously, while the fixed exchange rate regime guaranteed a severe contraction a la Mundell–Fleming. Before the authors can dismiss demand, they need to look more carefully at the real side; the paper needs an analysis of the components of aggregate demand, i.e. consumption, investment, government spending and the net contribution of the rest of the world.

A third remark concerns the emphasis on credit, which is clearly an interesting idea and has already made a dent in the way we think about the supply side in Western economies. Whether the argument has the same force in Eastern Europe needs to be established. It is a shame that the authors do not try to estimate the relevance of credit in these economies. If they are willing to use the data, why not estimate a production function directly? This would be a simpler econometric exercise than in the West, since Poland's generalized excess demand prior to 1990 allows us to rule out the relevance of demand shocks in all markets.

It has been argued already in several papers that interfirm credit is an efficient market response to tight money, even if it does introduce a systemic form of risk. That its supply may respond to perceived central bank bailout policy is an interesting hypothesis which could have been more deeply investigated, perhaps via comparison with other countries in Eastern Europe. Again, we really don't know how unusual the Polish case is in terms of the normal levels necessary for business. Furthermore: are the loans ever repaid? What is their legal status? The real risk seems to be the systemic risk to those long in interenterprise debt. Since most firms can easily hedge by not paying their own bills, this means the commercial banking system, and therefore its depositors, ends up bearing the risk.

The 'borrowing from workers' story is only one of many explanations for the behaviour of the statistical real wage in first half of 1990. An alternative is that real wages generally fall when unemployment or its threat increases. Additional information is clearly necessary to make it consistent with the authors' model – which is based on the governance structure of socialist firms in Poland. It would be more convincing if we knew that private sector wages did not experience the 'dip' they did in the socialist sector. And besides, if workers were lending to their firms, why did they call in their loans so early in the programme? Finally, I am not sure that running up arrears to workers is so much cheaper than not paying bills to suppliers: it is well known that attrition from the lower wage socialist enterprises to private sector firms is high (Lipton and Sachs, 1990) and probably costly.

More generally, I would underline the message of Appendix C about problems of using data to analyse Eastern European economies. The authors should be much more circumspect in basing radical conclusions (and policy prescriptions) on published wage, price and output statistics. Economists have a tendency to follow the data, even if they are quite bad. It reminds me of Zvi Griliches' remark about the similarity between second year graduate school econometric papers and sausage from the neighbourhood butcher: in either case you really don't want to know what went into it. To the problems identified by the authors I would add that the price indices used to compute real wages in Poland place excessive weight on consumption of highly subsidized goods like basic foodstuffs; energy was underpriced relative to market economies, and was overweighted in the households' CPI. The dismantling of these subsidies led to spectacular price rises, the welfare implications of which might have been mitigated by turning down thermostats rather than opening windows in winter.

In conclusion, I don't think the authors have proved their case. That the drop in notional demand was more important than supply seems hard to deny; everyone who has ever visited Warsaw notes the absence of shortages and queues. The evidence for inventories in Western countries as a production-smoothing device is weak, so falling inventories (also in the light of firms' adjustment to positive real interest rates at the same time) does not represent conclusive evidence against the demand shock either.

Grzegorz W. Kolodko
Warsaw School of Economics and Research Institute of Finance

There are by now quite a few papers on the Polish stabilization and transition to a market economy. The contribution by Calvo and Coricelli casts important light not only on the situation in Poland but also on the general problems faced by all post-communist economies. Their analysis of the recession and continuing inflation (running in 1991 still at 70–80% per annum) is based on an investigation of three main potential contributing factors: a technologically-based supply shock; a supply shock due to a credit squeeze and a household demand shock. They conclude that supply-side factors were principally responsible, especially the credit squeeze.

In effect, the Polish economy has shifted from a situation in which there was a tradeoff between inflation and shortage, to one of a tradeoff between inflation and excess supply.

In a number of ways, Poland's experience during 1990 was quite surprising. In particular, the budget surplus in the first half of that year was due principally to temporarily high profitability of the state enterprise sector (a result of the unloading of inventories and selling hard currency accumulated earlier) and to high profits earned by the banking sector. The profits of the enterprise sector owed a great deal to the overshooting of the exchange rate devaluation, while the banking sector profited from the excessive levels of nominal interest rates.

1991 has, however, proved to be very different from the experience of 1990. Public finances have been deteriorating ever since the second half of 1990. By the end of 1991 the state budget was in dire straits; the deficit is equal to about 5% of GDP (or 17% of expenditure). I do not think such developments are surprising. They are the natural outcome of the institutional changes typical of transition to a market economy: the State's ability to raise revenue is weakening, and the claims on its expenditure cannot be reduced at the same rate during a recession (due particularly to the need to meet unemployment compensation). These problems will be hard to solve, and would have occurred to some degree whatever policies were followed. But policy mistakes (particularly on the demand side) have undoubtedly exacerbated them.

General discussion

A number of panellists underlined the discussants' skepticism about the paper's dismissal of demand-side factors. Jeffrey Sachs pointed to the tightening of fiscal policy, the accumulation of money balances and the disappearance of shortages as evidence that demand conditions had dramatically changed. Martin Hellwig wondered why movements in goods prices should necessarily be considered as resulting from either a demand or a supply shock. There might be marketing problems; alternatively, Paul Seabright and Jaroslaw Gronicki suggested that changes in the price-setting behaviour of enterprises, enjoying unaccustomed freedom to exploit monopoly power, might precede and partially explain changes in quantities traded. However, Irena Grosfeld provided a defence of supply-side explanations for the behaviour of inventories. Much inventory accumulation had had the character of speculative hoarding, so that reductions in inventories as shortages eased might simply be the consequence of a perceived improvement in the reliability of supplies.

There was also some discussion of explanations for the behaviour of wages during the stabilization. Peter Bofinger wondered why wages had undershot the ceiling imposed by the wage policy in the first few months of the programme. It might have been due, he suggested, to difficulties in foreseeing the inflation rate and therefore to an undershooting of compensating wage claims. Enterprise profitability was then higher than expected, due (among other things) to the low *ex post* real interest rate; workers then took the opportunity to compensate for their earlier mistake. Guillermo Calvo thought there was also an element of the changing credibility of a tight policy. At first there had appeared to be a widespread belief that firms which conceded large wage increases would go bankrupt; subsequently the belief grew that policy would be relaxed, and this belief may have fuelled the large increases in nominal wages that continued even after price inflation had fallen dramatically.

In conclusion, Martin Hellwig emphasized the difficulty of drawing conclusions about precise explanations when it was clear that so many of the data used for analysis were highly unreliable.

Appendix A: Estimates of credit tightness in Poland in 1990

Table A1 presents three alternative definitions of the credit/liquidity concept: (1) bank credit for working capital, (2) bank credit for working capital + interfirm credit and (3) bank credit for working capital + interfirm credit + enterprise currency and demand deposits. The data concern the socialized industrial sector and correspond to the model discussed in Section 6 and Appendix B. Each of the alternative definitions is divided by average production costs for 1989. To estimate *required* credit/liquidity for January 1990 we multiply the 1989 credit/liquidity ratio by production costs in January 1990, as given by Table A1.[14]

Definition (1) assumes, implicitly, that firms' regular operations are entirely financed by bank credit. In practice, firms also hold some liquidity of their own (e.g. currency and demand deposits). Including these items in definition (1) creates the risk of double-counting, so what we present are lower-bound estimates. Definitions (2) and (3) include interfirm credit. There is again a risk of double-counting. For example, if firm A lends 100 zlotys to firm B and, in turn, firm B lends 100 zlotys to firm C, then, on account of those operations, interfirm credit equals 200 zlotys. However, if there were no delay between firm's B receipt of A's credit and firm's B loan to firm C, firm B would be a *pure* intermediary between firms A and C. The credit/liquidity requirement should be 100 zlotys. However, frictions and, in particular, imperfect information about the financial well-being of enterprises, make the two interfirm credits quite different assets (from the point of view of the credit market and of each one of its several actors). Thus, the inclusion of interfirm credit could turn out to be a better approximation of credit requirements. As seen in lines C1 to C3 in Table A1, the credit/liquidity ratios vary widely (from about 2 to 6) across the different credit/liquidity

---

[14] These are not actual costs. They are an estimate of the cost of production using the same (average) quantity of inputs as in 1989. As pointed out in footnote of Table 7, this estimate is obtained utilizing the index of producer prices as a proxy for the index of material-inputs prices. This procedure underestimates costs for January 1990, as prices of material-inputs such as coal increased by about 400%, while producer prices increased by about 100%. Therefore, the liquidity gaps in Table 7 underestimate the 'true' ones.

Table A1. Liquidity and costs

		1989	1990		
		Actual	Required	Actual	Gap
			(In bn. zlotys)		
A.	Average monthly costs	5,647	31,133[1]		
B1.	Bank credit[2]	10,661	58,776	19,479	39,297
B2.	Total credit[2 3]	28,574	157,533	72,209	85,324
B3.	Liquidity[2 4]	33,304	183,373	87,528	95,845
C.	Credit and liquidity ratios				
C1.	B1/A	1.90	1.90		
C2.	B2/A	5.06	5.06		
C3.	B3/A	5.89	5.89		
D.	Liquidity gaps (in bn. US dollars)				
B1.					4.1
B2.					9.0
B3.					10.1
	Inventories (average stock in January 1990)[5]				7.2
	Enterprise foreign currency deposits (end-1989)				2.3

Source: B. Wyznikiewicz (1990)
Notes: [1] $31,133 = 5,647 \times 5.51$, where 5,647 is the corresponding entry for 1989, 5.51 is the ratio of January-1990 unit costs to average unit costs during 1989. Moreover, unit costs are calculated as a weighted average of (1) material input prices (proxied by overall producer prices) and (2) unit wages, where the weight for material input prices is 0.82.
[2] For 1989 it is calculated as the geometric average of December 1988 and December 1989 stocks.
[3] Defined as bank credit for working capital + interenterprise credit.
[4] Liquidity defined as bank credit + interfirm credit + enterprise currency and demand deposits.
[5] Arithmetic average of the stock at end-1989 and the same stock revalued on the basis of the producer price increase in January 1990.

definitions. According to these estimates, in January 1990 there was a credit/liquidity shortage ranging from 40,000 bn. zlotys to 95,000 bn. zlotys. These are relatively large numbers. The smallest credit/liquidity gap is about twice as high as the actual stock of bank credit for working capital in January 1990.

Among the alternative credit/liquidity sources that firms could have mobilized in order to cover those gaps is the stock of foreign currency-denominated deposits. By Table A1, the liquidation of the *entire* stock of those deposits held at the end of 1989 would have amounted to slightly more than 55% of the lowest estimate of the gap. The remaining shortage could have been partly financed by inventories. The lowest estimate of credit/liquidity shortage (line B1 in Table A1) is equivalent to about 25% of the stock of inventories (or about US$1.8 bn.) in January 1990.[15] For inventories to actually be a credit/liquidity resource, it must be either that households are induced to hold them, or that they are exported, and in practice that means exports. Although exports have increased by a substantial amount, that was well short of the gap during the first few months of the programme.

Under definition (1) there is ample room for disagreement on whether there was a liquidity crunch. The finding that liquidation of foreign currency deposits and/or inventories could have been enough to cover the credit/liquidity gap, assumes that all firms had similar stocks or that the credit market could allow for interfirm transfers. Foreign currency deposits were held by export firms exclusively and, as noted above, effective liquidation of inventories implies that firms had good access to international trade markets. It is likely that firms in the exportable sector (involving convertible currencies) were relatively flush with liquidity. Since the exportable sector constitutes about 15% of sales of the whole industrial sector, avoidance of a liquidity crunch for the remaining 85% could have implied a sizable increase in the interfirm credit market. The expansion of interfirm credit in January 1990 was about US$300 mn., a small fraction of the required interfirm credit. This amount increased substantially in February 1990 (to about US$1.7 bn.). Even then, as stated above, this interfirm transfer of dollar deposits leaves a sizable credit/liquidity gap. If the credit/liquidity gaps are measured according to definitions (2) and (3) (lines B2 and B3 in Table A1), the case for tight credit conditions is further strengthened. For example, if the gap is measured as in line B2, recovery of credit/liquidity conditions prevailing in 1989 would have required the liquidation of the entire stock of foreign exchange deposits and inventories held by the enterprise sector.

Appendix B: The credit-market view: a simple framework

This appendix presents a model which highlights the role of credit/liquidity factors and exhibits the phenomenon of 'stagflation'. Stagflation models, while familiar (Bruno, 1979; Taylor, 1980; van Wijnbergen,

---

[15] Inventories and foreign exchange deposits available for conversion into liquid assets were actually much less than the revalued stock of those assets, because firms were subject to a capital gain tax that ranged between about 25 and 50%.

1982), typically rely on some form of price/wage stickiness. This does not strike us as a natural assumption in the case of a 'big-bang' programme like that in Poland (even though Coricelli *et al.*, 1990, find evidence of sluggishness in retail prices). The models presented here have perfectly flexible prices and wages and emphasize the role of credit/liquidity for both enterprises and households.[16] The next section lays out the basic model and examines the case in which households are not liquidity-constrained. Section B.2 relaxes the latter assumption, and studies the Kaldorian case in which labour income is fully spent. Finally, section B.3 analyses the implications of interest rate policy.

B.1. The basic model

We assume two types of goods: tradables and non-tradables. The international price of tradables is given and will be assumed equal to unity in terms of foreign currency. To simplify, we assume that the domestic output of tradables (e.g. coal) is exogenous and, thus, it is not affected by the stabilization programme. In contrast, production of non-tradables requires the input of tradables. To capture credit/liquidity constraints in the non-tradables sector, we assume that firms in that sector are subject to a liquidity-in-advance constraint of the form:[17]

$$x_t \leq z_t \tag{B1}$$

where x stands for the quantity of tradables used in the non-tradables sector, and z stands for liquidity (in terms of tradables) available to firms in the non-tradables sector. In general, z may include cash, bank deposits, inventories and even bank credit held or available to firms. In Appendix A, we showed that a case could be made for z being a binding constraint during the programme's execution.

To simplify the exposition, we will focus on the case in which firms hold no inventories (hence, x_t stands for both input at time t and purchases of tradable goods at time t), and liquidity, z, is just cash (zlotys). Aside from intermediate goods, production of non-tradables requires labour.[18] To capture the rigidity of the Polish labour market, the number of workers attached to a given enterprise is fixed. Actual employment at a given firm may vary and, thus, unemployment is possible.

---

[16] Wages were not fully flexible in Poland. Our models shed light on the possible reasons for wages to have lagged behind the programme's wage ceilings during the period of January to October, 1990.

[17] For simplicity, firms are assumed to be identical. Thus, there is no loss of precision by specifying the liquidity constraint for the whole non-tradables sector (as done below), instead of specifying such a constraint for each firm individually.

Each firm is managed by a Workers' Council so its objective is to maximize the welfare of each and every (identical) member of the firm's pool. If there were no unemployment compensation, no worker would be left unemployed and, if the marginal productivity of labour is always positive, all members of the pool will be employed at the firm. With unemployment compensation, it may be optimal to lay off some workers, particularly if there is an income-sharing rule among workers. The number of unemployed workers will depend on the characteristics of unemployment compensation, and on the income-sharing rules. These are important issues, but their inclusion would take us far astray from our main objective. In what follows we examine the case of no unemployment compensation and, consequently, focus on the case in which labour is a fixed factor.

Then the production function of non-tradables is written as $f(x)$, where x is input of intermediate goods. Function f is assumed to exhibit a positive derivative everywhere, and to be strictly concave. The firm is assumed to be liquidity-constrained, so condition (B1) holds with equality, and output of non-tradables is given by $f(z)$. Letting ω denote total labour income at the firm, and assuming a constant exchange rate, we get:

$$\dot{z}_t = p_t f(z_t) - z_t - \omega_t \tag{B2}$$

where p stands for the price of non-tradables in terms of tradables; p is exogenous to the firm, since we assume that all firms behave in a competitive manner.

Consider first the polar case in which households have perfect access to international capital markets. Thus, letting r stand for the (constant) international interest rate, it is natural to assume that the Workers' Council will try to maximize the present discounted value of labour income in the non-tradables sector, i.e.

$$\int_0^\infty \omega_t e^{-rt} dt \tag{B3}$$

subject to the liquidity-accumulation equation (B2), initial liquidity stock z_0, and the expected path of relative prices, p. A quick look reveals that, for given p, there exists (at most) one optimal steady state for liquidity, where $pf'(z) - 1 = r$; i.e. the net marginal productivity of liquidity (or, intermediate inputs) in terms of tradables, $pf'(z) - 1$, equals

---

[18] In general, the liquidity constraint (B2) would have to include the wage bill, in one way or another. Its inclusion, however, would not significantly affect ensuing results.

the international rate of interest, r. If z_0 is below such critical level for $p = p_0$ (the relevant case for Poland), then the optimal policy is to try to reach the optimal steady state at the maximum possible speed. This would imply setting ω as small as possible. The intuition is clear, if z_0 is less than the optimal steady state for liquidity then, due to strict concavity of the production function, $p_0 f'(z_0) - 1 > r$. Thus, one more unit of liquidity in the hands of non-tradable-goods firms yields more than in the hands of its workers (who get only r). In the present context lowering ω is equivalent to 'borrowing' from workers and, if $p_0 f'(z_0) - 1 > r$, offering workers an interest rate higher than the market rate, r. Therefore, we see here the effect stressed in the text, namely, that a liquidity crunch could lead firms to 'borrow' from workers.

As discussed in Calvo and Coricelli (1990), the above problem does not yield a well-defined solution unless, for example, one imposes a lower bound on wage income, ω. Such formal solution is unsatisfactory in the absence of a theory explaining such lower bound on labour income. A possibility is that labour income cannot fall below a certain level since, otherwise, some workers may also become liquidity-constrained, and thus unable to borrow any further in international markets.[19] Hence, a more plausible model should also take into consideration liquidity constraints on the part of households. We sketch such a version of the model in what follows. Among other things, the model can potentially explain inflation persistence.

B.2. Liquidity-constrained households

Let us consider the polar case in which, at each point in time, households' expenditure is constrained by labour income. Specifically,

$$\omega_t + y_t = p_t h_t + s_t \tag{B4}$$

where h and s denote, respectively, consumption of non-tradables and of tradables, and y is labour income in the tradables sector (assumed constant for simplicity). The 'direct' utility function depends on h and s. Thus, the indirect utility function can be expressed as $u(\omega + y, p)$. Let δ denote the households' subjective rate of time preference. Then, under these circumstances, workers' utility is given by:

$$\int_0^\infty u(\omega_t + y, p_t) \, e^{-\delta t} \, dt \tag{B5}$$

---

[19] Households' ability to borrow in international markets may sound like a farfetched assumption for Poland. However, recall that households are known to hold large foreign exchange-denominated balances (both cash and deposits). Thus, households would actually be 'borrowing' in international markets by merely lowering their foreign exchange-denominated holdings.

The optimization problem for the Workers' Council now consists of maximizing workers' utility (B5), subject to the liquidity-accumulation equation (B2), initial liquidity stock, z_0 and the path of relative prices, p. As an interesting illustration, consider the case in which the direct utility function is Cobb-Douglas and it is represented by $h^\alpha s^{1-\alpha}$, $0 < \alpha < 1$. Then, the indirect utility function satisfies:

$$u(\omega, p) = A(1/p)^\alpha (\omega + y) \tag{B6}$$

where $A = \alpha^\alpha (1 - \alpha)^{1-\alpha}$. Notice that the above form is linear in labour income, as in the perfect-capital mobility example. However, utility now depends also on the relative price of non-tradables with respect to tradables, p. The (undiscounted) Hamiltonian for this optimization problem is:

$$A(1/p)^\alpha (\omega + y) + \lambda [pf(z) - z - \omega] \tag{B7}$$

where λ is the co-state variable. Hence, interior optimal solutions require:[20]

$$A(1/p)^\alpha = \lambda \tag{B8}$$

$$\dot{\lambda} = -\lambda [pf'(z) - 1 - \delta] \tag{B9}$$

To close the model, we assume that households are the only consumers of non-tradable goods. Since (given the Cobb-Douglas utility function) households' demand for non-tradables is $\alpha(\omega + y)/p$, we have, at equilibrium:

$$f(z) = \alpha(\omega + y)/p \tag{B10}$$

By Equation (B8), we have

$$p = p(\lambda) \equiv (A/\lambda)^{1/\alpha} \tag{B11}$$

Thus, substituting Equations (B10) and (B11) into dynamic Equations (B2) and (B9) we get the following fundamental dynamic system characterizing this economy:

$$\dot{z} = p(\lambda)f(z)(1 - 1/\alpha) + y - z \tag{B12}$$

$$\dot{\lambda} = -\lambda [p(\lambda)f'(z) - 1 - \delta] \tag{B13}$$

The phase diagram for the above system is shown in Figure B1. The system exhibits saddle-path stability. The steady state corresponds to

---

[20] Time subscripts are dropped in what follows.

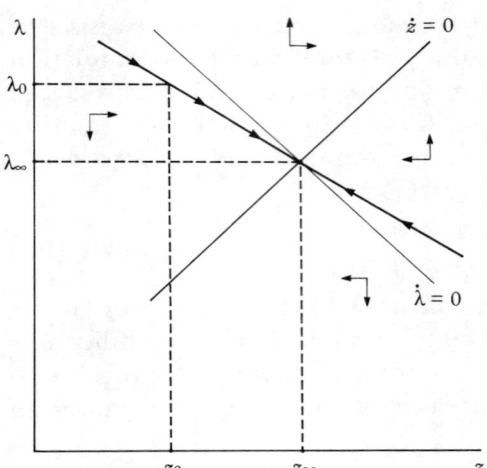

Figure B1. Determination of equilibrium

the point $(z_\infty, \lambda_\infty)$, and the saddle path is the heavy arrowed line going through the steady state. It can be verified that along the saddle path firms and households maximize their objective functions and the market for non-tradables is in equilibrium at all points in time. If the economy starts in the 'liquidity shortage' region (i.e. to the left of z_∞), at a point like z_0, the initial λ, λ_0, exceeds λ_∞. Afterwards, both z and λ move monotonically toward their respective steady states. Consequently, the initial liquidity squeeze lowers output. Henceforth, output rises over time. By Equations (B10) and (B11), the real wage in terms of non-tradables and the relative price of non-tradables with respect to tradables also rise. Thus, the model predicts a real appreciation of the domestic currency which, since the exchange rate is constant, implies inflation persistence. Furthermore, during the liquidity-shortage phase, $\dot{z} > 0$, implying that firms will exhibit positive profits. All of these implications are in accordance with developments in Poland after January 1990.

Let TB denote the trade balance and, for the sake of concreteness, let us assume that labour income in the tradables sector, y, equals output of tradables (thus, profits in that sector are zero). Then the trade balance satisfies:

$$TB = y - z - (1-\alpha)(\omega + y) = y - z - (1-\alpha)pf(z)/\alpha \qquad (B14)$$

Thus, the trade balance is the difference between the output of tradables, y, and the demand for tradables originating in non-tradables firms, z, and in households, $(1-\alpha)(\omega + y)$. The rightmost equality in expression (B14) follows from using Equation (B10) to substitute for total labour income, $\omega + y$. By Equations (B12) and (B14) it follows that[21]

$$\dot{z} = TB \tag{B15}$$

The trade balance will be in surplus as enterprises accumulate liquidity, which again, is in accordance with developments in Poland after January 1990.

B.3. Interest rates and credit ceilings

To introduce bank credit explicitly, let r_b denote the interest rate on bank credit to enterprises. We assume that r_b can be directly controlled by the monetary authority. Let b denote the amount of bank credit. We assume that bank credit is of instantaneous maturity, and that its presence modifies the liquidity constraint equation (B1) as follows:

$$x_t \le z_t + b_t \equiv l_t \tag{B1'}$$

Thus, firms' expenditure on intermediate goods require cash in advance on the portion that is not financed by bank credit. Furthermore, the liquidity accumulation equation (B2) is assumed to satisfy:

$$\dot{z} = pf(l) - l - r_b(l - z) - \omega \tag{B2'}$$

where $l - z = b$.

Previous analysis assumed that liquidity was entirely composed of own liquidity, z; thus, $l = z$. This is equivalent to saying that bank credit to enterprises is constrained to be zero. Actually, the Polish programme entailed upper limits to bank credit that were, of course, different from zero. Let $\bar{b} \ge 0$ denote the credit ceiling imposed by the monetary authority. Thus, in the present context firms are allowed to get credit from the banking system provided it does not exceed the credit limit, $\bar{b}$.[22] Formally, l is constrained to satisfy the following condition:

$$l - z \le \bar{b} \tag{B16}$$

We first note that if credit ceilings are binding then the model is formally similar to the one above. Equation (B2') becomes:

$$\dot{z} = pf(z + \bar{b}) - (z + \bar{b}) - r_b\bar{b} - \omega \tag{B17}$$

As expected, the above equation becomes Equation (B2) if $\bar{b} = 0$, and the analysis is identical to that of previous subsections. In general,

---

[21] Equation (B15) implies that, ultimately, firms in the non-tradables sector acquire liquidity by surrendering hard currency to the Central Bank.
[22] To simplify the exposition, we assume $\bar{b}$ to be constant over time.

taking into account the market clearing condition (B10), and noticing that (B8) remains unchanged, we obtain the following alternative dynamic system:

$$\dot{z} = p(\lambda)f(z+b)(1-1/\alpha) + y - (z+b) - r_b b \tag{B12'}$$

$$\dot{\lambda} = -\lambda[p(\lambda)f'(z+b) - 1 - \delta] \tag{B13'}$$

It is easy to verify that all the dynamic properties of the no-bank-credit model discussed above hold here if the rate of interest on bank credit is constant over time. It can also be shown that similar dynamic implications for p (the relative price of non-tradables) are obtained if r_b is expected to decline over time (as in the Polish programme, see Table 5) and, furthermore, if initially liquidity is less than steady-state liquidity corresponding to the future lower interest rate. Furthermore, if the high-interest period is expected to be relatively short, then the initial output fall may be followed by further output contraction and further fall in real wages (in terms of non-tradables), until the lower loan rates take effect. Henceforth, the economy exhibits all the characteristics discussed in previous subsections (i.e. p, ω/p and output rise over time).

As noted in the text, however, at the beginning of the Polish programme credit ceilings were not binding. A common interpretation is that lending rates were set too high. We show that the dynamic implications of the model with binding credit ceilings carry over to the case of initially nonbinding credit ceilings.

If (B16) is not binding, then it is clear that if (B2') holds with equality (a maintained assumption), then firms will choose l so that

$$pf'(l) - 1 = r_b \tag{B18}$$

i.e. the net marginal productivity of liquidity, $pf'(l) - 1$, equals the marginal cost of liquidity, r_b. Thus, at optimum, there exists a function $L(p, r_b)$ such that:

$$l = L(p, r_b), \quad L_p > 0 \quad \text{and} \quad L_r < 0 \tag{B19}$$

Therefore, by Equations (B2'), (B10), (B11) and (B19), we get

$$\dot{z} = p(\lambda)f(L(p(\lambda), r_b))(1-1/\alpha) + y - L(p(\lambda), r_b)$$
$$- r_b[L(p(\lambda), r_b) - z] \tag{B20}$$

Moreover, one can show that the co-state variable, λ, satisfies

$$\dot{\lambda} = -\lambda(r_b - \delta) \tag{B21}$$

First, let us consider the case of constant r_b. To ensure existence of a steady state, we further assume that $r_b = \delta$. Thus, λ is constant over time, a fact that can be used to show that all variables are constant over time. Second, consider the case in which $r_b = \bar{r} > \delta$ during the first T periods of the programme, and $r_b = \delta$ after time T. This interest rate configuration is closer to the Polish case. By Equation (B21), λ declines during the interval $[0, T]$, and remains constant afterwards. By Equation (B11), the latter implies that during the transition, i.e. from time 0 to time T, p goes up. In other words, inflation inertia also occurs under non-binding credit ceilings. Furthermore, by Equations (B10) and (B18), output and real wages also expand during the transition.

It is quite clear that in all of these models, output and labour productivity move in the same direction, while the models exhibit no employed-workers idleness. A more realistic scenario for Poland-1990 would be one in which there is no credit rationing during the first few months of the programme (due to high interest rates), and rationing afterwards. Thus, instead of the system coming to a complete halt at time T, as in the no-credit-rationing case, output and wages would continue rising, accompanied by positive inflation. A still more realistic model should incorporate inventories and anachronistic price setting.

Appendix C: Measurement problems

The reliability of official statistics is doubtful for three main reasons: (1) the coverage of production, employment and price statistics may largely underestimate private sector activities; (2) Gerschenkron-type index numbers problems may arise as a result of large relative price changes; furthermore, the presence of shortages, hence non-market-clearing prices, before stabilization creates additional index problems; (3) accounting methods, particularly in the field of national accounts, may be very imprecise. As regards the first issue, official statistics include an estimate of the private sector which is believed to be largely underestimated. This perception arises from anecdotes or casual observation of booming street trade, expansion of private surface transportation and so forth. However, at this moment there is no hard evidence pointing to the fact that a proper accounting of private sector activities could reverse the outcomes provided by official statistics. The second point may be more serious because with large changes in relative prices – starting from disequilibrium prices – there can be index number problems leading to an overestimation of the decline in output and an overestimation of the increase in prices (Osband, 1991). Output and price indices can be very misleading when base period prices are not market-clearing. Without denying the importance of the problem, two facts have to be stressed. First, January 1990 does not represent the date of price liberalization in Poland. Abstracting from energy, housing rent and other fees on public services, most of the adjustment in relative prices of final goods took place before January 1990. Second, all industrial sectors contracted in January 1990.[23]

When moving from a shortage economy to an economy where prices are market-clearing there are also problems in measuring real wages and real incomes. One could actually argue that the relevant price level for measuring real income and wealth will show little change in January 1990, since it incorporates the cost of waiting/searching for goods in a shortage economy. Therefore, deflating wages by the CPI and comparing observations belonging to two distinct regimes tends to grossly overestimate the decline in real 'real wages'. Unfortunately, available data do not allow us to construct a reliable time series of real wages. However, some information can be obtained if one is prepared to make the (strong) assumption that the dollar's black market rate could be taken as a proxy of the equilibrium price level. When so deflated wages display a significant increase during 1990, casting some doubts on the significance of the sharp fall in the statistical real wage.

Finally, accounting problems for inventories appear quite serious in periods of high inflation.[24] We present inventory series obtained by using moving averages, consistent with an average accounting method which seems to be widely used by Polish enterprises. As seen in Figure 3, all our estimates show a decline of inventories after the programme was implemented.

To conclude, measurement problems could be quite serious. However, we could find no strong evidence against the hypothesis that output suffered a precipitous fall, and that inventories declined after January 1990. The behaviour of real wages is much less clear.

References

Allen, M. (1991). 'Fund-Supported Adjustment Programmes in Eastern Europe', in *Central and Eastern Europe: Roads to Growth*, International Monetary Fund.

Bernanke, B. S. (1983). 'Nonmonetary Effects of the Financial Crisis in the Propagation of the Great Depression', *American Economic Review*.

Blanchard, O., R. Dornbusch, P. Krugman, R. Layard and L. Summers (1991). *Reform in Eastern Europe*, The MIT Press, Boston.

Blanchard, O. and S. Fischer (1989). *Lectures on Macroeconomics*, The MIT Press, Boston.

Blanchard, O. and R. Layard (1991). 'Post-Stabilization Inflation in Poland'.

<hr>

[23] Schaffer also argues that serious index problems could also be reflected in trade data. However, a comparison of trade data in constant zlotys with dollar value does not indicate large discrepancies. He reports information from surveys on physical output of enterprises which confirms the presence of a large output decline.

[24] Official data are obtained by deflating the nominal stock of inventories by the current-month price index. If firms use average price methods and are characterized by turnover periods longer than a month, the method misrepresents the behaviour of real inventories.

Bruno, M. (1979). 'Stabilization and Stagflation in a Semi-Industrialized Economy', in R. Dornbusch and J. Frenkel (eds.) *International Economic Policy: Theory and Evidence*, Johns Hopkins University Press, Baltimore.

—— (1990). 'High Inflation and the Nominal Anchors of an Open Economy', NBER Working Paper No. 3518, November.

Bruno, M. and J. Sachs (1985). *Economics of Worldwide Stagflation*, Blackwell, Oxford.

Calomiris, C. W. and R. G. Hubbard (1989). 'Price Flexibility, Credit Availability, and Economic Fluctuations: Evidence from The United States, 1894–1909', *The Quarterly Journal of Economics*.

Calvo, G. A. and F. Coricelli (1990). 'Stagflationary Effects of Stabilization Programmes in Reforming Socialist Economies: Enterprise-Side vs. Household-Side Factors', *World Bank Economic Review*.

Calvo, G. A. and J. A. Frenkel (1991a). 'Transformation of Centrally-Planned Economies: Credit Markets and Sustainable Growth', in *Central and Eastern Europe: Roads to Growth*, International Monetary Fund.

—— (1991b). 'Obstacles to Transforming Centrally-Planned Economies: The Role of Capital Markets', in *Transition to a Market Economy in Central and Eastern Europe*, proceedings of the OECD–World Bank Conference, Paris.

Calvo, G. A. and C. A. Vegh (1990). 'Credibility and the Dynamics of Stabilization Policy: A Basic Framework', WP/90/110, November 1990, International Monetary Fund. To appear in the Proceedings of the VI World Congress of the Econometric Society, Cambridge University Press.

Collins S. and D. Rodrik (1991). *Eastern Europe and the Soviet Union in the World Economy*, Washington, Institute for International Economics.

Commander, S., F. Coricelli and K. Staehr (1991). 'Wages and Unemployment in the Transition to a Market Economy', in *Central and Eastern Europe: Roads to Growth*, International Monetary Fund.

Coricelli, F., L. de la Calle and B. Pinto (1990). 'Poland: Macroeconomic Policy in the Second Phase of the Reform Programme', mimeo, The World Bank, December.

Coricelli, F. and R. Rocha (1991). 'Stabilization Programmes in Eastern Europe: A Comparative Analysis of the Polish and Yugoslav Programmes of 1990', in V. Corbo, F. Coricelli and J. Bossak (eds.) *Reforming Central and Eastern European Economies: Initial Results and Challenges*, The World Bank.

Frenkel, J. A. and A. Razin (1987). 'The Mundell–Fleming Model a Quarter Century Later: A Unified Exposition', *IMF Staff Papers*.

Frydman, R. and S. Wellisz (1991). 'The Ownership-Control Structure and the Behaviour of Polish Enterprises during the 1990 Reforms: Macroeconomic Measures and Microeconomic Response', in V. Corbo, F. Coricelli and J. Bossak (eds.) *Reforming Central and Eastern European Economies: Initial Results and Challenges*, The World Bank.

Frydman, R., S. Wellisz and G. Kolodko (1990). 'Stabilization in Poland: A Progress Report', in E. M. Classen and R. Mundell (eds.) *Exchange Rate Policies in Developing and Socialist Countries*, International Center for Economic Growth, San Francisco.

Gertler, M. (1988). 'Financial Structure and Aggregate Economic Activity: An Overview', *Journal of Money Credit and Banking*.

Gomulka, S. (1991). 'The Causes of Recession Following Stabilization', *Journal of Comparative Economic Studies*.

Hinds, M. (1990). 'Issues in the Introduction of Market Forces in Eastern European Socialist Economies', The World Bank, *EMENA Discussion Papers*, No. IDP-0057.

International Monetary Fund (1989). 'Economic Reform in Poland since 1981'.

Kiguel, M. and N. Liviatan (1989). 'The Business Cycle Associated with Exchange-Rate-Based Stabilizations', mimeo, The World Bank.

Kolodko, G. (1991). 'Transition from Socialism and Stabilization Policies: The Polish Experience', mimeo.

Kolodko, G. and W. McMahon (1987). 'Stagflation and Shortageflation: A Comparative Approach', *Kyklos*.

Kornai, J. (1980). *Economics of Shortage*, North-Holland, Amsterdam, New York, Oxford.

Lane, T. (1991). 'Inflation Stabilization and Economic transformation in Poland: The First Year', Carnegie-Rochester Conference Series on Public Policy, 36, forthcoming.

Lipton, D. and J. Sachs (1990). 'Creating a Market Economy in Eastern Europe: The Case of Poland', *Brookings Papers on Economic Activity*.

Osband, K. (1991). 'Index Number Biases during Price Liberalization', International Monetary Fund.

Rosati, D. (1990). 'Poland: Economic Reform and Policy in the 1980s', Foreign Trade Research Institute, Discussion Paper No. 14.

Schaffer, M. E. (1991). 'A Note on the Polish State-owned Enterprise Sector in 1990', Centre for Economic Performance, Working Paper No. 36.

Taylor, L. (1980). 'IS–LM in the Tropics: Diagrammatics of the New Structuralist Macro Critique', in Weintraub, S. and W. R. Cline (eds.) *Economic Stabilization in Developing Countries*, The Brookings Institution, Washington.

Van Wijnbergen, S. (1982). 'Stagflationary Effects of Monetary Stabilization Policies, a Quantitative Analysis of South Korea', *Journal of Development Economics*.

West, K. (1986). 'A Variance Bounds Test for the Linear Quadratic Inventory Model', *Journal of Political Economy*.

Wyznikiewicz, B. (1990). 'Poland: Recent Developments in the Financial Situation of Industrial Subsectors', mimeo, World Bank.

Economic Policy   April 1992   Printed in Great Britain

Hungary

Paul Hare and Tamás Révész

Summary

Among Eastern European countries, Hungary's great advantage is that it began economic reforms in 1968, and slowly introduced the institutions of a market economy during the 1980s. These measures laid the foundation for a gradual transition to the market, without the need for any sharp break with the past.

Policy mistakes were, of course, made. The most serious, extending over several years, was the 1970s investment boom funded by foreign capital, which contributed to Hungary's large debt burden. Despite this, the government accounts are not now in substantial deficit and the balance of payments on current account is in modest surplus; nevertheless, managing the external debt is now the most difficult of Hungary's problems. It is important that Hungarian joint ventures and privatization are now attracting significant quantities of foreign capital.

Given the quite rapid pace of liberalization since the late 1980s, the government's commitment to further changes, and a reasonably satisfactory macroeconomic balance (though inflation is worrying), there is no case for a 'big-bang' approach in Hungary. Such a shock could only disrupt established market relationships and expectations, with little benefit. The most valuable forms of 'aid' for Hungary would be debt relief and unrestricted access for Hungary's products to EC markets.

Hungary's transition to the market: the case against a 'big-bang'

Paul Hare and Tamás Révész

Heriot–Watt University, Edinburgh, and LSE; Budapest University of Economics

1. Introduction

Despite serious economic problems, Hungary is remarkably well-placed to carry through its transition to the market more rapidly, and more smoothly, than elsewhere in the region (except the special case of the GDR). Paradoxically, it will do so without the 'big-bang' strategy applied in Poland and the CSFR, and advocated elsewhere.

Hungary has the advantage of past experience of reform and (reasonable) political unity. Against this, it has the highest per capita external debt in the world, declining output due to internal and external shocks, rising unemployment and inflation in the mid-thirties per cent. Far from collapsing under the weight of these massive problems, Hungary is flourishing. Trade with the EC is rising fast, private sector activity is buoyant and substantial foreign investment is already being attracted; moreover, the country's economic administration is exactly what is needed – unexciting but pretty competent, making effective use of external advice.

Under these conditions, a 'big-bang' could only be damaging, by disturbing the already well-formed expectations of domestic and foreign investors. Nor would a big-bang solve the toughest problem, Hungary's external debt. For Hungary the best solution for this latter problem would be for Hungary to maintain its existing resolve to service the debt, but for Western governments and banks unilaterally to offer generous debt relief. This, and free access to EC markets, would be the most beneficial forms of 'aid' for Hungary. But we wonder whether the West is sufficiently bold to make such a gesture for a small,

We are grateful to the editors for very detailed comments and suggestions on earlier drafts of this paper, and to discussants and participants at the Prague *Economic Policy* Panel. Remaining errors are our own.

'unimportant' country. Yet, a success story in Hungary could demonstrate opportunities in the transition for other countries more effectively than any number of official reports.

1.1. Hungary's situation: a short summary

Unlike the rest of Eastern Europe, in managing the transition to the market Hungary's democratically elected government[1] can draw on two decades of prior economic reforms.[2] These reforms established many of the institutions and practices of a market economy in Hungary long before such reform was seriously considered in such countries as Czechoslovakia, the former GDR and Bulgaria. Nevertheless, many large distortions remained in Hungary at least up to the end of the 1980s, when the old, communist-dominated political structures finally began to relax their grip on the economy. As a result, at least among the larger state-owned enterprises (SOEs) which dominate production in most branches, market forms were often not accompanied by market behaviour.

At the same time, under the surface of communist rule, profound changes were taking place in the economy and society. In particular, the 'second economy' and, from the early 1980s onwards, legal small-scale businesses grew very rapidly (Hare, 1983). The new businesses were sometimes entirely private, sometimes in symbiotic relationship with existing SOEs. In either case, they provided opportunities for hard-working people with the right skills to earn high incomes; they also contributed towards the economy's supply-side flexibility in ways which, unfortunately, are not well captured in official statistics (which even by 1991 had little to say about private economic activity). Nevertheless, while some prospered during the 1980s, others – those lacking access to such opportunities, or reliant on state incomes (e.g. government employees and children) – did relatively badly. Hungarian society became more polarized. Given the extreme equality during much of the communist period, such a shift is unsurprising but may give rise to social tensions during the early period of the transition.

First, although Hungary has the advantage of substantial reform experience, it also faces severe problems and has to make some difficult

---

[1] Elected in Spring 1990, the government is led by the centre-right Democratic Forum, in coalition with the Christian Democratic Party and the Smallholders Party (whose one serious aim is restoration of rural land to its original owners or their descendants).

[2] Systemic change in Hungary would have been impossible but for *perestroika*. On this, see Aganbegyan (1988), Hewett (1988) and Tedstrom (1990); on the political upheavals in Eastern Europe in 1989–90, see Hawkes (1990), Rollo (1990), Batt (1991); on the ensuing economic issues, see van Brabant (1990), CEPR (1990), Collins and Rodrik (1991) and Kemme (1991).

policy choices. The most pressing is a gross external debt which in 1990 already exceeded $20 bn., easily the highest in Eastern Europe in per capita terms (OECD, 1991a). Unlike Bulgaria and Poland, both of which defaulted on their hard currency debt obligations,[3] Hungary has consistently insisted that it will continue to service its hard currency debt. The merits of this policy can be questioned; it certainly constrains Hungary's policy options in other spheres.

Second, trade policy is proving difficult, largely because of the unexpectedly rapid collapse of CMEA trade, especially that with the USSR. In Hungary's case, this trade 'shock' has been offset to some extent by the surprisingly good performance in exporting to Western markets in the last two years. Nevertheless, some analysis is required to assess prospects of further growth, the sectors in which Hungary is likely to prove competitive, and the extent of barriers to trade expansion (especially in the EC).

A third problem is adequate living standards. Even until the late 1980s, Hungary's living standards continued to rise or at worst stagnate. Hungarians, accustomed to rising consumption, are likely to prove far less willing than Poles to tolerate substantial falls in living standards during the transition period. Moreover, most ordinary people care little about esoteric problems such as the debt burden. Everyday perceptions focus more on whether consumer goods markets function reasonably well, whether most goods and services are readily available (with a few notable exceptions like private telephones, some household equipment and furniture, and good quality housing), and whether or not there is a 'visible' economic crisis. It is very important for the government to manage the transition without threatening perceived living standards too drastically.

Turning from problems to policies, five areas require special attention: inflation control and nominal anchors, fiscal policy, reform of the financial system, labour market policy and policies for privatization and structural change. There can be little doubt that Eastern Europe will achieve the transition to the market. The questions are *what type* of market economy, *how rapid* a transition and *by what methods*? Unlike Poland and Czechoslovakia, Hungary has preferred a gradualist, step-by-step approach to a 'big-bang' approach to economic reform. In our view, this choice is the correct one for Hungary, and our aim in this paper is to justify that conclusion.

Essentially, big-bang would jeopardize unnecessarily many of Hungary's achievements to date: a relatively high living standard,

---

[3] Bulgaria suspended payments in March 1990. Poland has paid neither interest nor principal since the early 1980s. Yugoslavia was effectively bankrupt in 1991.

international banking credibility, political and personal freedom, and at least partly functioning market institutions and enterprises. Of course, a gradualist approach also has its dangers: the mismanagment, waste and corruption (rent-seeking) connected with existing state ownership. Many such losses stem from the antagonistic coexistence of old and new regulations (or the absence of both!) during the transition.

To minimize such losses, proper sequencing is at least as important as speed. Transition, like a chess game, has no assured winning formula or strategy, but a limited number of fairly general, conditional behavioural rules, as we explain later. In our view, the most important of these rules for Hungary is this: that the government should advance step-by-step as far as possible, and only resort to 'shock therapy' when it meets impenetrable barriers. This process will not relegate Hungary to a boring sideshow. Resistance to change is frequently fierce and sophisticated; as soon as one privilege (distortion) is eliminated, there is strong pressure to resurrect it in a new guise. It is easy to make a long list of new hidden (implicit) subsidies and financial privileges.[4] Such distortions, and its lively, rapidly developing market environment, make Hungary an astonishing country.

1.2. Structure of the paper

Section 2 briefly reviews the history of the Hungarian reforms. Section 3 then examines certain key aspects of Hungary's economic performance, especially in the 1980s, which highlight the nature of the crisis now being faced. Taken together, these sections help to define an agenda for policy-makers. Sections 4 and 5 examine specific policies against this background. Section 4 discusses macroeconomic issues, Section 5 microeconomic issues (recognizing that a strict separation of macro and micro is not always possible). Section 6 relates economic issues to the political and social environment in Hungary.

2. Brief history of Hungarian reforms

In theoretical terms, the contradictions of the socialist management system were well understood long ago (Nove, 1983; Lavoie, 1985; Brus, 1970; Sik, 1967 and 1972; Kornai, 1959; Cave and Hare, 1981; Hare, 1991c, among many others), though communist regimes were not inclined to take much notice, or to deal with them effectively in practice.

---

[4] For example: toleration of overdue tax and social security payments, or of tips for government employees in preference to wage reform; allowing users of state property improperly to consume the assets.

In most of Eastern Europe the communists were never able to gain the confidence of a majority of the people, especially in those countries where foreign troops helped them to gain power in the first place, and their power could be sustained only by force.[5]

A characteristic feature of the traditional, Soviet-type economy was the virtually complete nationalization of the economy, partly to eliminate so-called reactionary classes (capitalists, intellectuals, the peasantry), and partly as the foundation for highly-centralized economic planning. Thus enormous wealth came into the hands of a largely uneducated and inexperienced state apparatus, whose staff were increasingly selected according to political not professional criteria. It was beyond their capacity to manage effectively.

The bureaucracy tried to moderate the resulting waste of public property, and to counteract the widespread indifference to the way in which it was used, in two ways: moral exhortation and an ever-increasing stream of different decrees and regulations. The latter often stopped the very activities which would otherwise have been favourable, and led to a quantitative approach to economic control (output targets, input requirements, etc.).

While this centralized model generated quite respectable growth rates in much of Eastern Europe, especially in the 1960s and 1970s, it also led to serious distortions. At first these problems appeared to be short-term, related to poor incentives at enterprise level and distorted prices, but later on they assumed more serious forms. It became clear that many investment decisions were also being affected by price distortions, by the isolation of these economies from the world market, and by lagging technology. In several countries, shortages became endemic.

To overcome increasingly severe indications of economic disfunction, Eastern European governments experimented with a variety of economic reforms, while seeking to avoid any fundamental threat to the dominant position of the Communist Party. Commonly, such partial reforms were reversed or counteracted by later measures within a short time.

Table 1 sets out the main economic (and, more recently, political) reforms, and retreats from reform, in Hungary since the mid-1950s[6]. After failing to adapt the domestic economy to the two oil price crises of 1973 and 1979, and having engineered an investment boom which had raised Hungary's external hard currency debt to dangerous levels

---

[5] Kaser and Radice (1986) is extremely useful background. Berend and Ranki (1985) addresses Hungary specifically.

[6] For a fuller account, see Hare *et al.* (1981), Hare (1983, 1981a, b), Marer (1986a, b, 1989), Kornai (1986), Berend (1990) and on agriculture Swain (1985).

Table 1. Economic reform in Hungary

1956	End of delivery obligations for farmers and cooperatives
1962*	Formation of trusts and large enterprises; agricultural collectivization completed
1964	Introduction of resource taxes (wage-related tax, and capital charge)
1968	*The New Economic Mechanism*: Plans no longer broken down to enterprise level; partial autonomy of SOEs in making contracts, distributing profits, choosing product mix, foreign trade, investment. Start of private agriculture
1971*	Partial recentralization, especially for large enterprises
1972	Start of 'wage-fund control' for enterprises, an incentive to limit or reduce employees
1980	Price reform simulating 'world prices'
1981	Small private firms legalized
1982	Closer links to international financial institutions and EC. Unified tourist and commercial exchange rate, start of bond market
1985	Introduction of self-governing companies (enterprise councils)
1986–87	Operation of commercial banks separated from the National Bank
1988	Tax reform (PIT and VAT), extensive price liberalization
1989	Import liberalization, export licences extended to companies; the communist party removed from workplaces; trade union privileges restricted; open unemployment acknowledged
1990	Communist factions lose parliamentary and local elections, their privileges gradually withdrawn; some enterprise leaders lose jobs; autonomous local councils set up; privatization begins
1991	Price import and export liberalization almost complete; drastic cuts in subsidies to firms and households; rouble trade stops

Sources: See main text; also, on price reform see Hare (1976), Swaan (1989); on banking and financial reforms see Blejer and Sagan (1991).
Note: * Denotes a period of retreat from reform.

without achieving the expected returns in terms of higher exports, the Hungarian government became increasingly defensive, and was obliged to accept some compromises on economic reform.[7] After 1979 reformers were able to press for further liberalization, but its introduction was in stages and piecemeal: only towards the end of the 1980s did a consistent pattern of economic management re-emerge. The market-oriented reforms implemented in Hungary during the 1980s were the most far reaching in the socialist world, with the possible exception of China. Of the many reforms of this period, two are singled out for separate discussion, small businesses and the tax system.

Hungary was the first country in the region to allow new private or cooperative businesses (and various types of business association) to be established (without the need for high-level ministerial permission), to

---

[7] After the 1956 restoration of communism, the Hungarian government was more open, and hence willing to listen and change direction.

Table 2. Hungarian enterprises, by type (thousands)

	1988	1989	1990	1991
Corporate bodies with a legal personality				
State enterprises	2.4	2.4	2.4	2.4
Cooperatives	7.4	7.5	7.6	7.7
Economic associations				
Associations	0.1	0.1	0.2	0.2
Joint enterprises	0.3	0.3	0.2	0.2
Joint stock companies	0.1	0.3	0.6	0.9
Limited liability companies	0.5	4.5	18.4	30.9
Undertakings without legal personality	31.4	34.3	36.6	45.8
Private sector				
Industrialist	162.2	174.8	240.0	310.0
Trader	34.5	39.6		
Farmer	1,375.0	1,435.0		

Sources: *Statisztikai Havi Közlemények, 1991/7*, Budapest; *Világgazdaság* (6/8/1991);
Gazdaság és Társadalom, 1991/1; *Statisztikai Évkönyv 1989*, Budapest.
Note: 1991 data are for June.

lease out shops, restaurants and other establishments to their managers, and to accept that such activity should be legal and taxed, rather than illegal and untaxed as was the case everywhere else. The enabling measures date from 1981, though subsequently the rules were relaxed further. Thousands of new businesses were formed during the 1980s, mostly in services but also in small-scale industry, agriculture and construction. Under the 1988 enterprise law (effective from January 1989), many of these new firms became limited liability companies, along with a further round of new business formation. Thus in Hungary it is not hard to start a firm, adequate procedures have been in place for at least a decade, and thousands of people have taken advantage of the new rules of the game (including, more recently, a large number of foreign firms, or joint ventures). By 1990 a business survey estimated that small firms were producing about 10% of industrial output. Table 2 presents recent data on small firms and other types of business.

This small business sector was allowed to flourish with remarkably little political interference, and little attempt to regulate incomes or prices. Its development was often seen in a very positive light, providing goods and services which were otherwise in short supply, and providing services for the large state firms; it also gave many people extensive experience of operating in a market environment. This is a huge advantage for Hungary: in the rest of the region such activities were discouraged or even illegal until the end of the 1980s.

Hungary is also fortunate in its tax system. Profits taxation was introduced in 1968, with uniform rates across almost the whole economy. This replaced the traditional arrangement in central planning which removed above-plan profits into the state budget, a 100% marginal tax rate which is a poor incentive in any system. Yet the correlation between pre-tax and post-tax profits, and between profits and investment, remained very weak in Hungary: the central authorities were reluctant to let enterprises use their profits freely. A huge range of special taxes and subsidies was devised to protect weak firms and cream off income from the stronger ones, a mechanism studied in great detail by Kornai and Matits (1987). Thus as the tax structure moved towards that of a market economy, it was still possible to maintain much of the old control system; highly differentiated taxes and subsidies replaced old-style direct instructions (Hare, 1990). One aim of the most recent reforms is precisely to remove most of these distortions.

Until this is done, it could be argued that the introduction of profits taxation in Hungary is a pure formality. Much the same could be said about the introduction of a general value-added tax (VAT) and a personal income tax (PIT) in 1988. If the government can decide how much revenue to extract from each enterprise via special taxes or subsidies, why does it need a VAT? If it directly controls personal incomes in the socialist sector, why bother with a PIT? These are interesting questions. Hungary was the only country in the region to introduce these taxes before the collapse of communism, and it certainly did not do so because it anticipated that collapse.

One answer is that even in the 1980s Hungary was preparing itself for closer links with Europe and with international agencies like the GATT, the IMF and the World Bank. Hungary came under increasing pressure to adopt a less distortionary, more Western, tax structure, which it eventually did. Yet it is doubtful whether the new taxes can have had much effect on resource allocation prior to 1990 (Newbery, 1990). However, with VAT and the PIT in place, Hungary can now contemplate both the complete dismantling of the old tax/subsidy system, and large scale privatization, without fearing that government revenues are at risk. This gives Hungary an immense advantage over other countries in the region, where market-oriented tax structures are not yet properly established.

Since about 1988, the critical situation facing the economy, the failure of previous partial reforms, and the scope available to a new political leadership no longer constrained by what Kadar might be prepared to tolerate, led the government to embark on more comprehensive reforms. Although the new package was presented as if Hungary was still building socialism, it was becoming clear that socialism was no

Table 3. Growth of GDP and its components (% per annum, constant prices)

	1970–80	1980–85	1986	1987	1988	1989	1990
Output (GDP)	4.8	1.8	1.5	4.1	−0.1	−0.2	−5.9
Industry	5.7	2.4	−0.5	3.2	−1.5	−3.4	−9.5
Construction	5.8	−1.4	0.1	7.8	−5.5	1.5	−1.9
Agriculture	0.8	3.0	3.5	−3.0	7.9	−1.8	−8.4
Domestic expenditure	4.0	0.1	3.9	3.2	−2.9	−0.3	−5.2
Consumption	3.8	1.5	2.4	3.3	−2.8	−0.7	−5.4
Investment	4.3	−3.8	8.6	3.2	−3.3	0.9	−4.8

Source: Statistical Yearbook 1989, Budapest; 1990 data from *Az 1991. évi gazdasági prográm háttérszámitásai*, Pénzügyminisztérium, Budapest.

longer the issue: the government was fighting for its own political, and the country's economic survival. As it soon turned out, these were no longer indissolubly linked.

The new measures included the fundamental tax reforms cited above, and a programme to remove most distorting taxes and subsidies, to liberalize prices and to liberalize the bulk of imports over a three to four year period. Elsewhere, such a programme was only started in 1990 or later, but in Hungary it has been largely accomplished, and the former Price Office has become the new Competition Office. What few price controls remain are in areas such as public utilities, and a limited number of key consumer goods. In 1990, therefore, Hungary's democratic government was fortunate to be able to take power with many of the requirements of a market economy already in place.

3. Hungary's economic performance and current situation

Table 3 shows that economic growth was at quite respectable rates in the 1970s, with a marked slowdown thereafter as Hungary's leaders sought to restrain domestic demand to restore external balance, and actual decline in the last three years. Both in the 1970s and more recently, domestic spending (consumption plus gross investment) grew more slowly than GDP. For much of the period, this reflected a proper attempt to shift resources into net exports. Unfortunately, since the terms of trade (especially in dollar trade) declined over much of the period (see p. 12, Table 5(b)), this attempt was less effective than it might have been (part of this adjustment, of course, was Hungary's delayed adaptation to higher world oil prices).

For much of the 1980s, total investment was falling, but from a high initial level; and, a substantial part of the decline can be explained by the decline in extremely inefficient, large state investments. Industrial

Table 4. Structure of GDP (%)

	1987	1988	1989
Output:			
Industry	36.7	36.2	35.2
Construction	6.9	6.5	6.6
Agriculture and forestry	19.5	21.1	20.8
Transport and telecoms	9.0	9.2	9.5
Trade	9.6	8.4	8.7
Other material activity	2.8	2.9	3.2
Material branches	84.5	84.3	84.0
Non-material branches	15.5	15.7	16.0
Expenditure:			
Private consumption	63.5	60.6	59.7
Public consumption	10.3	11.2	10.8
Fixed capital formation (installed)	22.8	19.1	18.4
Uncompleted investment	2.0	1.8	1.8
Increase in stocks	2.0	4.5	5.9
Trade surplus	−0.5	2.8	3.4

Source: *Statistical Yearbook 1989*, Budapest.

growth held up well up to the mid-1980s but growth rates have been extremely low in recent years, and increasingly negative since 1987. The industrial decline mirrors exactly what is now happening in the other Eastern European countries, and it is obviously of great concern to the government. However, on a more positive note, it is likely to be accompanied by the long-delayed, long expected and necessary restructuring of much of the economy.

The structure of GDP is summarized for the late 1980s in Table 4. The table shows that a little under 60% of GDP is consumed by individuals, and a further 11% is public consumption, leaving about 26% for gross investment (fixed capital formation plus stock changes), the balance being the trade surplus. Provided that such a high share of GDP can be saved and invested in the future, Hungary's growth should not be held back by insufficient investment; what is critical is its quality not its quantity.

Tables 5 show basic data on Hungary's foreign trade. For much of the 1980s, the structure of trade by region was surprisingly stable. There was a very gradual trend towards a higher trade share with market economies, a slightly higher growth rate of dollar trade than of rouble trade. Since 1988, however, change has been far more rapid, with the (former) CMEA share of Hungary's trade dropping sharply every year, and even more rapidly in 1991: in volume terms, Eastern trade will have fallen by over 60% in 1991. The resulting increase in the market economies' share of Hungary's trade is almost entirely

Table 5(a). Hungary's trade in the 1980s (%)

| | CMEA and economies in transformation | Market economies | | |
		EC	other developed	LDCs
Imports				
1981	52.6	23.8	16.9	6.7
1983	58.0	21.3	15.6	5.1
1985	55.8	21.8	17.5	4.9
1987	53.0	25.1	16.6	5.3
1988	49.3	25.7	18.3	6.7
1989	44.3	29.0	20.7	6.0
1990	36.9	31.0	22.1	10.0
Exports				
1981	59.9	17.4	11.1	11.6
1983	59.4	15.9	11.8	12.9
1985	60.4	15.7	13.3	10.6
1987	56.5	20.1	15.1	8.3
1988	51.2	22.6	17.5	8.7
1989	47.3	24.8	19.3	8.6
1990	37.7	32.2	21.8	8.3

Source: *Külkereskedelmi Statisztikai Évkönyv 1990*, Budapest.

Table 5(b). Trade growth, trade balances and terms of trade in the 1980s

| | Rouble trade | | | | Dollar trade | | | |
	Exp	Imp	T. Bal	T.o.T.	Exp	Imp	T. Bal	T.o.T.
1981	3.8	−3.7	−0.4	−3.9	4.4	5.9	−0.1	2.2
1983	7.9	3.1	−0.5	−2.7	5.3	−1.0	0.6	−2.4
1985	8.3	−0.4	0.4	−0.7	2.5	15.8	0.2	−1.1
1987	1.5	4.0	0.2	0.0	5.0	0.8	−0.3	−0.1
1988	0.4	2.9	0.2	3.3	12.2	−2.8	0.5	1.8
1989	−6.0	−6.9	0.5	3.7	5.0	7.2	0.5	2.2
1990	−26.1	−17.8	0.0	5.5	9.2	1.5	0.9	−1.4

Sources: *Statistical Yearbook 1989*, Budapest, and as Table 5(a).
Notes: Exp and Imp refer to annual growth rates for exports and imports; T. Bal. indicates trade balance (in billion roubles and $ bn.); T.o.T. is the % annual change in terms of trade.

accounted for by a very rapid increase in exports to the EC, accompanied by a rather smaller increase in imports from the EC. Given the trade structure shown in Table 5(c), much of these extra exports to the West must be materials, semi-finished products and spare parts. Hungary's success in reorienting trade towards Western markets has greatly mitigated the impact of the dramatic loss of CMEA markets. In the longer

Table 5(c). Commodity structure of Hungary's trade, 1986 and 1990 (%)

		Energy	Materials, semi-finished, spares	Machinery, vehicles, capital goods	Industrial consumer goods	Food and food industry
Rouble trade						
Imports:	1986	30.9	33.8	18.6	13.1	3.5
	1990	27.4	35.9	14.8	16.9	5.0
Exports:	1986	0.6	22.4	46.1	16.7	14.3
	1990	0.3	20.8	43.9	19.2	15.9
Dollar trade						
Imports:	1986	2.3	59.9	15.6	10.4	11.8
	1990	5.9	52.3	19.5	13.2	9.1
Exports:	1986	3.3	38.9	14.5	16.4	26.9
	1990	3.1	44.0	11.6	15.6	25.7

Source: As Table 5(a).

term Eastern trade should stabilize again, since the countries of the region are natural trading partners producing complementary products (Hughes and Hare, 1991c; but c.f. IMF, 1991, p. 26, which wrongly asserts the opposite view).

Trade with the rouble area in deficit at the start of the 1980s and in modest surplus thereafter, with the terms of trade first declining (as oil price increases came into effect in CMEA trade) and then improving. In 1991, with the transition to dollar payments and world prices in trade with former Eastern partners, a further substantial fall in the terms of trade has occurred. At the same time outstanding rouble balances, particularly with the USSR, need to be converted to dollars. It has been reported (OECD, 1991b) that a rate of $0.92 = R1.00 was agreed between Hungary and the USSR, but the timing of the settlement is still not finalized.

In Western trade, Hungary's terms of trade were declining for much of the 1980s, reflecting changes in energy prices, problems of market access, and increasing pressure on Hungarian firms to export to the West (at a time when Hungarian products were not being modernized very rapidly). Restrictive macroeconomic policies, and significant surpluses on tourism and travel, helped underpin positive dollar trade balances. Nevertheless, servicing the large hard-currency debt has forced the overall current account into deficit in most years, but so far the country has managed to continue to meet its commitments. Table 6 shows external debt, and some indicators of the debt burden. Cohen (1991) argues that Hungary is the most indebted country in Eastern Europe in terms of the real burden imposed, and questions

Table 6. Indicators of debt and the debt burden

	1985	1987	1989	1990
Debt in convertible currencies				
Gross ($ bn.)	13.8	19.6	20.6	21.7
Net ($ bn.)	11.5	18.1	19.4	20.3
Distribution of debt (%)				
Official and guaranteed	13	11	9	—
Unguaranteed banks	55	54	47	—
IMF/BIS/World Bank	8	9	9	—
Other	24	26	35	—
Indicators of debt burden (%)				
Net debt/exports ratio	275	358	302	343
Debt service ratio	58	52	49	65

Source: OECD (1991a).
Note: 1990 data is provisional.

the wisdom of continuing to service the debt. We return to this issue later.

Hungarian living standards are not easy to assess: necessary data on second jobs and income from private businesses is not readily available, and increasingly people have such additional (or alternative) sources of income. But published data still provides a broad guide (see Tables 7).

Table 7(a) shows that real incomes stagnated in the 1980s, and are now declining. For much of the decade pensioners appear to have done well, despite popular belief to the contrary.[8] The change in the structure of outlays since 1985 (Table 7(b)) shows the effect of the new income tax, and increases in other contributions by households. Hence, consumption rose more slowly than incomes; with real income now falling, consumption is now in sharp decline. Finally, notice that household savings out of disposable income are rather low.

Declining living standards not only endanger political stability, but also threaten economic reforms. The new democratic government was forced to raise the state guaranteed minimum income at a time when net real wages were falling steeply. Already wages were burdened with a 53% social insurance contribution (45% from employers, 10% from employees). In July 1991 this was increased by a new unemployment contribution, initially 2% of the wage, rising in January 1992 to 6% (of which 1% is paid by employees).[9]

---

[8] By 1991 net pensions had risen to about 70% of net wages, which is both generous and a heavy burden on the economy. With a low retirement age and very low birth rate, every third voter in Hungary is a pensioner.

[9] The following illustrates the burden on enterprise labour costs. The gross wage is 100. After deductions of 10 (pensions contribution) and 17 (PIT), the net wage is 73. Also the enterprise must pay 43 (social security) and 2 (unemployment contribution).

Table 7(a). Annual change in real incomes, and annual inflation (%)

	Real income growth of			Average inflation
	Workers	Agric. coop. workers	Pensioners	
1975–80	0.7	0.5	5.9	6.3
1980–85	−0.8	−0.8	1.3	6.7
1986	1.9	2.5	1.2	5.3
1987	−0.4	−1.8	0.5	8.5
1988	−4.9	−2.4	0.9	15.7
1989	0.9	−4.3	0.8	17.0
1990	−8.4	—	—	29.7

Source: *Statistical Yearbook 1988* and *Statisztikai Évköny 1989*, Budapest; and as Table 5(a).

Table 7(b). Population income and expenditure (Fts bn., current prices)

	1985		1989	
	Fts bn.	%	Fts bn.	%
Wage income	395.3	48.2	640.5	42.2
Small business income	148.5	18.1	311.8	20.5
Total income from labour	543.8	66.5	952.3	62.7
Social security income	137.3	16.7	257.3	16.9
Other money income	46.5	5.7	119.6	7.9
Non-income receipts	92.6	11.3	189.6	12.5
Total receipts	820.2	100.0	1,518.8	100.0
Small business outlays	95.2	11.6	200.8	13.2
Taxes & social security payments	49.5	6.0	183.7	12.1
Other deductions from income	84.7	10.3	236.9	15.6
Net disposable income	590.8	72.0	897.4	59.1
Purchased consumption	509.6	62.1	791.2	52.1
Housing investment	43.0	5.2	68.6	4.5
Monetary savings	38.2	4.7	37.6	2.5

Source: *Statisztikai Évkönyv 1989, 1990*, Budapest.

Living standards depend both on wages and consumer prices. Increases in the latter have of course been exacerbated by price liberalization and subsidy reduction. So far in 1991, inflation (about 35%) has remained below the planned and expected level (about 38%), and in some areas firms are unable to pass on cost increases to their customers as in the past. Since many of the most significant subsidies have now been removed, inflation may begin to decline from 1991 onwards. The level of subsidies was still rising as recently as 1987. Since then both consumer and producer subsidies have fallen back sharply. Thus

Table 8. Government income and expenditure (Fts bn., current prices)

	1985	1987	1989	1990
TOTAL INCOME, of which:	632.8	760.6	1,063.7	1,279.0
Payments by enterprises	407.5	469.4	443.2	488.7
Taxes on consumption	92.2	122.3	230.7	255.0
Payments by the population, of which:	61.5	79.3	209.4	248.9
Personal income tax	—	—	94.2	126.8
Social security	33.6	42.8	67.4	84.2
Payments by budget supported organizations	51.0	63.7	138.8	181.0
International and other income	20.6	25.9	41.6	105.4
TOTAL EXPENDITURE, of which:	646.1	795.0	1,112.4	1,279.5
Investment outlays	82.4	99.9	115.5	125.3
Purchases by budget supported organizations of which:	204.9	242.7	368.5	541.4
Health	27.4	32.7	59.3	—
Education	43.2	49.6	90.1	—
Defence	37.6	45.4	62.0	—
Transfers:				
Subsidies to enterprises	119.1	150.7	115.7	98.2
Consumer price subsidies	50.2	66.7	44.1	36.8
Social security outlays	204.9	242.7	386.5	293.0
Debt service and other international outlays	58.5	80.3	181.1	185.0
GOVERNMENT SURPLUS	−13.8	−34.4	−48.7	−0.7
GDP	1,033.7	1,226.4	1,706.0	2,079.0
Government purchases/GDP (%)	27.8	27.9	29.4	32.1
Domestic transfers/GDP (%)	36.2	37.5	32.0	20.6

Sources: *Statisztikai Évkönyv 1989, Ministry of Finance Budget Report.*

although subsidy reductions are being phased over several years, and started quite slowly, they are now being pursued with some vigour.

Government expenditure on social security grew much faster than other spending until 1990. Pensioners became more numerous, pensions more generous, and more recently unemployment has increased. Even so, total transfers as a proportion of GDP are slowly declining. Table 8 sets out the government accounts in recent years. There has usually been a modest deficit, reaching 2.9% of GDP in 1989, but falling almost to zero in 1990. Table 8 indicates that the budget is pretty well under control; taking account of off-budget liabilities (e.g. housing finance, social security, local authorities), the picture is less satisfactory.

Finally, we turn to the labour market (see Tables 9). Table 9(a) shows the main labour force trends. With a static population, there has been a small fall in the economically active population. Over three-quarters

Table 9(a). The labour market in Hungary

	1976	1981	1988	1989
Population (million)	10.6	10.7	10.6	10.6
Population of working age	6.2	6.1	6.1	6.1
Inactive, of working age	1.4	1.3	1.3	1.4
Economically active: Men	2.9	2.8	2.6	2.6
Women	2.2	2.3	2.2	2.2

Source: *Statisztikai Évkönyv, 1989,* Budapest.

Table 9(b). Employment and productivity growth by sector

	1989 employment		Productivity growth 1980–89 (% p.a.)
	% of 1980	000s	
All industry	86	1,356	3.27
Mining	82	93	1.09
Electricity	112	42	1.37
Metallurgy	81	72	3.81
Engineering	86	442	4.58
Building materials	83	61	3.13
Chemicals	102	110	1.59
Other, light	79	332	3.18
Food	101	203	1.36
Construction	82	259	0.83
Agriculture	83	627	4.37
Forestry	101	49	
Transport	88	281	
Post and telecoms	114	76	
Domestic trade	94	416	
Foreign trade		24	
Water supply	102	78	
Other material branches		44	
Material branches – total		3,211	
Non-material branches		1,249	
TOTAL		4,460	

Source: *Statisztikai Évkönyv 1989*, Budapest.

of the fall since 1981 is accounted for by men; women's participation fell less than 2%.

Table 9(b) shows changes in the structure of employment. Employment in industry fell by 14% between 1980 and 1989. Despite productivity improvements, output stagnated. The same conclusion applied at sectoral level: the largest employment declines were in the sectors with the fastest productivity growth.

Table 9(c). Unemployment and vacancies (thousands)

	1989	1990	1990II	1990III	1990IV	1991I	1991II
Unemployed:							
Men	7.3	12.1	21.6	33.1	53.4	82.5	118.5
Women	4.8	8.3	14.8	23.2	35.9	48.2	73.7
Total	12.1	20.4	36.4	55.3	89.3	130.7	192.2
People seeking work					66.3	136.5	185.5
Reported vacancies					17.2	13.6	14.9

Source: *Statisztikai Havi Közlemenyek*.
Note: Data on those seeking work and reported vacancies in 1990IV is in fact for November 1990.

Table 9(c) shows unemployment. Officially almost unknown before 1989, initially it rose slowly, but is now rising at about 20,000 per month; by Autumn 1991, it reached 6.6% of the labour force. Unemployment 'within the factory' was always a major problem in Hungary and is coming out into the open. Rapid structural change cannot occur without an accompanying increase in unemployment, occurring as a result of natural labour turnover.

The current economic situation in Hungary (in late-1991) can be summed up as mixed. GDP for 1991 is expected to fall by over 5%; industrial output in June 1991 was only 76% of the level in June 1990 (a fall of 6.4% in energy, 23.3% in basic material production, and 28.1% in manufacturing). Industrial productivity is now declining, while gross industrial wages are just keeping up with consumer prices (hence, with the new income tax, net wages are down). Inflation was 36% (Jan–June 1991, compared with the same period in 1990), but public sector wages were limited to a 20% increase in 1991, a policy which may prove unsustainable. Nevertheless, it is clear living standards will have fallen again in 1991.

In the first half of 1991, Hungary's trade with other Eastern European countries was only 22% of its imports and 20% of its exports. Trade with developed market economies continued to grow, and the current account of the balance of payments was better than expected. But servicing the external debt remains a severe burden.

Domestically, the government was, as expected, in deficit but only within the forecast limits. Monetary policy, too, was continuing along cautious lines, though, as elsewhere in Eastern Europe, this was partly undermined by unplanned inter-enterprise lending and delayed tax payments and social security contributions. The Forint exchange rate against the major Western currencies has been adjusted to maintain adequate competitiveness (see OECD, 1991b).

4. Macroeconomic reforms

The gevernment's economic strategy has short, medium and long-term components, summarized in Table 10. In the long run, the aim is preparation for EC entry. Much of the medium-term policy is micro-economic and structural, including development of institutions. Short-term policy is more conventionally macroeconomic.

The role of macroeconomic policy is to maintain a suitable balance between tax revenues and government expenditure; to achieve a sufficient trade surplus to service the debt and raise adequate new foreign capital; and to control inflation. As elsewhere in Eastern Europe, until a market economy and its accompanying institutions are fully established, some aspects of macro policy may not function as in a Western textbook.

In the absence of a major domestic market for government securities, monetary policy is necessarily closely tied to the government deficit: deficits tend to be monetized. Hence, it is more than usually important for Hungary both to control public spending and to ensure adequate tax revenues, and to keep the two roughly in balance. Even after a bond market does develop, large government deficits will remain undesirable. Savings and credit will increasingly be needed for private investment. Such government discipline has not been encouraged by the practice of allowing the government to pay extremely subsidized rates of interest on its own debt. Nevertheless, Hungary's tax system is already modernized, revenues remain strong even in the present recession, and public spending is under control. Financial discipline may further be enhanced by the central banking law currently before Parliament.

Inflation is influenced both by monetary policy and the market conditions in which firms find themselves. In the past, firms were either told what prices they could set, or were presented with strict rules based on cost-plus pricing, combined with wage controls and a stiff tax on wage increases. Now substantial liberalization of prices and imports has removed most central control of prices, while the removal of subsidies and the switch to world prices in Eastern trade are raising many domestic prices relative to the wage. Hence, there is strong pressure for money wages to rise in order to maintain real wages, or stem their decline. Many SOEs are unwilling or unable to resist such pressure. This is why the tax on wage increases is still needed, though for private firms (including SOEs now privatized) it will not be applied. Unfortunately, the government is bowing to pressure from firms to rescind the tax, which may disappear early in 1992, thereby removing one anchor on inflation.

Table 10. Government policy in Hungary

Horizon	Aim	Policy
Short-run	Macro-economic balance	Balancing the budget; tight money; competitive real exchange rate; continue debt service
	Liberalization	Further subsidy reductions and removals; relax import restrictions; but new privileges emerge
	EC Association	Conclude negotiations for better market access; agreement signed December 1991
Medium-run	Institutional development	Develop banks, insurance, pension funds, bond and equity markets. Competition policy (where plans still unclear)
	Ownership change	Privatization of small business, large firms, land, housing; restitution/compensation of ex-owners (mainly farmers, small business)
	Labour market reform	Develop new trade union structures, new wage bargaining arrangements
	Prepare for EC membership	Adopt EC guidelines, policies (e.g. in accounting) from 1992
Long-run	Join the EC	No specific policies on this yet. Depends on Hungary's performance in next decade

Note: On the EC, see Angresano and Sinkovics (1991).

1991 inflation, expected to be 38%, was in fact 35% and the government now projects a fall to 20–25% in 1992, falling gradually in later years. This is plausible given that remaining subsidies will disappear slowly (no large official source of sharp price increases), provided wage controls hold (now less likely than before) and monetary policy is tough. Here the government faces a difficult dilemma. Sooner or later it will have to let tight credit conditions force firms into bankruptcy; only then will there be appropriate incentives to resist wage increases which firms cannot afford. Yet the government is understandably nervous about increasing unemployment any faster.

In the past, the Hungarian government relaxed domestic constraints by borrowing abroad. Ostensibly, this was for investment which would subsequently yield additional (hard currency) export earnings, but in the event much of the investment proved unprofitable (though less disastrously so than in Poland). Such borrowing remains possible provided Hungary can run trade surpluses to service both old debt and new borrowing. Exchange rate policy is therefore to maintain a low real value of the Forint, though over the last two years nominal depreciation has not fully offset high Hungarian inflation. Thus there has been a small real appreciation, though from a low initial real level.

Table 11. Two-sector model of Hungary: summary of results

	Consumption (% of 1988)	Trade surplus (Fts bn.)	Industry output (% of 1988)	Other output (% of 1988)
Exports constant	0.95	0.51	0.98	0.97
	0.90	14.17	0.96	0.94
	0.85	27.84	0.93	0.91
	0.80	41.51	0.91	0.88
Exports down 10%	1·00	−49.45	0.96	0.98
	0.95	−35.78	0.94	0.95
	0.90	−22.11	0.91	0.92
	0.85	−8.45	0.89	0.89
	0.80	5.22	0.87	0.86
Exports up 10%	1.00	23.13	1.04	1.02
	0.95	36.80	1.02	0.99
	0.90	50.46	1.00	0.96
	0.85	64.13	0.98	0.93
	0.80	77.80	0.95	0.91

Source: Own calculations, based on 1988 input–output table for Hungary.

This exchange rate policy has a number of advantages. First, a highly competitive exchange rate smooths the transition, giving many domestic firms time to adjust to new market conditions. Second, the more recent real appreciation means that the competition faced by many firms is slowly intensifying. Third, the profitability of exports has generated a sustained, export-led boom, whose timing could scarcely be better for Hungary.

Though stimulating trade through a low real exchange rate, the debt burden also has adverse effects. In particular, it influences both the extent to which real incomes must fall during the transition and the rate at which resources can be switched into the domestic investment, essential for long-run economic growth. Since these are crucial issues, we report some simple calculations based on a two-sector model (industry, everything else) of the economy, derived the 1988 input–output table. On the assumption of constant import coefficients both in intermediate demand and in final demand, and a constant exchange rate, some tradeoffs between domestic consumption and the trade balance can be calculated. The main results are presented in Table 11.

In reading Table 11, note that the exchange rate was about Fts 50/$1 in 1988, and Hungary's debt service is about $2 bn. a year in interest and about the same again in repayment of principal (though the latter may be financed by new loans). The simple message is that substantial trade surpluses (to service debt) must generally be accompanied by substantial declines in consumption. Thus unless Hungary's exports rise remarkably or the country receives substantial debt relief, drastic falls in living standards are almost inevitable, raising serious political questions about the viability of the government. This is simply a legacy of the past. It is not the result of the new reform programme. But if it is not somehow resolved, the debt burden will certainly delay the time when Hungary's impatient consumers start to see the benefits of the transition.

5. Microeconomic reforms

The most important areas for microeconomic reform are privatization, industrial policy, the capital markets and the labour market. Although desirable and necessary steps towards a market economy, these reforms have not yet had a dramatic effect on resource allocation. There are three reasons.

First, former distortions, though pervasive, were less serious than in other Eastern European countries. Hence, gradual removal or reduction of distortions has a smaller effect in Hungary than elsewhere, especially since many firms had begun adjustment before the present government came to power. Second, Hungary's exchange rate, grossly undervalued on any reasonable PPP basis, has sheltered domestic firms from import competition, preserving employment but delaying structural adjustment. Third, the failure to break up the large monopolies and cartels in Hungary has enabled many firms to exploit their market position to the disadvantage of their customers (high prices) and their employees (unemployment). In time, this should be alleviated by imports, joint ventures and other forms of new entry, and the actions of the competition office (when it finally discovers its proper role). But the process is likely to be slow.

Privatization of the overextended state sector is difficult, both technically and politically. Lack of relevant technical skills (asset valuation, preparation and auditing of company annual reports, marketing, legal services), and the overloading and potential for corruption (e.g. via lobbying) of privatization agencies make it inevitable that there will be serious losses in the process. Will Hungary's badly managed operation lead to unnecessary waste and damage? A more desirable process may prove infeasible because various lobbies will fight to preserve their wealth and power.

In the early stages, entrusting privatization to the managers gave rise to many dubious practices. Managers could use their own funds to establish a limited liability company (under Hungary's enterprise law of 1988 or the 1989 transformation law), which then bought shares in the original SOE in return for bonds. The state lost any rights of managerial control and became entitled only to a low interest rate bond of the firm. A second device was a joint venture, again allowing assets of the SOE to be transferred to the new business at an unduly low price. By way of 'thanks', the foreign partner (behind whom there was often hard currency already in Hungarian ownership, deposited in the West) not merely retained the manager, it often raised his income substantially (for a detailed analysis of the early Hungarian privatization, see Grosfeld and Hare, 1991).

These problems aside, Hungary has made much progress in privatization. Institutionally, it has a State Property Agency (SPA) to supervise the process, and has decided generally to favour a fairly conventional approach to privatization: conversion of firms to joint stock companies, then sale of shares (by private bargain with a single buyer or by public offering). It does not plan any form of free distribution of shares or vouchers as envisaged in Poland and Czechoslovakia (c.f. the arguments favouring free distribution in Blanchard *et al.*, 1991; and those against in McKinnon, 1991), though some shares will be assigned to pension funds and other financial intermediaries as part of their initial capital. Banks are now becoming major shareholders, replacing debt with equity in their portfolios; employees, too, may receive up to 20% of the equity in many firms, financed by low-interest credits. Some shares will also be assigned to local authorities, and firms providing local services will be transferred to local authority ownership. Small businesses are being privatized quickly, through sale or lease (many have been leased since the early 1980s); for larger firms the process will be slower.

Of Hungary's 200 largest firms, 34 had been transformed into limited liability or joint stock companies by early 1991 (reported in *Figyelö*, 4.7.91), and such changes were gathering pace. An SPA report to Parliament indicated that by mid-1991 privatization had already affected 2,200 firms with a book value of Fts 1,890 bn. (*Figyelö*, 11.7.91). Many cases were incomplete, but the foundation for faster privatization has now been laid.

The government intends to privatize about half the existing state assets, including most of industry, within about three years. For the larger firms, the SPA itself will offer many to the market in a series of blocks (10–20 firms in a block). For others, firms themselves will be free to make their own proposals, and potential buyers (foreign and domestic) may submit proposals to the SPA which may agree to privatize even without the consent of the SOE (not unlike a hostile takeover in the West).

The programme is ambitious and one must question both its administrative demands and the capacity of domestic and foreign capital markets to fund it. It may yet prove necessary virtually to give away many of the firms. Despite that, the 1991 budget envisaged that privatization would provide state revenues of at least Fts 20 bn. (some estimates were as high as Fts 50 bn.). But a preliminary report of the 1992 budget (*Figyelö*, 31.10.91) suggests that it will be zero in 1991 and only Fts 20 bn. in 1992. Unsurprisingly, the Finance Ministry is considering ways of accelerating privatization.

Several problems require very careful treatment. These include property restitution to former owners (either physical return of original assets, or financial compensation), the issue of enterprise and bank balance sheets and the treatment of outstanding debts, the ownership and management structure of newly privatized firms, and fiscal aspects of privatization (a smaller concern in Hungary than in the other Eastern European countries).

Restitution of land to cooperative farm members or other former owners was virtually the only policy of the Smallholders Party (a small party in the governing coalition). Early legislation to implement this policy was rejected by Hungary's constitutional court on the grounds that it discriminated between different types of asset, and between different economic agents. The version finally passed by the Parliament met these points, making restitution (usually in the form of financial compensation) possible for all assets nationalized after 8 June 1949. In practice, this applies to land and small business: most larger businesses had been nationalized before 1949. Property is also being returned to the church. Although claims will take some time to settle, it is unlikely that this issue will greatly delay Hungary's privatization.

From the former system many firms carry over large burdens of debt which now they cannot service. Correspondingly, the main commercial banks have large amounts of virtually worthless loans on their balance sheets. No private owner will take on such debt; as enterprises are prepared for privatization, much will have to be written off. For the banks, assets cannot simply be written off without also writing down deposits, likely to be unacceptable. It is more likely that bank assets will be replaced either by equity in certain firms, by public debt, or by rights to shares in future privatizations.

Although there is a strong impetus towards the market in Hungary, there is little recognition yet that markets themselves, and some firms within them, require regulation. This is partly a reaction to years of excessive state control, now perceived as damaging, partly because the new Competition Office has not yet worked out what to do or how to do it (here technical assistance is useful), partly because those firms most obviously requiring regulation are still SOEs and likely to remain so for some time. What is important is to design a suitable institutional framework and to choose sensible instruments: in this respect, the experience of the UK and several other Western countries can be very helpful for Hungary.

Monopoly remains a problem for two reasons. First, the economy is too small to allow both scale economies and many firms; for this foreign competition is needed to enlarge the market. This was limited under the CMEA and, even since liberalization, remains hampered by the undervalued rate needed for debt service, by high customs duties, and by wholesale and retail monopolies. Second, many artificial monopolies were created under central planning to simplify state management and provide covert channels for redistribution of income. Partial liberaliz-ation has thus given monopolies the opportunity to set very high prices, an opportunity they have taken.

Some large SOEs have been broken up into smaller units, but in practice there has been no effective way to prevent the formation of informal cartels (a point acknowledged by Ferenc Vissi, head of the Competition Office). The legal, technical, informational and political conditions to regulate monopoly and encourage competition are not yet present. In the immediate future, greater competition is more likely to be a consequence of growing competition from abroad.

As this occurs, it will soon become clear which sectors and/or enter-prises can remain viable and compete effectively in world markets. Some indication of this at a sectoral level is provided in Hughes and Hare (1991a, b), which uses 1988 input–output data and information on the ratios between world prices and domestic prices to rank industries according to their profitability at world market prices.

In the short term, firms which might be viable in the longer term could encounter liquidity problems, while others basically unable to compete nevertheless survive because they have accumulated assets from the subsidies received in the past. Hence, it is vital that the government and/or the banks be guided by a clear view about the *long-term* prospects of any given firm, when deciding whether to extend further credit. This raises many issues, mainly about the functioning of the capital markets. We begin with banks.

Throughout Eastern Europe priorities are extensive retraining of bank staff (especially those in lending departments), computerization, and development of the most basic services taken for granted in the West. Both firms and banks need to introduce Western accounting conventions for business. In Hungary, new accounting systems based on EC directives come into effect in January 1992, but have already been criticized for failing to make any provisions for inflation accounting.

The financial sector needs both institutional and product develop-ment. Hungary still has to develop adequate private pension funds, and many new forms of insurance contract. These developments take time, but will help provide essential depth to a capital market that, banks aside, comprises only a limited bond market and a tiny equity market. The former, opened in 1982, basically collapsed when inflation accelerated in the late 1980s; the latter, opened in 1990, is very volatile, and as yet does little business. As elsewhere in Eastern Europe, at this stage a stock market is largely symbolic. But it is also dangerous: its unavoidable volatility is bound to undermine domestic investors' confidence in the equity market.

Finally, a few remarks on the labour market. The old mechanisms for determining wages (including the tax on wage increases) are disappearing rapidly. What is not clear is what will replace them: trade unions are weak and, as unemployment climbs, their bargaining power is steadily eroded. Their position is complicated by the existence of several competing organizations in many firms, and by the fact that legal protections and privileges for the old, communist-dominated unions have not yet been removed (or extended to the new unions). Hence, there are no longer any clear rules as to who should be recognized in wage bargaining at enterprise level. In practice, managers in the non-privatized firms are weak, and sometimes dominated by the Workers' Councils; unions are also weak.

The strongest demand from workers is usually for wage increases to match inflation. Interestingly, in the first half of 1991, those branches or firms which offered the largest wage increases were those in the weakest financial position, probably because they expected to go into liquidation and wanted to put their workers in a favourable position (redundancy payments, unemployment compensation and pensions all depend on the final wage). Such adverse incentives can be removed only by amending the social security laws.

6. Social and political issues: conclusions

To assess Hungary's economic prospects, we must understand the legacy of the old system, especially its impact on the quality and availability of manpower, and on the country's political life (Csaba, 1990). The old system wasted and even damaged human resources. Cultural life was largely nationalized, and traditional career paths for the well-educated were subject to new forms of 'selection' based on social origin, political conformity, or personal contacts with the leadership. Objective and open assessments of the quality of intellectual work were rare. Thus human capital, already scarce because of underinvestment in so-called non-productive sectors like education, was used inefficiently. Censorship and secrecy compounded the problem. In addition, many people preferred the 'brain-drain' to the 'brain-wash': during 1963–88, net emigration was 121,000, of whom 71,000 left illegally.

In purely quantitative terms the educational system did show results, but the quality of the intellectual elite was eroded. The sorts of knowledge and skill required to operate a market economy and democratic political institutions become extremely scarce. Most people found themselves working longer and longer hours (mainly in the second economy) simply to maintain their living standards.

Such a legacy helps explain several political and institutional obstacles to a smooth path of reform. The prevailing intellectual confusion reveals itself in a confused constitution which allows the constitutional court, asserting its law-making powers, to block government actions; in the infrequent elections;[10] in the apparent inability of the government to take strong decisions and stick to them, because of its worries about holding together the present coalition; the freezing of a political structure disproportionately favouring the present large parties for the next four years, though in society at large enormous changes are expected and desired.

The damaging effects of state paternalism can still be seen.[11] Many enterprises and many individuals still look to the state for solutions to their problems, unable to accept that the state, unlike Santa Claus, can only give what it has taken. Such illusions are even reinforced by the present government, as for instance when, in connection with the proposed World Exhibition in Budapest, it forgets that provision of state funds and credits for that project must entail higher taxes, interest rates and unemployment in other areas.

The egalitarianism practised in many spheres (despite numerous privileges of the apparatus) distorts people's understanding of many economic matters. Thus workers believe (even more than before) that factories rightfully belong to them, that they should get free shares in their enterprises and have the right to manage them (though fortunately these pressures are weaker than in Poland and the CSFR). Similarly, those who rent flats are convinced that they should become their owners, without any payment. Debtors are less and less inclined to service their debts, and primitive notions of a general hostility to interest payments are becoming widespread again.[12] More and more allegedly needy people, or people requiring compensation, come forward with

---

[10] The possibility of recalling parliamentary representatives has been abolished, the scope for voting for individuals has been drastically reduced in favour of party lists, voting for different bodies has been synchronized and the president is elected indirectly. The present structure of representation will be unchanged for four years (from 1990).

[11] See Kornai (1980) on paternalism and its relation to shortages.

[12] More and more credits now bear negative real interest rates, while the state, by imposing a 20% tax on deposit interest and dividend income, is effectively imposing an 8% wealth tax on savers.

demands, and absurd subsidies surpass even what the former communist government would have accepted.

Given its inexperience, it is not surprising that the government's approach to many problems is evolving, and that its proposals remain to be fully developed. Despite the dangers discussed above, there are many positive features in Hungary today. Twenty years of market-oriented reforms, including a decade of legal private business, have accustomed the population to varying prices, to the idea of profit as a desirable performance indicator, to the idea of private initiative (despite the above remarks on state paternalism). In all these crucial respects, Hungary is unique in Eastern Europe. This is why everyone is convinced that, despite present difficulties, there can be no going back to the old centralized model. If anything Hungarians are now impatient with government indecision (often reflecting clashes between different interest groups), rather than reluctant to accept change.

Thus, of the former communist states of Eastern Europe, Hungary is now best placed to carry through a successful transition to some form of market economy. Completing this transition may take up to two generations. All one can hope for in the next decade is to set the country moving in the right direction, with a broad consensus that this direction is correct, and with at least the first signs that the economy is starting to recover from the severe shock and dislocations occasioned by the early stages of the transition.

Could or should Hungary attempt to achieve the transition more rapidly? In our view it should not. Larger disturbances to production would impose even greater burdens on the living standards of the present generation, burdens which the world's capital markets would do nothing to alleviate, especially in a country which already has an enormous external debt. Nor is it obvious those who attempt a more rapid transition than Hungary will in fact succeed: the sheer complexity of the whole process sets definite limits upon its feasible pace. Although proceeding in a step-by-step manner, Hungary may be close to the maximum realistic speed of transition.

Can the other countries of Eastern Europe learn from Hungary's gradualist approach? Since none of them has the option of repeating Hungary's 20 years of market-oriented reforms, the answer can only be a qualified 'yes'. Yet there are some useful lessons. One is the central importance of tax reform (which Hungary introduced in 1988 as a substitute for more comprehensive reforms and under pressure from international organizations). Government revenues are fragile during the early stages of transition, a time when they must be especially secure. Poland and the CSFR have yet to implement modern tax reforms; in the former this has already led to large government deficits once again.

Table 12. Supporting Hungary's transition

Action by Hungarian Government	
Informational measures	Develop accounting and business information systems; small business advisory services; legal advice on business
Market regulation	Protection of quality and standards, consumer and credit protection; action against cartels; financial discipline
Strengthening tax collection	Remove exemptions, clarify rules, speed up collection
Reduce social subsidies	Restrict to individual cases of proven need; greater use of credits (e.g. for education)
Encourage savings	Develop pension funds, life insurance. Support for individuals in buying bonds and shares
Privatization	Continue privatizing as fast as possible; encourage new businesses; support domestic and foreign investors
Financial system development	Train staff, improve regulation, restructure balance sheets and move to commercial lending; support loans for small firms
Labour market reforms	Improve training, retraining, education; clarify unions' role; develop wage regulation system

Actions by external agencies	
Technical assistance	EC and individual government programmes in operation or being considered
Transitional support	Support for e.g. the unemployed to reduce the burden on the budget or ease the pain of adjustment; the case for such support is not strong
Debt relief	Controversial. Hungary has maintained debt service but the burden is severe. Unilateral relief from creditors would help considerably
Direct foreign investment	Although discouraged by high debt, has developed well and far higher than elsewhere in the region; needed to bring in technology and management
Market access	EC still restricts access for food, textiles, steel and other items. Some relaxation under the Association Agreement but progress is slow. For Hungary the most important form of 'aid'

A second lesson is that massive external debt need not be as crippling as it appeared in Poland. Of course it imposes immense costs, but an economy capable of responding more effectively to market signals can find ways of adapting to the constraints of its debt burden, as with Hungary's exceptionally good trade performance in 1991, despite the collapse of USSR trade. Even the old SOEs, which still produce most of Hungary's output, have adapted to the market in ways, and at a speed, previously judged impossible. Other lessons involve the stability of the economic 'rules of the game', the rules about ownership change (which in Hungary alone are not enshrined in a single privatization law), and exchange rate and monetary policy. We lack the space for a detailed discussion, and several of Hungary's policies are effective precisely because of its past history of reform; the same policies might be less effective elsewhere. Hence, the qualified 'yes'.

Our analysis shows that gradual transition is both feasible and desirable for Hungary provided that the country receives substantial help with its external debt and in its trading links with the EC. There will not be a 'big-bang' in Hungary, essentially because there is no need for it, but with the help of continuing, strong external pressure on the government, and substantial technical assistance, there will be a successful transition.

What is being done by the government and other agencies in Hungary, and what external agencies can do, are summarized in Table 12, which brings together many of the points discussed more fully above. One final, but crucial point: all economic agents in Hungary expect that transition to come about. Consequently, provided that existing policies are substantially maintained, these expectations will not be disappointed. Even in Hungary the acceleration of reform, following two decades at a more sedate pace, is a shock to those who believed that their privileged positions would always be protected (e.g. members of the former elite). But nobody seriously believes that the government, for all its faults, will lose its nerve and try to stop the transformation!

Discussion

Petr Aven
International Institute for Applied Systems Analysis, Vienna

The gradualism of the Hungarian reform programme had the consequence that there was no fundamental questioning of the main feature of a centrally planned economy: the responsibility of the state for the delivery of goods to the market. Although there was a significant increase in the autonomy of enterprises, their freedom was constrained by a system of *ad hoc* taxes and prices and by static control over the nomination of managers. Labour and capital markets were very underdeveloped.

The system had the advantage of stability, though social peace was partly due to the memory of 1956. The main difference between the Hungarian reform process after 1968 and the USSR reforms after 1985 was that the former saw the consolidation of the political leadership while the latter saw the complete collapse of the traditional administrative structures (including the Communist Party)

Social peace and stability had their price. Although the national economy became more efficient, political constraints made certain desirable changes infeasible. The most important was decisive privatization. This bias seems to be reflected in the authors' own discussion. According to them, spontaneous privatization is 'unfair' and gives unreasonable privileges to the old nomenclatura. But economic efficiency has nothing to do with fairness. Only with substantial managerial cooperation will it be possible for auditors to obtain proper information on the value of enterprises, and for outside investors to evaluate their worth. The need for rapid privatization means that concerns about fairness are a serious obstacle to reform. In fact (and unlike in Czechoslovakia and the former USSR) there is a strong case for saying tht the appointment of enterprise managers owed more to ability than to political orthodoxy. The tradeoff between fairness and efficiency in these circumstances may not even be very high.

Fairness comes up again when we consider the question of debt, bearing in mind the change in political regime. Debts were incurred mainly by the former communist regime, were spent without the approval of the population and have now to be repaid by the democratically elected government. Is this fair? Since the burden of debt may threaten the whole reform process, efficiency as well as equity considerations militate in favour of debt relief.

Gábor Oblath
Kopint-Datorg, Budapest

I like the paper by Paul Hare and Tamás Révész for two reasons. First, it provides a comprehensive, accurate and balanced overview of Hungary's past and present economic situation, while pointing to the major challenges the country has to face in the coming years. Second, I fundamentally agree with the basic message of the paper: Hungary does not need a 'big-bang'.

Hungary differs from the other East European countries in two main ways. First, it has a long history of economic reforms. These have been limited in many respects and rightly criticized for having been half-hearted. However, it cannot be questioned that they went a long way towards establishing the institutional framework of a market economy. Second, relatively high living standards have been achieved, at least in comparison to those of its neighbours. For example, over the last decade there have never been signs of a serious 'monetary overhang'; consumer goods were generally available. Therefore, unlike in Poland, Rumania or Bulgaria before the 'big-bangs', Hungarian households have a lot to lose: the population could not be persuaded that things are so terribly bad that very serious short-run sacrifices have to be made in order to improve the general prospects of the economy. To be more precise: people in Hungary have undergone a significant decline in living standards as well as a sharp increase in unemployment in recent years. But these developments are related to exogenous (external) shocks, rather than to bangs designed by policy-makers.

There are a number of looming future difficulties. First, the growing budget deficit is becoming a major macroeconomic problem. The over-spending of the government exceeds the targets for 1991; the deficit is very likely to increase in 1992. This is because tax revenues are likely to fall, partly due to the recession, partly as a result of increasing tax evasion of the private sector (at a time when privatization is to accelerate). Meanwhile expenditures related to establishing the social safety-net as well as the expansion in unemployment benefits are certain to lead to a significant growth in the outlays of the government.

The second main problem is the exchange rate. Imports have been almost totally liberalized in a relatively short time span (since 1989) without the tariffication of previous explicit and implicit quantitative restrictions. This fact should have called for a real devaluation of the Hungarian currency. The switch-over from a clearing arrangement among Eastern European countries to hard currency payments would also have required a real devaluation of the domestic currency, since reorientating exports to Western markets entails additional costs. However, exchange rate policy since 1989 has resulted in a real appreci-ation of the domestic currency that is clearly unsustainable.

External debt is the third major problem. But while debt relief might be very welcome if offered by foreign creditors, it would be very dangerous for the government to give the impression that it is less than fully committed to repaying its debts. In the short run there is no difficulty in servicing them. This is mainly due to the much larger than anticipated inflow of foreign money and investment into the country. Although it is not clear whether this inflow is only transitory or a sustainable trend, at this point any explicit change in the country's debt strategy would probably lead to a temporary halt in the interest of private investors in the country.

The Hungarian economy is in a very fragile position. It can enter into a virtuous, or a vicious, circle. If keeping out of the war on the borders of the country is possible, if foreign investment continues to flow at least at the present scale and if getting public finance under control is feasible, then prospects involving a recovery and sustained economic growth accompanied by the deceleration of inflation are by no means unrealistic.

On the other hand, the possibility of a vicious circle of declining production and increasing inflation cannot be ruled out either. Which of these prospects is realized may depend as much on good luck as on good management.

Hans-Werner Sinn
University of Munich (CES) and NBER

There was an old communist joke to the effect that Poland had the longest queues, East Germany the most impressive statistics and Hungary the highest living standards. There was a lot of truth in it – despite the problem of external debt and the usual problems of socialist countries, over the last 20 years Hungary has been a success story. Below the surface of the communist state, privatization advanced considerably in important sectors of the economy, and there is exceptional prosperity not caught by any statistics, which is clearly visible to an observant visitor.

Paul Hare and Tamás Révész give an impressive account of the success story. In the Introduction the authors say: 'Hungary has preferred a gradualist, step-by-step approach to a big-bang approach. . . . Our aim in this paper is to justify that conclusion'. This is a strong and clear view, but it is stated rather than argued. How might we assess the case for and against a big-bang?

This year's Nobel Prize winner Ronald Coase made what was in effect a very strong case for a big-bang. You have to establish property rights quickly; how you do it is of secondary importance. Well-defined property rights and a firm legal framework that gives investors and other market agents reliable expectations for the future are essential for recovery and efficiency. Another argument is more political. Now, with the collapse of communism and the expulsion of a foreign occupying force, people's relief is so great that they are willing to sacrifice consumption and to tolerate hardship. Wise politicians know that this tolerance will not last for ever.

It may be feared that the big-bang approach overlooks the transactions costs of the transition to a market economy and enforces more rapid structural change than is advisable on efficiency grounds. I do not believe this fear is justified. Fast privatization and political reform do not necessarily mean fast structural change. If it is efficient to continue operating with the old structures in the transition phase until enough new plants are available, then this will also be profitable in a market environment. I have no particular reason to mistrust the invisible hand's ability to optimize the speed of transition. However, there are many reasons to mistrust the ability of the political decision-making process to do so.

The only important argument for a gradualist approach is the extreme change in income distribution which a big-bang brings about. This change has an intersectoral and an intertemporal dimension. As to the former, many people will lose their jobs and become poor, while others may become extremely rich. Since the overall cake is growing, this problem can be overcome by an active redistribution of incomes and property rights. These problems have been apparent even with Hungary's gradualist approach. The politicians have reacted by introducing progressive income taxation at an early stage, and by attempting to emphasize justice and fairness in the privatization process. The more difficult distribution problem is the intertemporal one. The faster the reform, the larger the consumption loss the current generation has to accept. When this generation's tolerance of such a loss is limited the speed of adjustment chosen by the market process may be larger than is politically tolerable.

In principle, the current generation's liquidity problem could be overcome by borrowing for consumption and shifting some of the burden of transition to future generations. However, in Hungary's case, the scope for such a policy is at present limited. Hungary has already a debt/GDP ratio that parallels that of highly indebted developing countries. This should encourage the West to help by significantly expanding its credit lines. Generous consumption loans for the Hungarians may help increase the speed of transition to a market economy and be strictly welfare-improving.

It is interesting to compare Hungary's transition with that of East Germany. Hungary has definitely been wiser about the restitution of old property rights. As in East Germany people whose property was expropriated after 1949 have a right to restitution, and also as in East Germany, this rule covers only a minor part of the expropriations that have occurred. Large-scale industry was nationalized before 1949. However, unlike in Germany, there is no restitution in kind in the sense that the previous owners are given back the same properties they lost. Typically they will receive cash or vouchers, and if they receive compensation in kind, they will receive similar, but not the same properties. From an efficiency perspective this is a very big advantage because disputes over property rights will not inhibit investment.

However, Hungary shares with Germany the problems posed by the attempt to sell state-owned assets in the market place. In the absence of a significant monetary overhang, domestic residents cannot afford to pay market prices unless sales of assets are used to cover the budget deficit. But this method cannot be quick. The Hungarian government has made use of this possibility by financing the budget deficit with money creation and then absorbing the money by selling state-owned assets. The policy is extremely slow, because the budget deficit is a flow while the assest to be sold represent a stock. Because of the stock-flow mismatch, sales to the domestic population can only occur gradually. The stock-flow problem may be the major reason why Hungary has chosen a gradualist approach. Selling state-owned assets to the domestic population is not compatible with a big-bang solution. If, as in Germany's case, rapid sale is nevertheless attempted, then the purchasers must be non-residents, or the sales prices must be so low that the assets are, in fact, given away rather than sold.

The disadvantages of the selling strategy can be avoided. The Czech voucher method is one way of privatizing the economy quickly without giving it to foreigners, though space forbids consideration of its merits here.

Finally, a major disaster in Germany's big-bang was the agreement between the West German trade unions and the West German employers' associations to prevent competition from the East by introducing Western wages there. It is clear that this will destroy East German industry. Fortunately no similar effects are operating in Hungary. Unless the Austro–Hungarian empire is reestablished and Austrians fix Hungarian wages, Hungary will be safe from the destruction that has been planned to be the destiny of the East German economy. This is a disadvantage of the special kind of big-bang exercised in Germany, not a disadvantage of the big-bang as such.

General discussion

Much of the discussion focused on how one could evaluate the merits or otherwise of a big-bang. Philippe Aghion pointed out that it would often make sense to move very fast in some areas (such as price liberalization) while being more gradualist in others (such as industrial restructuring, given the substantial costs of bankruptcy). Privatization was bound to be slow, and probably ought to be, given the need to train managers. Patrick Bolton registered a protest against Hans-Werner Sinn's characterization of the lessons of the Coase theorem. If it didn't matter how property rights were allocated they could simply be given to the government, and bargaining between the government and the private sector relied upon to produce efficient allocations. The fact that privatization was desirable at all was a sign that it did matter how property rights were allocated.

John Flemming pointed out that Hungary's privatization programme was in fact progressing faster than many had thought possible (though Tamás Bauer said there was no coherent strategy behind the programme). One difficulty, continued Flemming, was resistance to the transfer of enterprises to their managers, who might be good owners but were resented by others in society. Overall, he wondered why the costs of transition must inevitably be high: the fact that the planned economies were inefficient implied that there were potential Pareto improvements in resource allocation. If the answer lay in the timing of the gains, there was an obvious role for capital markets to play in smoothing consumption. He would have welcomed more explicit emphasis on the role of capital markets in the transition process.

David Begg wondered exactly which aspects of Hungary's experience might help policy-makers to choose how fast to undertake their reforms. It had been argued that Hungary's high external debt made consumption smoothing more difficult, but Begg doubted whether other Eastern European countries would find capital market access any easier. It had also been argued that Hungarians would be unwilling to take a fall in present consumption, but why should citizens of other countries be any more willing? Or did gradualism provide Hungary with a more credible means of commitment to the reform process? It was hard to see why this should be so.

Mervyn King wondered whether the paper had focused on the appropriate counterfactual. What mattered was not whether Hungary was better off than other countries as a result of having begun its reform programme earlier, but whether, once a programme was begun, it should be pursued more or less rapidly. There was plenty of evidence in the paper bearing on the former question, but not enough bearing on the latter.

References

Aganbegyan, A. (1988). *The challenge: Economics of perestroika*, Hutchinson Education, London.

Angresano, J. and S. Sinkovics (1991). 'Hungary and the European Community: Problems and Prospects', mimeo.

Batt, J. (1991). *East Central Europe from reforms to transformation*, RIIA/Pinter, London.

Berend, I. (1990). *The Hungarian economic reforms, 1953–1988,* CUP, Cambridge.

Berend, I. and G. Ranki (1985). *The Hungarian economy in the twentieth century*, Croom Helm, Beckenham, Kent.

Blanchard, O., R. Dornbusch, P. Krugman, R. Layard and L. Summers (1991). *Reform in Eastern Europe*, MIT Press, Cambridge, Mass.

Blejer, M. I. and S. B. Sagari (1991). 'Hungary: Financial sector reform in a socialist economy', World Bank Working Papers, WPS 595.

Brus, W. (1970). *Problemes generaux du fonctionnement de l'economie socialiste*, Francois Maspero, Paris.

Cave, M. and P. G. Hare (1981). *Alternative approaches to economic planning*, Macmillan, London.

CEPR (1990). *Monitoring European integration: The impact of Eastern Europe, A CEPR Annual Report,* Centre for Economic Policy Research, London.

Cohen, D. (1991). 'The solvency of Eastern Europe', *European Economy.*

Collins, S. M. and D. Rodrik (1991). *Eastern Europe and the Soviet Union in the world economy,* Policy Analyses in International Economics No. 32, Institute for International Economics, Washington DC.

Csaba, L. (1990). 'The bumpy road to the free market in Eastern Europe', *Acta Oeconomica.*

Grosfeld, I. and P. G. Hare (1991). 'Privatization in Hungary, Poland and Czechoslovakia', *European Economy,*

Hare, P. G. (1976). 'Industrial prices in Hungary', *Soviet Studies.*

—— (1983). 'The beginnings of institutional reform in Hungary', *Soviet Studies.*

—— (1990). 'Reform of enterprise regulation in Hungary – from "tutelage" to market', *European Economy.*

—— (1991a). 'Industrial reform in the socialist countries: Hungary', in I. Jeffries (ed.) *Industrial reform in the socialist countries,* forthcoming.

—— (1991b). 'Hungary', in D. Dyker (ed.) *The European economy, Volume 2: Country studies,* forthcoming.

—— (1991c). *Central planning,* Harwood Academic Publishers, Chur, Switzerland.

Hare, P. G., H. K. Radice and N. Swain (1981). *Hungary: a decade of economic reform,* Allen and Unwin, London.

Hawkes, N. (ed.) (1990). *Tearing down the curtain (The people's revolution in Eastern Europe by a team from The Observer),* Hodder and Stoughton, London.

Hewett, E. A. (1988). *Reforming the Soviet economy,* Brookings, Washington DC.

Hughes, G. and P. G. Hare (1991a). 'Competitiveness and industrial restructuring in Czechoslovakia, Hungary and Poland', *European Economy.*

—— (1991b). 'The international competitiveness of industries in Bulgaria, Czechoslovakia, Hungary and Poland', presented to RES conference 1991, Warwick University.

—— (1991c). 'Industrial restructuring in Eastern Europe: policies and prospects', *European Economic Review.*

IMF (1991). *World economic outlook: October 1991,* IMF, Washington, DC.

Kaser, M. and E. A. Radice (eds.) (1986). *The economic history of Eastern Europe 1919–1975,* vols. 1–3, OUP, Oxford.

Kemme, D. M. (1991). *Economic transition in Eastern Europe and the Soviet Union: Issues and strategies,* Institute for East West Security Studies Occasional Paper No. 20, New York.

Kornai, J. (1959). *Overcentralisation in economic administration,* OUP, Oxford.

—— (1980). *Economics of shortage,* North Holland, Amsterdam.

—— (1986). 'The Hungarian reform process: Vision, hopes and reality', *Journal of Economic Literature.*

Kornai, J. and A. Matits (1987). *A vállalatok nyereségének bürokratikus újráelosztása,* Közgazdasági és Jogi Könyvkiadó, Budapest.

Lavoie, D. (1985). *Rivalry and central planning,* CUP, Cambridge.

Marer, P. (1986a). 'Economic reform in Hungary: From central planning to regulated market', *East European economies: Slow growth in the 1980s,* vol. 3, US Congress Joint Economic Committee, Washington, DC.

—— (1986b). 'Hungary's balance of payments crisis and response, 1978–84', *East European economies: Slow growth in the 1980s,* vol. 3, US Congress Joint Economic Committee, Washington, DC.

—— (1989). 'Hungary's political and economic transformation (1988–89) and prospects after Kadar', *Pressures for reform in the East European economies,* vol. 2, Congress Joint Economic Committee, Washington, DC.

McKinnon, R. (1991). 'Financial control in the transition to a market economy', *Journal of Economic Perspectives,* forthcoming.

Newbery, D. (1990). 'Tax reform, trade liberalization and industrial restructuring in Hungary', *European Economy.*

Nove, A. (1983). *The economics of feasible socialism,* Unwin, London.

OECD (1991a). 'The international financial situation of the Central and Eastern European Countries', *Financial Market Trends.*

—— (1991b). 'OECD Economic Surveys: Hungary', Paris.

Rollo, J. M. C. (1990). *The new Eastern Europe: Western responses,* RIIA, London.

Sik, O. (1967). *Plan and market under socialism,* IASP, White Plains, NY.

—— (1972). *The bureaucratic economy,* IASP, White Plains, NY.

Swaan, W. (1989). 'Price regulation in Hungary: Indirect but comprehensive bureaucratic control', *Comparative Economic Studies*.

Swain, N. (1985). *Collective farms which work?*, CUP, Cambridge.

Tedstrom, J. E. (ed.) (1990). *Socialism, Perestroika, and the dilemmas of Soviet economic reform*, Westview Press, Boulder, Colorado.

Economic Policy   Issue 13   Erratum

Political and monetary institutions and public financial
policies in the industrial countries

Vittorio Grilli, Donato Masciandaro and Guido Tabellini

p. 351 Table 4 Political fractionalization

Amend columns (a) Democracy, and (b) Representatives, to read

Germany   Pa-R   na
Switzerland   Pr   na

In the Table as printed *Germany* was incorrectly classified as a
Majoritarian Democracy, with two representatives per district. This is
in fact true for half the representatives, but the actual division of seats
among parties is entirely decided by a proportional system, limited only
by the 5% threshold for a party to be represented in Parliament. Hence,
a better classification for Germany is as a Proportional Democracy, with
a large number of representatives per district.

Second, *Switzerland* also can not be classified as a Majoritarian Parliamentary Democracy, as there are about eight representatives per
canton (or half-canton). It can best be classified as a (multi-person)
Presidential system, rather than as a Parliamentary Democracy.

We are grateful to Ron Rogowski for pointing this out.

PUBLIC FINANCE/FINANCES PUBLIQUES

International Quarterly Journal founded by J. A. Monod de Froideville
Revue Trimestrielle Internationale Fondée par J. A. Monod de Froideville

Publisher / Editeur
Foundation Journal for Public Finance
Fondation Revue de Finances Publiques
(Stichting Tijdschrift voor Openbare Financien)

Editorial Board / Comité de rédaction
M. Frank, A. J. Middelhoek, A. T. Peacock
Managing Editor / Editeur Gérant: D. Biehl

Volume XXXXV/XXXXVième Année
No. 3/1990

Articles

The articles published in English, French, or German are followed by summaries in the three languages.
Annual subscription rate (3 issues): DM 142,50.

PUBLIC FINANCE / FINANCES PUBLIQUES
c/o Institut für öffentliche Wirtschaft, Geld und Währung
Johann Wolfgang Goethe-Universität
Postfach 111932
D-6000 Frankfurt am Main 11
Federal Republic of Germany

Journal of Transport Economics and Policy

Since 1967, JTEP has published articles on all aspects of Transport Economics and Policy, with contributions from authors all over the world covering the latest research in the field.

In September 1991, a special issue was produced under the guest editorship of David Starkie on the important and topical subject FINANCING INFRASTRUCTURE, including the following articles:

Privatised Infrastructure and Incentives to Invest
Dieter Helm and David Thompson

The Optimal Timing of Infrastructure Investment
Stefan Szymanski

The Prospects for Privatising Infrastructure
Jose A. Gomez-Ibanez, John R. Meyer and David E. Luberoff

Commercial Funding of Transport Infrastructure
Gordon Mills

Policy Notes

California's Private Infrastructure Initiative	**Yuval Cohen**
Airport Investment	**David Starkie**

Single copies may be obtained from the Journal Office at £14.00. A regular subscription (individuals £22.00) ensures that all future special issues will be received on publication.

JOURNAL OF TRANSPORT ECONOMICS AND POLICY
University of Bath, Claverton Down, Bath BA2 7AY
Telephone (0225) 826302   Fax (0225) 826767

INTERNATIONAL REVIEW OF ECONOMICS AND BUSINESS

Rivista Internazionale
di Scienze Economiche e Commerciali

October-November 1991, Vol. XXXVIII

J.W. DEAN: Inter-generational Effects of Deficits under Keynesian and Ricardian Assumptions – R.J. CEBULA and G. SCOTT: Budget Deficits, Debt Service, and Real Interest Rates in the United States – A.K. AL-SAJI: The Effect of Government Budget Deficits on Real Interest Rates: Empirical Evidence from Italy: 1960:1-1990:2 – M. ESPOSITO: Il numero dei fattori (latenti) nel mercato telematico dei titoli di stato – R. FIORENTINI: Equilibrio ed efficienza nel mercato dei cambi. Un'analisi della parità del potere d'acquisto ex ante – R. TAMBORINI: The Exchange Rate as an Asset Price and the Imperfect Information Hypothesis – M. BASSETTO: Rischi di cambio e di inflazione in un problema di scelta di portafoglio – R. ROJ and A. RASSOULI: A Note of International Capital Movements in an Overlapping Generations Model – G.A. WOLFE, S.P. FERRIS and R. SANT: Information Asymmetry and the Dealer's Bid-Ask Spread: The Case of Initial Public Offerings of Common Stock – G.A. KARA-THANASSIS and N. NIARCHOS: Athens Stock Market: Recent Developments and Future Prospects – K.C. ROY and R.K. SEN: On the Domestic Debt and Its Effects on LDC's Internal and External Balance – A.M.A. GHAMDI: Foreign Aid, Foreign Interest Rates, and the Demand for Money in Developing Countries: The Case of Jordan

December 1991, Vol. XXXVIII

M. KADHIM: The Japanese Road to Modernization – G. FODELLA: I fattori alla base della competitività giapponese – T. FURUKI: Urban Planning under the Micro-electronic Revolution in Japan – S. PIGRUCCI: Politica economica e sviluppo dell'industria automobilistica giapponese e coreana – H. TAKEYA: Industrial Restructuring and Agricultural Organization in Japan – L. JIA: Industrialization and Technological Linkage between Agriculture and Industry in China. Comparable Experience in the Early Japanese Industrialization

A monthly journal. Subscription rate: Lire 170.000 (Italy); Lire 220.000 (abroad). - Complete set of back issues available (1954-1990). Address: R.I.S.E.C. - Via Teuliè 1 - 20136 Milano (Italy).